Barry Ferguson

SCHOOL DISTRICT BUDGETING

William T. Hartman
Pennsylvania State University

SCHOOL DISTRICT BUDGETING

ALLYN and BACON
BOSTON LONDON TORONTO SYDNEY TOKYO SINGAPORE

Library of Congress Cataloging-in-Publication Data

HARTMAN, WILLIAM T.
  School district budgeting.

    Includes index.
    1. School budgets—United States.   2. School
districts—United States—Finance.   3. Schools—United
States—Accounting.   I. Title.
LB2830.H35   1988   379.1'1   87-29142
ISBN 0-13-792292-2

Editorial/production supervision: *Edith Riker*
Cover design: *Lundgren Graphics*

Printed in the United States of America

10 9 8 7 6 5 4 3   95 94 93

ISBN   0-13-792292-2   01

CONTENTS

FIGURES AND TABLES

PREFACE

This is a book about school district budgeting. Unlike other available texts, it is devoted exclusively to the budgeting process in school districts. As such, it allows an in-depth treatment of both conceptual and practical aspects of budgeting in a single volume. The book was written out of necessity: the fragmentation of appropriate materials to teach about school budgets and budgeting made it difficult to put together a comprehensive picture of the subject. By default, the state education accounting manual became the primary text, supplemented by state department of education memoranda and data and by school district budget documents and related materials. This book was developed to remedy this situation.

The school budget has always been of crucial importance to school administrators but has received relatively little attention to date. Increasing costs, changing enrollments, lack of public support, and demands for new program directions all combine to place educational budgets and administrators under a great deal of pressure. Public scrutiny of district budgets requires more convincing justification of expenditure requests. Traditional revenue sources are less stable. Administrators are being asked to accomplish more with fewer resources. In short, a thorough knowledge of the budget process and the ability to use it effectively are essential competencies for school administrators.

Understanding the philosophy behind budgeting is as important as knowing the proper techniques. Budgets are not an end in themselves, but rather a means to implement appropriate educational programs for the district's students. The perspective underlying this book is that budgeting is one of the most important management tools possessed by school administrators; one that should be used to further the district's educational goals and accomplishments—not hinder them.

The budgeting process is arguably the single most important planning and political process in a school district. Developing the budget requires that administrators plan in detail what programs, services, and activities they will operate for the upcoming year and what their costs will be. Concurrently, the revenues to support these operations must be estimated and expenditure levels adjusted, sometimes dramatically, to meet available funding. Once prepared, the budget must be approved, an undertaking that may involve an election campaign. Finally, the approved budget is used to manage the district's fiscal operations. A smooth functioning budget process requires a great deal of effort and skill from school administrators, but it also results in an efficient, well-run school district. Conversely, a poorly managed budget process is a constant drain on administrators' time and energy and diverts their efforts from instructional activities.

The primary use for this text is intended to be for graduate courses in educational administration, particularly those in business management, business administration, and school finance. It can also serve as a reference book for practicing administrators, as well as the basis for inservice training programs.

The book contains eight chapters, each devoted to a separate aspect of school budgeting. Chapter One provides the introduction to budgets and budgeting. Both the steps in the budgeting process and the specific contents in the budget document are discussed. Chapter Two continues the introductory material with a discussion of the different budgeting approaches that have been used in education. The budget calendar, which provides a timeline for all related budgeting activities, is also reviewed. The final topic of this chapter deals with alternative organizational arrangements for school district budgeting, ranging from a centralized structure to a decentralized school site approach.

School accounting is the topic of Chapter Three. The focus is on fund accounting, expenditure and revenue accounts, and financial statements that are the aspects of the school accounting system most relevant for administrators dealing with budgets. While individual state accounting systems will vary in details, most are based on the model accounting structure developed by the National Center for Education Statistics, which is used in this book, and have sufficient commonality to be discussed generally.

Chapter Four is the heart of the book. Through descriptions and examples the procedures for developing budget estimates are illustrated.

This is the practical, nuts and bolts aspect of creating the numbers that go into the budget, which is rarely discussed. Beginning with student enrollment projections, the chapter describes how to translate these into personnel requirements. Estimation procedures for each type of budget expenditure are reviewed—salaries, benefits, outside purchased services, supplies, and capital outlay. Revenue estimating procedures for each revenue source are also presented. With this information administrators can develop their district (or school) budget.

Chapter Five presents a procedure for evaluating and explaining the changes in the budget from one year to the next. Called a baseline budget analysis, this technique separates the budget increases and decreases into those caused by changes in workload, changes in the prices paid for resources, and changes in educational program standards established by the district. A section on cost analysis is also included. Concepts such as total and unit costs, variable and fixed costs, direct and indirect costs, and average and marginal costs are discussed in educational contexts.

The subject of Chapter Six is budget adjustments; these are changes to the original budget at some point during the budgeting process. While budget reductions are the most common adjustments, increases to the budget and transfers from one budget section to another are also included.

Chapter Seven is about budget elections and will be relevant only to those states that allow or require districts to present their budget (or some part of it, such as the amount of local taxes to be levied) to the voters for approval. In this stage the budget process becomes overtly political. A considerable part of this chapter is devoted to description of the elements and activities of a successful campaign strategy.

The last stage in the budget process is discussed in Chapter Eight on budget management. Use of the budget to monitor expenditures, transfers among budget accounts, and financial reports are all elements that are part of this component. A final section on the use of microcomputers provides examples and suggestions on how to utilize these tools effectively throughout the budget process.

The type of material covered in this book cannot be adequately learned by only reading about the various budgeting procedures. To develop mastery of the techniques, it is essential that students actually apply them. To this end, each chapter has a set of realistic problems that require students to utilize the concepts and techniques presented in the text.

The author wishes to thank a number of people for their assistance in creating this book. The students in the educational administration program at the University of Oregon, where most of the material was developed and tested, were both patient with early versions and helpful in their suggestions for improvement. I received many insights into the budget process and solid examples of applications from local school administrators, particularly Don Jackson and Charles Hamby of Eugene School District and Jim Cyphert of Springfield School District. Phil Rice and Al Shannon of the Oregon Department of Education were a constant source of technical information about the budgeting process and of inspiration for completion of the project. The people at Prentice Hall were very supportive and helpful throughout the endeavor: Susan Willig and Shirley Chlopak for their confidence in the initial concept and their faith that the manuscript would finally be completed; and Edie Riker for her excellent editorial assistance. Most importantly, I want to thank Peggy Hartman, my wife, for her constant support and encouragement and for her insightful comments which improved the clarity and organization of many chapters.

William T. Hartman
State College, Pennsylvania

1

BUDGETS AND BUDGETING

CONCEPTS OF BUDGETS AND BUDGETING

Introduction

The school district budget is central to the successful operation of the educational enterprise. Educational programs cost money—without it even the best conceived program cannot function. Since money allows educators to provide instructional programs and services to students, administrators should view the budget as a device for accomplishing the districts' educational goals and objectives. Put another way, administrators should know how to use budgets and the budgeting process to establish and carry out district and individual school educational priorities.

The primary purpose of the budget is to translate the district's educational priorities into programmatic and financial terms. This must occur in the context of available fiscal resources and legal constraints. Although the final decisions on choice and emphasis of the district's overall educational program will be made by the school board, school administrators can and do exert significant influence on these decisions. This is because administrators, by and large, have the responsibility for preparing the budgets for review and approval; as a result, they have control over most of the items and amounts included.

1

This book, designed for administrators, emphasizes the managerial uses of school district budgeting. Subsequent chapters will discuss how to organize, prepare, analyze, modify, obtain approval for, and manage a school district budget. Underlying the specific procedures and techniques is the fundamental concept of this book: *The budget is much more than a collection of numbers; it is an important tool for school administrators to understand and to utilize in achieving their basic mission—educating children in the most effective and cost-efficient manner.* Consequently, administrators can and should view the budget as a powerful and, if used properly, reliable device to obtain sufficient resources for district educational programs.

From a managerial perspective, the budget serves as an important fiscal and program planning device. It can provide a systematic means for focusing the efforts of district personnel on district priorities.

> Budgeting is the process of planning the overall activity of the enterprise for a specified period of time, usually one year. An important objective of this process is to fit together the separate plans made for various segments of the enterprise so as to assure that these plans harmonize with one another and that the aggregate effect of all of them on the whole enterprise is satisfactory.[1]

The budget and the budgeting process can also be viewed as the major political process in a school district. The important decisions of who gets what are determined through this process. Key segments of this process include: the establishment of the district's objectives and priorities; the allocation of resources; public involvement through budget hearings, school board decisions, and other means of representative democracy; and budget elections. Results of the budgeting process reveal not only the goods and services to be purchased, but, more importantly, what priorities prevail and whose purposes receive the greatest allocations of the district's resources.[2]

Definitions of Budgets and Budgeting

To begin this study, it is necessary to define what is meant by a budget. Most everyone has some idea of what a budget is, and most school administrators have seen and worked with them. However, *budget* and *budgeting* can have different meanings to different people. Definitions of both terms will provide common meanings and avoid misinterpretation.

Budgets.   Three separate elements make up a budget: (1) a description of the total educational program to be provided by the school district; (2) an estimate of the expenditures needed to carry out the desired program; and (3) an estimate of the revenues which will be available to pay for the expenditures. Therefore, a school district budget is defined as:

> *A document which specifies the planned expenditures and anticipated revenues of a school district in a given fiscal year, along with other data and information relating the fiscal elements to the educational philosophy, programs, and needs of the district.*

To illustrate, a budget can be pictured as a triangle with each element as one side. This representation, shown in Figure 1.1, indicates that each element is connected to the other two and that the budget is not complete without all three elements.

The element portrayed as the foundation of the budget is a matter of perspective. Figure 1 shows educational programs as the base of the triangle. This implies that educational programs are the determining factor in the budget. In other words, once the desired programs are established, the necessary expenditures are determined and the required revenues are obtained.

Another equally valid perspective could have revenues as the base of the triangle. This would imply that revenues are the driving force in a budget; that is, the revenues that are available to a school district determine how much can be spent and what educational programs can be offered.

Expenditures could also form the base of the triangle. In some states, districts have expenditure limits which set maximum amounts. This limit effectively establishes the amount of revenues districts need to raise, and the educational programs which they can provide.

In practice, there is a great deal of interplay among the three elements—no single one is dominant. In establishing a budget, school districts must reach a balance between programmatic desires and fiscal possibilities.

Budgeting.   Budgeting in a school district encompasses more than the development of the budget document specifying expenditures and revenues. It includes the entire cycle of developing, approving, and implementing the district's budget. Budgeting, or the budgeting process, is defined as:

> The sequence of activities involved in planning the district's educational program, estimating the needed expenditures and revenues to implement these programs, gaining the necessary approval, and using the budget to assist in managing the district's operations.

Planning – W.S.

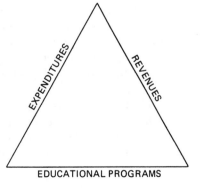

FIGURE 1.1
Budget Elements. *Source:* Carl Candoli et al., *School Business Administration: A Planning Approach*, 3rd ed. (Boston: Allyn and Bacon, 1984). p. 145.

The budget document itself is a detailed and complex work. It requires substantial time and effort on the part of school district personnel in its development. The development of the budget document and its approval should occur before the beginning of the budget year so the document is completed in time to direct the next year's operations. Consequently, work on the next year's budget must begin during the current year. The budgeting process begins in the early part of the preceding year with central office planning and organization. During the course of that year it includes developing the expenditure and revenue estimates, and obtaining public approval if necessary. Once completed, the budget is the major financial management tool used to monitor and control fiscal activities in the school district.

Business managers in school districts are fond of saying that budgeting is a year-round operation for many people in the district, not just a once-a-year activity by a small handful of administrators to pull some numbers together. It's true. A budget process in a school district which operates on the year-round principle will have the personnel trained and knowledgeable; the necessary data available; the policies, procedures, and forms in place to guide the activities which occur; and should have achieved the understanding and support of the school board for the needed budgeting actions in the district. Last minute efforts at communication, data gathering, and process instructions tend to be haphazard, rushed, and incomplete. The result can be mistakes in the budget and difficulties during the operating year. A well-planned budgeting process is no guarantee against omissions and errors, but they are less likely to occur than in an unstructured process.

Allocation of Resources

Allocation of resources among different programs in the district is a critical function of the budget. If funding were unlimited, there would be no need to make any choices among district programs and each program would receive all the requested resources. However, funds are limited and choices have to be made on how the monies will be spent. By establishing budget amounts for different areas of the district's operation, there is an explicit allocation process which favors some areas and de-emphasizes others. Within the confines of state and federal regulations which may require certain programs or services to be provided, the allocation decisions should represent the educational priorities of the district if the budget process is working properly.

The budget serves to implement the district's educational goals through the selection and allocation of *resources*. Resources are the building blocks of budgets. They consist of all of the personnel, supplies and materials, goods and services purchased from outside vendors, and capital items which the district uses to operate its educational program. However, resources represent costs and since the overall budget sets a limit on the total dollar amount available, the district must choose which resources it will purchase for the coming year. These choices include not only the *types,* but the *mix* of resources to be used and the *quantity* of each one. In reaching these decisions, both the need for the resource in a particular educational program and the *price* of the resource must be taken into account.

In economic terms, the budget can be viewed as the sum of all of the resources purchased by the district multiplied by their prices.[3] This relationship is shown in the equation below.

$$B = X_1 * P_1 + X_2 * P_2 + ... + X_n * P_n$$

where,

B is the total budget amount;
X_1 is the quantity of resource 1;
P_1 is the price of resource 1;
X_2 is the quantity of resource 2;
P_2 is the price of resource 2; and so forth.

This equation illustrates a simple, but important concept in budgeting. It is, that *within a given budget limit*, a decision to use more of one resource will require a reduction in another area. Similarly, a price increase for one resource will require a reduction in the quantity purchased of that resource or a reduction in another area to stay within a given total budget amount. If increases (or decreases) in the total budget amount are possible (or required), the same relationships among quantities and prices of the different resources hold.

For purposes of illustration assume that a district's educational program utilizes only two resources—teachers and microcomputers. If the budget called for hiring 100 teachers at an average salary of $20,000 each, and purchasing one hundred microcomputers at an average price of $1,000 each, the total budget would be $2,100,000, as shown below.

$$
\begin{aligned}
B &= \text{100 teachers} * \$20{,}000 + \text{100 microcomputers} * \$1{,}000 \\
&= \qquad \$2{,}000{,}000 \qquad + \qquad \quad \$100{,}000 \\
&= \qquad \$2{,}100{,}000
\end{aligned}
$$

Assuming that the total budget amount was fixed, if average teacher salaries increased by $1,000 the district would either have to reduce the number of teachers, eliminate the microcomputers, or reduce both the number of teachers and microcomputers.

$$
\begin{aligned}
B &= 100 \text{ teachers} * \$21{,}000 + 0 \text{ microcomputers} * \$1{,}000 \\
&= \quad\ \$2{,}100{,}000 \qquad + \qquad\qquad \$0 \\
&= \quad\ \$2{,}100{,}000
\end{aligned}
$$

or

$$
\begin{aligned}
B &= 95 \text{ teachers} * \$21{,}000 + 100 \text{ microcomputers} * \$1{,}000 \\
&= \quad \$2{,}000{,}000 \qquad + \qquad\qquad \$100{,}000 \\
&= \quad \$2{,}100{,}000
\end{aligned}
$$

or

$$
\begin{aligned}
B &= 98 \text{ teachers} * \$21{,}000 + 50 \text{ microcomputers} * \$1{,}000 \\
&= \quad \$2{,}050{,}000 \qquad + \qquad\qquad \$50{,}000 \\
&= \quad \$2{,}100{,}000
\end{aligned}
$$

To maintain both the number of teachers and the number of micro-computers after a price increase for teachers (or microcomputers) would necessitate an increase in the total budget amount.

$$
\begin{aligned}
B &= 100 \text{ teachers} * \$21{,}000 + 100 \text{ microcomputers} * \$1{,}000 \\
&= \quad \$2{,}100{,}000 \qquad + \qquad\qquad \$100{,}000 \\
&= \quad \$2{,}200{,}000
\end{aligned}
$$

In some instances, the use of microcomputer assisted instruction in class-rooms could reduce the number of teachers required. If this were a possi-ble adjustment which a district could make, the result would be an increase in a lower priced resource (microcomputers) and a decrease in a higher priced one (teachers) with a possible net reduction in cost to the district. For example, for the same total budget, a doubling of the number of microcomputers would reduce the number of teachers by five.

The purpose of this example is to emphasize that *the instructional strategy chosen by the district is directly reflected in resource requirements and costs, and that these are decisions which the district makes.* Even the choice of continuing past policies, such as limited use of microcomputers for instruction, and maintaining existing student/teacher ratios and support personnel stan-dards is a decision to utilize a particular mix of selected resources instead of an alternative one.

Through resource selection and allocation, the budget plays a crucial role in achieving a balance between what is ideal and what is possible. Most administrators, teachers, and other educators want the best possible pro-grams and learning environments for their students. They can envision nu-merous valid improvements to their existing programs, and understandably desire to implement them. However, as noted above, the funds to support the overall educational program of the district are limited. Thus, the budget is a vehicle for forcing choices—deciding to select one area over another (like buying four microcomputers for the math department instead of replacing a welding machine in the industrial arts shop). It requires educators, the school board, and the public to function with limited funding and to select resources within the available funds which they believe can provide the best possible educational program for students.

PURPOSES AND USES OF BUDGETS

The budget is one of the primary management tools for educational administrators. It is the major one in the fiscal area. As such, it has numerous uses and assumes many different roles during the year.

At the beginning of the development process, it operates as the principal *planning system* for the district, serving an educational function even more than a fiscal one. During this period, the district plans programs and services offered to students, educational program standards, support and central office activities, resources to be utilized, prices paid for the resources, and the total cost of the educational program—all within the constraints of available funding. This determines what the district is about and what it will do in the upcoming year.

The budget also serves as a vehicle for *public review and approval* of the educational and fiscal plans of the school district. This process can take many forms depending on state laws, ranging from school board approval in a nonpublic session, to the submission to the voters of the local property tax levy required to support the budget, or even a vote on the budget itself. In states requiring voter approval, a defeat at the polls means that the budget must be resubmitted, often after being reduced, until approval is obtained. This process has the related purpose of requiring the *justification of expenditure of public funds* at the proposed levels. It allows the public a forum in which to examine the rationale for the proposed spending plans and to approve them at an acceptable level.

Once approved by the school board, the budget is often a legal document. In this capacity it serves as the *legal basis for spending public funds.* With an approved budget the district has the authorization to expend its revenues (derived from local, state, and federal tax dollars) in the planned manner.

During the operating year, the budget functions as a management control document. It provides a basis for *control over school district expenditures.* The budgeted amounts for particular expenditures in individual programs or areas determine spending limits not to be exceeded without approval. By comparing the year-to-date expenditures in a budget category with the budgeted amount at regular intervals during the school year, administrators can watch for and prevent overexpenditures. Similarly, a regular comparison of the anticipated revenues with those actually received during the year allows administrators to monitor income. If there appears to be a shortfall developing in the district's anticipated revenues, early identification of this problem allows more time and flexibility to deal with it.

Another use of the budget is to *evaluate fiscal performance.* This evaluation can focus on different areas for different types of administrators. For example, the superintendent's performance in the fiscal management area can be judged by the functioning of the budgeting process itself, the accuracy of the budget, the quality and adequacy of the programs which are funded, and the control of expenditures throughout the year. A principal could be evaluated on a similar set of criteria, but focused at the school building level.

STEPS IN THE BUDGETING PROCESS

To accomplish the necessary goals of the budgeting process, five major steps need to be carried out. They are: development of guidelines; preparation of the budget document; modification of the original budget; approval of the budget; and management of the budget. Other descriptions of this process may combine[4] or expand[5] these steps, but the principal activities to be completed remain constant.

Development of Guidelines

Budgets do not come into being automatically. They have to be created by persons in school districts. Depending on the size of the district, the development process can involve from several people to hundreds. If all of these efforts are to be combined into a unified plan for the district, all persons working on the budget must follow the same directions. Consequently, the first step in the budget process is to develop guidelines for those preparing a portion of the budget.

The central office of the school district has this responsibility, and the task of preparing the specific guidelines is usually given to the business office. This involves 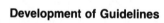 producing materials which will guide others in the school district who must develop their budget sections. The guidelines frequently contain items such as:

> A message from the superintendent providing the fiscal context within which the budget is to be developed.
> Directives or expectations from the school board concerning the size of the budget or its growth (or reduction).

Any limitations in expenditure requests in the new budget (for example, to maintain the current level of services, hold increases to 5 percent for inflation, forbid approval of new program requests, or forbid hiring of new personnel).

A schedule of events and dates in the budget process with emphasis on the timing for the budget proposals from individual district units.

Guidelines on staff and community participation in preparing the budget proposals, particularly at the school level.

Budget forms to be completed and accompanying instructions and worksheets.

Accounts, budget codes, and cost center descriptions to be utilized.

Cost estimating procedures.

Special instructions on particular account items (such as allocation amounts for supplies and equipment, calculation of salaries and fixed charges, and allowable purchased services).

Logistical procedures such as number of copies to be submitted, to whom, and when, and who to contact for further assistance.

Once prepared, the guidelines are distributed to the district's schools and central office departments for use in preparing their budget proposals. Distribution is usually carried out early in the school year to allow principals and district department administrators time to collect the necessary information, organize their staff, and inform them of the procedures and timelines established for budget preparation by the district. Frequently, the business office will hold informational meetings to discuss the forms and procedures, and will conduct training workshops for administrators and clerical staff to explain the content and format of properly prepared budgets. If the individual school and department budget submissions can be made uniform and accurate, substantial later work by the business office and the individual units to correct and standardize the budget proposals can be avoided.

Budget Preparation

Estimation of expenditures. The heart of budget preparation is estimating expenditures for the upcoming year. This estimation is not an exact science, but every effort should be made to make it accurate. However, keep in mind that school district personnel will be required to predict their expenditures more than a year in advance. What is needed is not 100 percent accuracy, but the best estimate possible with the data available.

Development of expenditure estimates is frequently a bottom-up process in which specific proposals for the next year are prepared by individual schools and district level departments under the guidelines of the district office. The schools and departments plan their activities and estimate costs within the programmatic and funding level constraints established by the school board and district office. The budget requests, completed in the designated format and on the standardized forms, specify the particular expenditure items and their planned costs for next year. Frequently, priorities are assigned to expenditure items so that if reductions are necessary, an order of deletion is established. Once completed, the individual requests from schools and district level departments are submitted to the business office. There they are reviewed for compliance with the development guidelines and for accuracy, and then compiled into a single expenditure proposal for the school district. This estimation process will be explored in detail in Chapter Four.

Workup revenues 1st
★

Estimation of revenues. The other side of the budget development process is estimating revenues that the district is expected to receive during the next year. In contrast to the frequently decentralized process for the specification of expenditures, the estimation of anticipated revenues is usually done in the central district office by the business office personnel. This is based on information from representatives of outside funding sources, historical trends, calculations or estimates of the amount available from local property taxes, and the business office's own assumptions about the future. This process is also one of trying to project how much money the school district will obtain more than a year in advance and it is subject to its own set of difficulties and uncertainties.

Revenues come from a variety of sources—local, intermediate, state, and federal. The most important local source is the property tax, but there are a number of other possible local sources. Intermediate governmental agencies, such as county education offices or regional educational service units, may also provide some funding for school districts, but the largest outside funding source for school districts is the state. Many states funding schemes provide aid to districts on an "equalized basis"—that is, more state funds are given to poorer districts and fewer funds are given to richer ones. The proportion of local and state revenues for a given district will depend on the general funding pattern in the state and the wealth of the district. Funds from the federal government for education are largely restricted to the support of particular purposes and programs. In total, the federal funds generally represent less than 10 percent of a district's total revenue, but in certain districts or in programs such as vocational education or compensatory education, they may be much more important revenue sources.

Combining expenditure and revenue estimates. Once the separate expenditure and revenue estimates have been made, the numerical parts of the budget are complete. The business office must then combine the separate cost estimates into a unified expenditure projection and combine that with the revenue projections to form a single document. This is not the end of the budget development process. Rarely will the first combination of expenditure and revenue estimates be adequate. Adjustments, readjust-

Guesstimates at best

ments, and modifications will be necessary before the budget is complete, but with the initial estimates of the desired expenditures and the anticipated revenues the process is well begun.

Budget Modification

The total revenue estimate for the school district is critical because it establishes the amount of money that the district can spend. Expenditures cannot exceed revenues: In almost all states, school districts are prohibited from deficit spending. Consequently, when the separate expenditure estimates are combined and compared with the projected revenues, the budget must balance; that is, the projected expenditure total must be equal to or less than the projected revenues. If the projected expenditures are greater than revenues, the difference between the two figures must be eliminated.

There are two basic ways of bringing the budget into balance: *reducing expenditures* to meet available revenues and *increasing revenues* to support the desired level of expenditures. Practically, some combination of these two methods is usually employed by school districts. Of the two, the most painful one for school districts is to reduce expenditures; however, this is the action over which districts have most control.

The conventional wisdom surrounding expenditure reduction is that cuts should be made as far from the classroom as possible.[6] This is not always possible, particularly if the required budget reduction is large. Personnel costs make up over 80 percent of the total budget for most districts, and the bulk of the personnel costs are for teachers. Consequently, the only place to realize large budget reductions is from personnel and that usually means teachers must be included. Chapter Six, Budget Adjustments, discusses the process, possible management actions, and the implications for budget reductions in further detail.

The revenue source over which the district has most control is the property tax levy. This, however, is not necessarily a solution to a budget imbalance as there are often practical and political considerations which will limit tax increases. Other local revenue sources usually offer limited opportunities for increased income. The other funding sources—state and federal—are not under the control of the school district. As a result, the best the school district can do is to lobby for additional support (usually a long run strategy) and to obtain the latest available estimates of the state and federal monies to incorporate into the revised budget.

Budget Approval

Once the budget has been prepared and proposed expenditures are in balance with expected revenues, it must be approved by some higher authority than the district superintendent. This usually means the district school board, although for some districts another public body such as a city council may have to give their approval also. Whatever the specific state and district requirements, the approval process requires convincing the appropriate governing body or bodies that the expenditures are necessary, that the other revenues will be forthcoming in the magnitude projected to balance the expenditures, and that the amount of local property tax required is acceptable to the public.

Once approved by the school board (and other public bodies as necessary), many districts face another, and increasingly difficult, hurdle—approval by the voting public. For those districts who must obtain voter approval of their budget, this requires holding and winning an election. In the face of increasing voter resistance to higher taxes as illustrated in recent and widespread property tax revolts in many states,[7] a successful fiscal election campaign generally requires a well planned and implemented campaign to turn out a majority of "Yes" voters. Due to its importance in some states, this topic is the subject of Chapter Seven.

Budget Administration

Once the budget has been approved by the necessary process, it becomes the major fiscal management tool during the school year. Administrators manage their operations throughout the year using the budget in a variety of ways: monitoring program implementation; expenditure control; keeping track of revenues; making corrections in expenditure plans to reflect changes in program plans or actual revenues; reporting on the fiscal operations to the school board and public. In Chapter Eight these budget management practices are examined in detail.

CONTENT OF BUDGETS

For many school districts the budget is a complex and multifaceted document, perhaps including several separate documents and hundreds of pages. While it contains many parts, there are six elements that should be included in some fashion in most all school district budgets.

Introduction

This first section of the budget document contains a variety of different elements to describe the budget process and to put the budget projections into context. Primary among these is the *Budget Message.* This component often fulfills many functions: explaining what the budget document is; describing the economic conditions anticipated in the district and other important planning assumptions which guided the development of the budget; outlining the major financial policies proposed for the upcoming year and explaining changes from prior years in these policies; relating the financial policies to the district's program standards and to the proposed expenditures and revenues in the budget; and discussing any significant changes in levels of expenditures and revenues anticipated in the next year.

Another element frequently found in this section of the budget document is the *Philosophy and Goals Statement* of the school district. This is a written description of what the district is trying to accomplish in its educational programs and how it is organizing and operating to achieve its goals. *School board members* and other individuals who may have had an official role in the budget development process can also be identified in this section along with the *Budget Calendar* and any *Legal Notices* which may be required.

Financial Summary Information

Most school district budgets today are lengthy documents which contain an enormous amount of information, much of it in the form of detailed expenditure and revenue estimates. While these are necessary in the development and justification of the budget, they can also be overwhelming to many school board members, district patrons, and district employees. To make the budget information manageable and understandable to the public it is useful to present the key financial elements in a summarized format. This would include such information as total expenditures by major purpose (such as instruction, support services, and non-instructional services), total revenues by source, and amount of local property tax required from local taxpayers. For proper context, all of these items should be compared with their values from past years. If individuals want additional information they can proceed to the detailed expenditure and revenue sections which document the aggregate amounts presented in the summary.

Expenditures

The bulk of the budget document will generally be devoted to this section. It consists of a detailed specification of the proposed expenditures of the school district for the upcoming year. The expenditure estimates are organized according to the state's school accounting system with the appropriate format and accounting codes. For example, state regulations may require that districts budget by major fund, by function (purposes of the expenditures) within each fund, and by object of expenditure within each function. To place the budget request amounts in context, comparable budget data from the two prior years and the current year may also be required to be presented. An expenditure page which illustrates how these requirements would be fulfilled is shown in Table 1.1.

TABLE 1.1 Sample Expenditure Page from Oregon School District Budget

OREGON DEPARTMENT OF EDUCATION
SALEM, OREGON 97310

GENERAL FUND
BUDGET DETAILED ESTIMATE SHEET
☒ REQUIREMENTS ☐ RESOURCES

JULY 1, 19___ TO JUNE 30, 19___

SCHOOL DISTRICT NO. ___
COUNTY ___

ACCOUNT CODE AND DESCRIPTION (1)	ACTUAL DATA FOR PRIOR TWO YEARS		BUDGET THIS YEAR 19 -19 (4)	BUDGET NEXT YEAR 19 -19		
	SECOND YEAR 19 -19 (2)	FIRST YEAR 19 -19 (3)		PROPOSED (5)	APPROVED (6)	ADOPTED (7)
					Same as column (5) except as noted	Same as column (6) except as noted
1000 Instruction						
1110 Regular Program—Elementary Schools						
110 Regular Salaries	$472,928	$486,237	$510,435	$576,230		
120 Temporary Salaries	8,276	9,488	10,000	10,000		
210 Public Employees Retirement System	36,664	42,924	52,190	66,338		
220 Social Security	25,123	27,962	31,290	35,936		
230 Employee Insurance	24,798	26,142	29,063	40,198		
310 Instructional Services	790	976	1,000	1,000		
340 Travel	2,705	2,674	2,800	2,890		
410 Teaching Supplies	19,321	23,842	24,500	25,000		
420 Textbooks	30,968	5,789	32,400	35,200	$ 24,000	$ 26,000
Total Regular Elementary Instruction	$621,573	$626,034	$693,678	$792,792	$781,592	$782,592

Source: Oregon Department of Education, *Program Budgeting and Accounting Manual for School Districts* (Salem, OR: Oregon Department of Education, 1980). p. 118.

14

Revenues

The revenues which the district is projecting to receive are specified in this section of the budget. Generally, they are identified first by accounting fund to which they belong, then as to the level of government providing the revenues—local, intermediate, state, and federal—and, finally, by the particular source within the level. Table 1.2 provides an example of this format of revenue estimates. It presents source-by-source revenue data for the two prior years and for the current year, along with the projections for the upcoming year.

Position Counts

While frequently not a separate section, the number of personnel to be employed by the district in the upcoming year is usually specified somewhere in the budget document. Personnel counts are usually expressed in full-time equivalents (FTE), which is the number of persons calculated as if all were working on a full-time basis. This means that part-time employees are figured as fractional FTE amounts (for example, a half-time instructional aide would be counted as 0.5 FTE). The number of FTE personnel are frequently either shown in the calculations section of the budget document or identified in parentheses along with the associated salary amounts in the expenditures section.

Explanation of Expenditure Calculations

This section of the budget document provides a description of the calculation process used to project the expenditures. It provides the assumptions, cost standards, enrollments, salary levels, FTE, and other cost estimating data used in developing the expenditure estimates in the budget. These calculations can be found in many forms: presented in the expenditure section (such as on the facing page of each expenditure); as an appendix to the budget document; or in a separate workbook. The format of these calculations is not as important as their existence. Without them, it is largely impossible for anyone other than the persons who did the actual estimations to evaluate the validity of the estimation process. An example format illustrating the derivation of the expenditure estimates for Elementary Education (Table 1.1) is shown in Table 1.3.

Additional Information

Content and format of individual district budgets will vary. Other items in addition to the six elements discussed above may also be included. For example, the table of contents of a school district budget document, which is shown in Table 1.4, illustrates the variety of additional information which may be provided in a school district budget: definitions of funds, expenditures and revenues; a long range plan; salary and benefit data; expenditure

TABLE 1.2 Sample Revenue Page from Oregon School District Budget

OREGON DEPARTMENT OF EDUCATION
SALEM, OREGON 97310

100 GENERAL ____ FUND
BUDGET DETAILED ESTIMATE SHEET
☐ REQUIREMENTS   ☒ RESOURCES

JULY 1, 19 ____ TO JUNE 30, 19 ____

SCHOOL DISTRICT NO. ____
COUNTY ____

ACCOUNT CODE AND DESCRIPTION (1)	ACTUAL DATA FOR PRIOR TWO YEARS		BUDGET THIS YEAR	BUDGET NEXT YEAR 19 -19		
	SECOND YEAR 19 -19 (2)	FIRST YEAR 19 -19 (3)	19 -19 (4)	PROPOSED (5)	APPROVED (6)	ADOPTED (7)
					Same as column (5) except as noted	Same as column (6) except as noted
1000 Revenue from Local Sources (except current taxes)						
1112 Delinquent Taxes	$ 39,892	35,624	40,000	40,000		
1311 Tuition from Individuals	8,450	8,625	1,425	1,680		
1312 Tuition from XYZ School District			9,000	9,000		
1411 Transportation Fees from Individuals			250	250		
1412 Transportation Fees from XYZ School Dist.	5,775	5,930	6,400	6,400		
1510 Interest on Investments	28,701	39,072	30,000	40,000		
1710 Admissions	38,074	41,518	42,000	42,000		
1740 Fees	4,806	4,920	5,000	5,000		
1910 Rental of Building	12,190	12,634	14,200	14,600		
1941 Services Provided Other LEA's Within State	9,162	9,541	10,000	10,000		
1990 Miscellaneous	216	289	300	300		
Total Revenue from Local Sources (except taxes)	147,266	158,153	158,575	169,230		
2000 Revenue from Intermediate Sources						
2101 County School Fund	39,693	39,841	40,680	40,000		
Total Revenue from Intermediate Sources	39,693	39,841	40,680	40,000		

16

3000 Revenue from State Sources						
3101 Basic School Support Fund—General Support	955,758	998,601	1,019,882	1,327,568		1,401,900
3102 Basic School Support Fund—School Lunch Match	6,019	6,121	6,400	6,500		
3103 Common School Fund	11,464	12,877	13,500	14,500		
3202 Handicapped Children	26,794	29,098	68,500	70,000		
3204 Driver Education	7,904	8,474	9,000	10,000		
Total Revenue from State Sources	1,007,939	1,055,171	1,117,282	1,428,568	1,428,568	1,502,900
4000 Revenue from Federal Sources						
4801 Federal Forest Fees	$ 4,175	3,274	6,500	7,000		
4802 Impact Aid—PL 874	1,826	1,998	2,000	2,000		
Total Revenue from Federal Sources	$ 6,001	5,272	8,500	9,000		
5000 Other Sources						
5200 Transfer from Capital Projects Fund	3,000					
5300 Sale of Equipment		1,029				
Total Other Sources	3,000	1,029				
Total Revenue and Other Sources Except Current Taxes	$1,203,899	$1,259,466	$1,325,037	$1,646,798	$1,646,798	$1,721,138
Beginning Cash Balance/Net Working Capital	201,121	194,719	200,000	200,000	200,000	250,000
Total Resources Except Current Taxes	$1,405,020	*1,454,185	*1,525,037	$ 1,846,798	*1,846,798	$1,971,138
1111 Current Year Taxes				2,527,492		2,477,492
Taxes Required to Balance Budget	2,064,380	*2,228,378	*2,230,402		*2,477,492	
Total Resources	$3,469,400	$3,682,563	$3,755,439	$ 4,374,290	$4,324,290	$4,448,630

Source: Oregon Department of Education, Program Budgeting and Accounting Manual for School Districts (Salem, OR: Oregon Department of Education, 1980). p. 123–24.

TABLE 1.3   Sample Expenditure Calculations

EXPLANATORY COMMENTS
1110 Instruction—Regular Programs—Elementary Schools

OBJECT CODE	EXPLANATION	CURRENTLY BUDGETED NO. OF POS.	AMOUNT	PROPOSED NEXT YEAR NO. OF POS.	AMOUNT
110	Position Title: Classroom teacher	40	$499,470.	40	$564,586.
	Teacher Aide	2	10,965.	2	11,645.
	Total		$510,435.		$576,231.
120	For substitute Teachers: 200 teaching days @ $50 per day $10,000.				
210	Employer contribution is 11.75% of regular salaries: $564,586. × 11.75% $66,338.				
220	Employer contribution is 6.13% of all salaries to a maximum annual salary of $25,900. Salaries for temporary employees are included. $586,231. × 6.13% $35,935.				
230	Insurance coverage for regular employees is approximately 7.12% of salaries paid. $564,586. × 7.12% $40,198.				
310	Admission fees for students to OMSI $ 1,000.				
340	Private car mileage for teachers traveling between teaching stations. 17,000 miles @ 17¢ per mile $ 2,890.				
410	Teaching supplies allowances: $25. per student per year. 1,000 students @ $25. $25,000.				
420	Three new textbooks adopted at an estimated cost of $35,200.				

Source: Oregon Department of Education, *Program Budgeting and Accounting Manual for School Districts* (Salem, OR: Oregon Department of Education, 1980), p. 117.

summaries by cost centers (schools and district-level departments); expenditures for capital outlay; detailed information on personnel allocations and costs; and expenditures for data processing.

Selecting information to be included in the budget and designing the presentational format should be guided by the goal of communicating the district's financial needs and resources in a clear manner. Important and summary information should be highlighted and easy to understand for the lay reader (which will often include many school board members). However, the expenditure and revenue specifications and supporting data needed by someone interested in examining a particular program or area in more detail should be available also. It is helpful in presenting and explaining the budget when information in the different sections is easy to locate. A useful practice is to color code each section of the budget document for ease of reference (for example, budget message printed on yellow paper, expenditures printed on green paper, revenues printed on blue, and so forth).

TABLE 1.4   Table of Contents from Beaverton, Oregon School District Budget

BUDGET DOCUMENT
1983–84
TABLE OF CONTENTS

Source: Beaverton School District, *1983-84 Budget Document* (Beaverton, OR: Beaverton School District, 1983).

On the other hand, it may create the wrong impression if the budget document itself appears to be lavish and expensive to produce; board members and voters may feel that a district which can afford a fancy, elaborate budget document is spending their money inappropriately and these same persons may be less inclined to support requests for additional monies. Finally, information in the budget should represent the district's best effort at explaining its educational programs and services, justifying their support, and estimating their costs in the upcoming year.

CONCLUSION

The budgeting process is one of the most important means of considering and making policy decisions for the school district. Developing the budget for the upcoming year affords the opportunity to think about and plan for the educational programs of the school district. The actual budget is a short-range document; it covers only the next year of operation for the district. It specifies the anticipated purposes and amounts to be spent during the upcoming year in great detail for all district personnel and the community to see. It forces the district and those preparing the budget to be specific about what resources they wish to purchase for next year, in what quantity, and for what purposes, and makes it possible to compare the stated educational goals and objectives of the district with the proposed use of the available funds. If there are important discrepancies they can be identified, debated, and rectified if desired. In its operation, the budget implements district policies which have been established throughout the budgeting process. As a result, final resource allocation decisions reflected in the budget give the strongest indication of the district's actual educational priorities.

The budget can also be a vehicle for introducing some long-range planning into the traditional short-range focus of school district planning. Certain programs may start small, but be expected to grow significantly in the future; if the early expenditures are not made with an eye to the future, wasteful and unnecessary costs may result. The introduction of microcomputers into the schools' curriculum is a prime example of this situation. Early hardware and software purchases should be both compatible with expected later purchases and useful in the anticipated future curriculum. This is a particularly difficult task given the rapidly changing and improving state of microcomputers in education, but a planning and budgeting process which asks for justification of requested expenditures will force some consideration of these difficult questions.

The budget is also the format for making the difficult allocation decisions in the school district. Whether it is at the district level with choices to be made between elementary, middle, or high schools; between regular and special education; at the school level with choices to be made between core academic or elective subjects; or between different academic programs, the necessity of completing the budget document requires those involved to resolve differences in opinions and educational priorities.

In the discussion of this chapter and throughout the book, it may appear as if the process and its associated activities are rational, well ordered, and logically structured. To some extent this is true, for there is a budget calendar giving dates, an assignment of responsibilities for specific tasks, an organizational structure, and a management strategy for carrying out the budget process. However, this order does not represent the whole picture. The budget process has many conflicting aspects which must be understood.

Rational and subjective: The budget process is a rational undertaking in which goals and objectives are identified and then resources assigned to particular programs to achieve the stated goals. However, the establishment of the goals and objectives is a highly subjective matter in which those involved will make their decisions based largely on personal beliefs and values. Principals, teachers, central office administrators, superintendents, school board members, parents, and special interest groups all have opinions of which activities are more important and strive to see them reflected in the district's budget.

Constrained and flexible: Districts are limited, among other things, by available funds from the state and federal government, by the local property taxes which can be raised, and by numerous statutes and regulations. However, there is frequently a great deal of discretion at the district and school building level on exactly how those revenues will be spent.

Reasonable and arbitrary: Many of the decisions in the budget process involve professional judgment and personal values. The variety of persons participating in the process generally keep the decisions from becoming unreasonable or too biased in one direction. However, there are often no definite right or wrong answers to questions such as the appropriate student/teacher ratio in elementary schools and sometimes such decisions have to be arbitrary.

Precise and uncertain: The budget has specific dollar amounts listed for each expenditure and revenue item. The columns of numbers in the document give an impression of precision and accuracy, particularly if in the form of a computer printout. However, those who have developed the budgets are aware that the numbers are largely estimates and represent their best guess at what will happen next year. Within the overall expenditure level, there is generally some "wiggle room" in most budgets; that is, monies can be shifted around from one program to another during the year to meet unexpected changes in operations or to take advantage of opportunities which may occur. Administrators should be aware of this possibility and knowledgeable about which budget categories or areas have potentially available funds which might be shifted to better uses.

Open and concealed: The budget document for school districts provides an enormous amount of financial information, but there is probably an equal amount that is not presented. The worksheets, planning assumptions, alternative spending plans are generally not included or made available to the public as these documents are too bulky, indecipherable, or technical for outsiders to understand readily.

Specialized and public: The document is prepared by educational specialists and represents their proposal of the amount and type of education that should be provided by the school district. However, the plan is reviewed, modified if necessary, and approved by the lay public, either represented by elected school board members or by the district voters. This creates an automatic tension between professional expertise and lay concerns over both program and costs.

Educational goals and political reality: The budget is a compromise between the desire for improving educational programs and the need to gain public support through acceptable spending and taxing levels. It is a continual balancing act for there are always many excellent proposals for new, better, more effective educational programs, but these programs cost money and often taxpayers and the school board have a strong interest in keeping costs down.

These conflicting aspects will never be fully resolved and will be present throughout the budget process. However, it is useful to make note of them and to think about how you would work to reconcile the differences and minimize the disruptions which they could cause.

Above all, the budget should be a useful document and the budget process should be one which aids the effective management of the school district. School administrators should recognize that the budget is ultimately a device for achieving educational goals. Consequently, they should understand the budget thoroughly and be able to use both the document and the process in positive ways to accomplish the educational purposes of their school, department, or district.

PROBLEMS

1.1   Obtain a copy of your school district's budget document and use it to:
  - a.) Identify the different sections of the document. Are all six described in this chapter present? Which, if any, are missing? Which, if any, additional sections have been included?
  - b.) If you are employed in the district, locate the budget entry which contains your salary. Locate the budget entry which contains the costs of the business office.
  - c.) What percentage of the expenditures are budgeted for instruction? What proportion of the instructional expenditures are for elementary schools, for middle schools, and for high schools? Do these represent all of the instructional expenditures of the district?
  - d.) What percentage of the revenues come from local, intermediate, state, and federal sources?

1.2   Prepare suggestions on how your district budget document could be modified to improve communication with school board members and the district patrons.

NOTES

  1. Robert N. Anthony, *Management Accounting Principles* (Homewood, IL: Richard D. Irwin, Inc., 1965), p. 5.
  2. A similar perspective is found in Charles H. Sederberg, "Budgeting," in L. Dean

Webb and Van D. Mueller, eds., *Managing Limited Resources: New Demands on Public School Management* (Cambridge, MA.: Ballinger, 1984).

3. Henry M. Levin, "The Effects of Different Levels of Expenditure on Educational Output" in R. L. Johns et al., eds., *Economic Factors Affecting the Financing of Education*, vol. II (Gainesville, Florida: National Education Finance Project, University of Florida, 1971), p. 177.

4. Walter I. Garms, James W. Guthrie, and Lawrence C. Pierce, *School Finance: The Economics and Politics of Public Education* (Englewood Cliffs, NJ: Prentice-Hall, 1978), p. 265 combines the first four steps into one called budget formation.

5. Sederberg, "Budgets," p. 61.

6. William T. Hartman and Jon Rivenburg, "School District Response to Fiscal Constraint" *Journal of Education Finance* 11 (Fall 1985), pp. 219-235.

7. Philip Piele, "Public Support for Public Schools: The Past, The Future, and the Federal Role," *Teachers College Record*, 84 (Spring 1983), pp. 690-707.

2

ORGANIZATION FOR BUDGETING

INTRODUCTION

The budgeting process is complex. It involves many people in all parts of the school district organization and in the community. A single budget cycle covers a period of almost two years and requires a multitude of activities. Throughout the entire process, numerous special interest groups, both inside and outside the school district organization, bring pressure to bear to see that their particular interests are met; frequently, the desires of these groups are in conflict. Both the revenue and expenditure amounts in the budget are subject to change and the budget process must regularly incorporate updated information to modify previously established figures. In short, it is a difficult process to manage effectively, but one that is of enormous importance to the well-being of the school district.

This chapter will provide an organizational context for the more technical and detailed material on budget accounting, preparation, analysis, reductions, elections, and management in the following chapters. Before a school district administrator can arrive at one of those phases, it is necessary to understand and to work within the organizational structure which the district has established for the budgeting process. This chapter will cover the basic questions of budget organization:

1. What type of approach to budgeting will be used?
2. What activities have to be carried out?
3. When do the activities have to be accomplished?
4. Who is responsible for doing the activities or seeing that they are accomplished both in the proper manner and on time?

To answer these questions, this chapter concentrates on three major topics: alternative approaches to budgeting; development of a budget calendar; and organizational structures for budgeting. These aspects are closely related. The budgeting approach chosen by the district provides the particular structure for the budget process and dictates, in general, the activities which will be required. The budget calendar designates what specific things have to be done and when. And the organizational structure identifies who is responsible for each activity and what other persons or groups should be involved.

APPROACHES TO BUDGETING

The approach to budgeting refers to the general methodology and format used in developing the budget estimates and preparing the budget document. The principal approaches to budgeting used by school districts are line-item budgeting, program budgeting, program planning and budgeting systems (PPBS), and zero-based budgeting (ZBB).[1] Other approaches, either recommended or in use, include performance budgeting,[2] school site budgeting,[3] and the local planning and budgeting model.[4]

These approaches reflect a variety of management objectives sought through the budget: cost control; organizational responsibility; program planning; output measurement and evaluation; political control; setting priorities; and reallocation of resources toward more efficient and/or desired areas. Each of the approaches relates to all of these objectives in some fashion, but they differ on the emphasis placed on the objectives and the format. Activities required during the budget process will also vary with the approach selected.

Line-Item Budgeting

Line-item budgeting is a technique in which line items, or objects of expenditure—personnel, supplies, contractual services, and capital outlays— are the focus of analysis, authorization and control.[5]

The line-item approach to budgeting was the most common approach through the 1960s. Its emphasis on identifiable items provided educational managers and trustees with a budget which was easily understood and controlled. As an historical example, the complete line-item budget for Springfield, Oregon for the school year 1922-23 is shown in Table 2.1.

With line-item budgeting, attention is given to the items which are purchased, rather than the purpose of the expenditures. Strict adherence to the line-item approach results in a format for budget information that is inappropriate for either planning or managing school districts which today are much more diverse and complex. The problem is that the same line items for different operations are aggregated to yield a single total amount. There is no provision for identifying or planning separate expenditures for different schools, different types of students, or different grade levels.

TABLE 2.1   Report of the School Clerk, District 19, 1922–23, Springfield, Oregon

DISBURSEMENT

EXPENSE OF GENERAL CONTROL		
Board & Clerk	$175.00	
Election & Census	$30.00	
Clerical	$2.50	
Miscellaneous	$2.12	$209.62
EXPENSE OF INSTRUCTION		
Teacher Salary	$22,098.92	
Stationery & Supplies	$476.70	
Miscellaneous	$195.96	$22,771.58
EXPENSE OF OPERATING SCHOOL PLANT		
Janitor Salary	$1,713.90	
Janitor Supplies	$89.51	
Fuel	$843.44	
Water	$115.02	
Light & Power	$175.27	$2,937.14
EXPENSE OF MAINTENANCE OF SCHOOL PLANT		
Building Repair & Upkeep of Grounds	$152.19	
Replacement & Repairs to Equipment	$521.20	
Insurance	$300.00	
Other Expenses	$36.45	$1,009.84
OUTLAY CAPITAL		
Equipment, New Building	$709.43	
Equipment, Old Building	$814.53	
Alteration, Old Building	$28.13	
Manual Training	$334.16	
Domestic Science	$170.63	
Interest	$1,987.99	
Miscellaneous	$24.02	$4,068.89
GRAND TOTAL		$30,997.07

SIGNED: J. M. COFFIN
        Clerk, District 19

For example, all teachers' salaries in the district would be combined into one total; no information would be readily available on the salary expenditures for high schools compared to elementary schools, instructional expenditures for regular students compared to handicapped students, expenditures for a particular school, or for any other useful category for managing district operations.

However, the line-item approach does provide useful and essential information. The solution is to use this approach in combination with another budgeting approach which will overcome its problems. In fact, all of the other budgeting methods use a line-item approach as a basic element in the organization and development of their data.

Program Budgeting

> Program budgeting is a technique in which spending plans are formulated and appropriations are made on the basis of the expected results of services to be performed by organizational units.[6]

The organization of the program budget is based on the program structure. This is the classification scheme which organizes the expenditures into categories according to their objective or purpose. If the line-item approach is the "what" to be purchased, then the program budget approach identifies the "why" of educational expenditures.

The most common approach to school district budgeting organizes the budget around the major functions in the district—primarily Instruction and Supporting Services. These functions are further divided into more specific subfunctions, such as high school instruction, programs for physically handicapped, guidance services, school administration, fiscal services, or operations and maintenance of physical plant.[7] By design this program structure closely matches the way in which responsibilities are assigned. *The program functions and subfunctions correspond to the organizational structure* utilized by most school districts. As a result, there is an individual who has both organizational and fiscal responsibility for every budget category.

Within each function or subfunction, the expenditures required to carry out the necessary activities are estimated and reported on a line-item basis. This provides budget information in two important dimensions—the objectives of the expenditure (function or subfunction) and the specific items purchased (object). This approach to budgeting is referred to as program budgeting. The combination of line-item specification of expenditures within each budget subfunction is the approach recommended by this book. The function/object specification is utilized by the accounting system to record and report budgeting and other fiscal data; Chapter Three describes how the accounting structure is used as an outline for the budget.

An excerpt from a program budget is shown in Table 2.2; the portion

TABLE 2.2 Sample Program Budget Excerpt

CODE	FUNCTION/OBJECT	
1110	HIGH SCHOOL PROGRAMS—REGULAR	
111	Regular Certificated Salaries	$9,556,963
112	Regular Noncertificated Salaries	393,975
122	Temporary Noncertificated Salaries	214
151	Extra Duty Increment—Department Head	8,596
155	Extra Duty Increment—Curriculum Development	4,175
	TOTAL SALARIES	$9,963,923
210	Public Employees Retirement System	$1,686,648
220	Social Security Administration	693,186
230	Employee Insurance	1,097,253
	TOTAL EMPLOYEE BENEFITS	$3,477,087
311	Instructional Services	$3,493
312	Instructional Program Services	2,220
319	Other Professional and Technical Services	5,336
341	Travel—Local	5,035
353	Postage	2,402
	TOTAL PURCHASED SERVICES	$18,486
410	Supplies	$239,371
420	Textbooks	130,914
440	Periodicals	1,100
	TOTAL SUPPLIES AND MATERIALS	$371,385
541	Initial or Additional Equipment	$24,060
542	Replacement Equipment	6,021
	TOTAL CAPITAL OUTLAY	$30,081
	TOTAL HIGH SCHOOL PROGRAMS	$13,860,962

is for the subfunction of high school instruction and presents the types of expenditures planned for the area. It is but a small part of a district's total program budget; the complete budget would have similar budgets for other areas of instruction, possibly by individual schools, and by each support and administrative subfunction. Chapter Four provides a detailed description of how the budget amounts are specified.

Program, Planning, and Budgeting Systems (PPBS)[8]

This approach is sometimes called PPBES, where the E stands for evaluation. It is another type of program budgeting, but one which focuses on:

1. A careful specification and a systematic analysis of objectives.
2. A search for relevant alternatives, the different ways of achieving the objectives.
3. An estimate of the total costs of each alternative—direct and indirect costs, initial costs and those to which the alternatives would commit the organiza-

tion for future years, and dollar costs and those costs which cannot be measured in dollar terms.

4. An estimate of the effectiveness of each alternative, of how close it comes to satisfying the objective.

5. A comparison and analysis of the alternatives, seeking the combination that promises the greatest effectiveness, for the resources in achieving the objectives.[9]

In this approach the budget is organized around educational objectives which the district establishes. The expenditures are grouped by corresponding objectives, rather than by the organizational structure of the district. Consequently, expenditures in a single budget category can cut across organizational boundaries.

Two primary problems have emerged in the efforts to apply PPBS to educational budgeting: the complexity and difficulty of establishing a program structure with objectives useful for managing educational operations; and the mismatch between the budget categories in the program structure and the organizational structure responsible for operating the programs.[10] As a result, there has not been widespread use of the PPBS approach in school district budgeting.

There are many features of PPBS which are useful, however, and can be incorporated into the budgeting process. These include specification of the educational objectives of the district, identification of alternative means of reaching the objectives, multi-year cost estimates of the alternatives, selection of the most cost-effective alternative, and an evaluation of the outcomes for use in future years' decision making. These features, however, are not the exclusive property of PPBS and can be utilized by any budgeting approach without having to use the sometimes cumbersome PPBS program structure.

Zero-Based Budgeting

Zero-base budgeting is a process in which "decision packages" are prepared to describe the funding of existing and new programs at alternative service levels, both lower and higher than the current level, and funds are allocated to programs based on rankings of these alternatives.[11]

This approach is yet another way to organize a budget. The basic concept is to build and justify the entire budget each budget cycle. It attempts to avoid incremental budgeting, in which the existing budget is not questioned and attention is focused only on the new amounts or additions to be added each year. Rather, zero-base budgeting considers the entire budget and requires comparisons among all budget areas.

Obviously, zero-base budgeting is a time consuming process if practiced completely. It forces comparisons of and choices among programs and activities which are sometimes very difficult to compare adequately.

Further, it is known at the outset of the budgeting process that many of the educational programs will continue from year to year; consequently, it is not necessary to go through the exercise of justifying them annually.

Zero-base budgeting has not been widely adopted by school districts. Similar to PPBS, however, there are useful concepts, such as a periodic full scale review of operations (on a rotating basis), an analysis of alternative means of accomplishing an objective, or an examination of the consequences of not funding a given activity, which can be usefully incorporated into a district's budget process, particularly in times requiring budget cutbacks.

Conclusions

In reality, the state educational accounting manual and associated regulations may dictate the format in which a district's final budget is reported. However, there is usually sufficient flexibility for district administrators to select a particular approach for building their budgets. The choice will be influenced by the economic and political conditions facing the district. A district needing to reduce its budget to match falling revenues may wish to incorporate a ZBB approach to evaluate and compare the effects of cutbacks in various program areas as an aid in establishing budget priorities. Another district, involved in reformulating its educational objectives, could include some aspects of a PPBS approach to link the programmatic and fiscal planning activities. However, without any strong pressures to the contrary, a program budgeting approach is usually appropriate.

BUDGET CALENDAR

A budget calendar for a school district is a listing of all of the activities which are required during the budgeting process, arranged chronologically by month. The level of detail included in the calendar will depend upon how and by whom it will be used. For example, the school board will need and want a listing of the major activities to be carried out throughout the year (for example, January—first presentation of the school district budget request to the school board at the regular board meeting). The business manager, on the other hand, would need a much more detailed specification of the important tasks and subtasks which are required (like, complete the revenue estimates by individual source, print the required number of copies of the school district budget request document, publish notices informing the public of the budget meeting(s) ten days before the meeting is scheduled). In fact, several versions of a district calendar can be created, each with levels of detail appropriate to different groups or persons in the organization.

The budget calendar has several important purposes. First, it schedules all critical budget related activities at the time when they should be properly done, and establishes deadlines for their completion. This step, which requires a careful review and specification of all budget related activities, should include all important budgeting activities. A second purpose of the calendar is to allow districts to plan and carry out their budgeting processes efficiently. A third purpose is to create a device to monitor the critical activities of the budget process to make sure that they are completed at their scheduled times. The budget calendar also serves as a communication device within the district. The monthly list of activities informs members of the school district organization and community about the major events that are scheduled during the year (like deadlines for schools' submission of budget requests to district office, public budget hearings, school board meetings for budget approval, budget elections).

The timetable provided by a well-prepared budget calendar informs districts when they have to begin work on various budgeting activities to have them finished at the required time. If the interconnected activities are identified and arranged in an efficient and feasible time sequence, the budgeting process will proceed smoothly; otherwise, last minute rushes with their inevitable mistakes and omissions will plague the process.

Content of the Budget Calendar

What goes in the budget calendar? The general answer is: all important activities in the budgeting process; the dates on which they are started and/or completed; and, perhaps, the person or position who is responsible for the activity. This answer, however, begs the question of what activities are important enough to be included in the budget calendar. There is no uniform definition of what is "important enough;" what might qualify in one district could be omitted in another. The test is whether the district administration feels that the activity should receive attention and be identified separately as a necessary and significant task to be accomplished during the budget process.

It is possible, however, to specify the types of activities that are generally included in budget calendars. The major categories are described below.

Planning and preliminary steps. These are activities concerned with organizing and planning the budget development process. Included are such activities as: budget planning and orientation meetings for the school board, administrators, and the community; development of the budget calendar; data collection; and development of guidelines, materials, and instructions for budget preparation.

Budget development. Activities in this area are directly related to developing the expenditure and revenue estimates and other components of the budget document. Examples of activities which might be included in a budget calendar are: enrollment projections; development of school and district department expenditure requests; revenue estimates; and preparation of the budget document.

Review and approval.   These are primarily activities or actions which involve the school board, other public bodies, and the voting public. While the school district personnel are primarily responsible for the development of the budget requests, the proposed uses of public funds generally require some form of public review and approval. Common activities would include: receiving, reviewing, and approving the proposed school district budget; budget elections; appropriations for spending in the upcoming year; and property tax levy declaration.

Beginning a new budget year.   After the budget has been approved there are still some logistical steps necessary to start the new year properly and accurately. These include: closing accounts for the old year; opening accounts for the new year; and distributing approved budget spending limits to administrators.

Developing the Budget Calendar

How does a school district develop a useful budget calendar? As most districts have some form of budget calendar in use, the logical beginning point is the current year's calendar. It should be examined for adequacy and accuracy, and any dissatisfactions with it noted for possible modification in next year's calendar. Anticipated changes in the district's budgeting process, or state requirements which would change the budgeting activities or timing for the upcoming year, should also be included in the new calendar.

Creating a new budget calendar for the upcoming year, whether a simple modification of the current year's budget calendar or the development of an entirely new one, can be carried out in five steps. If the procedure is primarily to modify the existing budget calendar, then many of the decisions called for will already have been made. Nevertheless, it is useful to review them to make sure that they are still appropriate.

1. Determine level of detail.   As a first step in establishing a budget calendar, it is necessary to decide upon the level of detail to be specified. General activities (like estimate expenditures) provide little guidance for the actual work to be done or its timing. On the other hand, detailed activities create a bulky budget calendar which is time consuming to prepare, and difficult to use.

How do district administrators decide what is the appropriate level of detail for their district's budget calendar? It depends on who will use the calendar and for what purposes. For example, a single page calendar outlining activities of the school board in budget development may be appropriate for keeping the board informed of the overall process and alerted to the actions required of them. (The lack of detail in the calendar for this group can also keep board members properly focused on policy considerations and away from the day-to-day operating activities of developing the budget.)

On the other hand, the business manager needs a more detailed listing to organize the specific activities necessary to complete the budget accurately and on time. Other participants in the process, such as building principals, will be heavily involved in only parts of the budget development. For them, a partial, but detailed calendar covering their involvement and responsibilities along with the overall major activities could be appropriate.

For a given district the basic information contained in these different calendars will be the same, but only provided in a different level of specificity or covering only a part of the process. This suggests the creation of a master detailed calendar used by central administrators to monitor and direct the overall process, and a series of nested sub-calendars developed by condensing or segmenting the master calendar. An alternative to sub-calendars could be separate documents providing information on the budgeting activities and their timing, or a series of budget memoranda to the participants. In either way, a necessary coordination among the related budgeting activities can be achieved.

2. Identify activities.   There are two methods for identifying the necessary activities to be carried out in the budget process during the year—activity-oriented and time-oriented. The activity method is based upon identifying series of related activities and then arranging them by date. The major categories of budgeting activities for the upcoming year are identified and then the sub-activities are specified at a predetermined level of detail. All major activities and their respective sub-activities are then combined in chronological order and shown by month on the calendar.

The time-oriented method focuses on a time period, generally a month, and identifies all of the activities that should occur during that period. This approach is useful when some of the activities are specific to a particular date (such as school board member elections on the first Tuesday of May).

In practice, a combination of the two methods is useful, relying on the activity-oriented method to think through the sequence of activities and supplementing those with date-specific activities through the the time-oriented method.

3. Specify dates.   In addition to the particular activities, it is also necessary to specify the dates that they occur. Frequently, this information is developed at the same time as the activity specification.

Two types of dates can be included in the budget calendar: the date on which an activity should begin; and the date on which the activity should be completed. Both are useful in managing the budget process; the beginning date notifies administrators and others of the time when work on the task should start and the ending date gives a deadline to ensure that the budget process is not delayed. For some activities, the duration of an activity is known or can be estimated (for example, schools and district level departments require six weeks to develop their budget requests). That information, combined with either the beginning or ending date, will give the other missing date (ending or beginning) for the budget calendar.

Some activities may have dates which are mandated by statute or regulation. For example, state law may permit a district to hold budget elections only on specified dates during the year, or a budget meeting may have to be announced in the local newspaper ten days before it is held. The mandated dates for activities such as these can be utilized directly in scheduling events in the budget calendar.

Other dates are more at the district's discretion and are established so that activities can be completed within the overall budget cycle. For example, if individual schools are supposed to submit their budget requests to the district office by January 1, and they are expected to need six weeks to develop their requests, then they must be provided with the forms, instructions, and necessary data by the middle of November in order to finish on time. This, in turn, has implications for the timing of the earlier development of the school level forms and other materials by the business office.

Depending on the overall schedule, the district may have some leeway in timing certain activities. This allows flexibility in planning for these activities; for example, the district may decide that it wants to complete certain activities early to get them out of the way, or it may decide to schedule activities across several months in order to smooth out workloads, or it may decide to delay certain activities to wait until additional information may become available. The best choices for some of the discretionary dates may be known in advance by administrators based on past experience, but others will only become apparent by trying to fit all of the necessary activities into the budget calendar.

4. Identify responsible personnel.   The *who* of an activity is as important as the *what*. That is, the person or position responsible for carrying out the given activity should also be identified. This serves to communicate to others whom to hold accountable for completion of the activity. It also indicates the person to contact to obtain more information about the activity, to coordinate related activities, to ask questions about the activity, to provide relevant data, and to deal with for other necessary interactions.

A variety of people or positions can be involved in the budgeting process in one fashion or another. Obviously, the superintendent, business manager, and directors of personnel and of research and planning will be heavily involved, as will other central office staff such as those responsible for elementary and secondary curriculum, special education, and pupil personnel services. At the school level, the building principals and their administrators and secretaries will have work to do in developing their budget requests. Depending on the grade level of the school and the management strategy utilized by the principal, academic department heads, teachers, classified staff, students, and perhaps a parent or community advisory committee may also become involved in the process.

It may be useful to identify not only the person with primary responsibility for an activity, but also those persons or groups which should be informed or consulted about the activity. More broadly, districts can identify the type of involvement that various persons or groups should have with each activity on the budget calendar. At this point, however, the budget calendar may become cluttered with too much information.

To avoid overloading, districts may want to develop a separate linear responsibility chart for the budget process to be used in conjunction with the general calendar.[12] This is a specific technique for identifying the level of involvement and interactions among different groups. For each activity, the linear chart identifies the person responsible to do the actual work, any persons or groups who must be consulted, the persons or groups who are to receive the report (if any), and the persons or groups who should be notified about the activity. The linear responsibility chart provides a more detailed specification of activities along with the relationships of those involved in each activity. As such, it can provide more guidance for daily operations than a general budget calendar.

5. Construct calendar. The final step is to put together the pieces which have now been assembled. The first task is to put the fixed dates on the calendar—those which are thought to be inflexible. Next, take the date of the last event (like the school board adoption of the budget) and place it on the calendar. Now, select a series of activities which must be accomplished immediately prior to this final event and begin working backwards to place them in the calendar. To establish the starting and completion dates for each activity in the series, use known dates directly or use the estimated time needed to accomplish each activity combined with either the starting or ending date. Follow this same procedure for each series of activities. When all activities are entered on the calendar the district will have a rough first draft of the budget calendar.

Developing the budget calendar is an iterative process in which the first draft represents the district's initial estimate of when it would prefer things to occur and how long each activity is expected to take. Then the results are examined for any unacceptable results—completion time beyond latest allowable date, overlap of activities which have to be completed sequentially, not meeting mandated deadlines, or insufficient time allowed for certain activities. Where possible, completion or beginning times are changed or the time allowed for activities is modified and the calendar adjusted until an acceptable solution is achieved.

A completed example of a budget calendar for a school district for one year is illustrated in Table 2.3. In this sample calendar, the preliminary steps, such as data gathering, development of guidelines, enrollment projections, and preparation of budgeting materials for schools and district offices are scheduled during the first part of the school year. These are followed by the development of the budget requests in December and submission to the business office for consolidation in January. February is devoted to preparation of the budget document which is presented to the school board in March. This allows the board time to review the overall district budget, receive the latest revenue estimates, conduct budget elections if necessary, and to adopt the budget, appropriate funds, and levy the property taxes to support the budget by the beginning of the new school year.

PERT charts. Districts which want or need a more detailed specification of activities should consider developing and using a PERT (Planning, Evaluation, and Review Technique) chart.[13] This technique establishes a detailed list of activities necessary to carry out the budget process, charting those activities to illustrate their sequence and relationships, estimating the time required to accomplish each activity, and determining the time required for completion of the overall budget process and the critical path through the chart (the sequence of activities with the longest elapsed time through the complete budget process). Computer programs are available which will carry out the calculations involved, but the specification of activities, their relationships, and time estimates all must be established by district personnel. Creating and using a PERT chart can involve a considerable effort and represent a significant investment for the district. However, it forces a thorough examination of all of the activities required for the budget process and can provide a very useful instrument for monitoring and controlling.

Conclusions

One final point to remember about budget calendars (and linear responsibility charts or PERT charts if they are used) is that they are management tools. They should be useful and improve both the efficiency and effectiveness of a school district's operation. They should not get in the way or act as a strait jacket for administrators. If the original calendar is not working—deadlines are being missed, selection of activities is not helpful, interrelated activities are not adequately coordinated—then either the calendar should be changed or updated to reflect the actual situation more accurately or the budget process itself should be carefully reviewed for

TABLE 2.3 General Budget Calendar for 19XX–XX School Year

AUGUST
Business office begins gathering student, personnel, program, cost, and economic data.

SEPTEMBER
Superintendent and other district administrators hold planning/orientation meeting(s) with school board and any other groups directly involved with the budget process.
Superintendent, district administrators, and principals hold input sessions for district patrons.
Superintendent and business office develop proposed budget calendar.

OCTOBER
School board approves budget calendar.
Superintendent and senior district administrators (including business manager) develop cost and program guidelines for the upcoming year.
Superintendent and personnel office plan and conduct collective bargaining negotiations, if necessary.
Research and/or business offices make enrollment projections for upcoming school year and distribute them to the schools and district departments.

NOVEMBER
Business office develops and distributes budgeting forms, instructions, guidelines, and other materials for school and district staff.
Business office holds training sessions or workshops for all administrators and clerical staff involved in budget development.

DECEMBER
Schools and district level departments prepare their expenditure requests.
Business office develops revenue estimates by source of revenue.

JANUARY
Business office consolidates expenditure estimates to develop the overall district totals.
Superintendent, business office, and other district administrators review expenditure requests and adjust if necessary to balance with available revenues.

FEBRUARY
Superintendent and business office prepare complete budget message, budget document, and appropriate supplementary information for presentation to school board.

MARCH
Superintendent presents the completed budget document to the school board for their review and approval.
School board holds hearings on the proposed budget of the school district.

APRIL
Business office updates revenue estimates as new information becomes available from the tax assessor, state legislature, state department of education, and federal government agencies.

MAY
School district holds budget election(s), if necessary.

JUNE
School board adopts the budget for the upcoming school year, makes the appropriations of monies for the school district by major fund and budget category, and declares and certifies the property tax levy required to balance the budget.

JULY
Business office closes out the accounts for the year being completed, enters the appropriations for the new year into the books of account, and opens the new accounts for the new year.

AUGUST
Business office distributes the approved budget amounts for each cost center to the administrator responsible for its operation.

operating deficiencies and modified to provide better management direction and control.

ORGANIZATION FOR BUDGETING

Many people in the school district are involved in budgeting to some extent. To avoid an uncoordinated, ineffective, and potentially disruptive process, it is necessary to make clear the roles and responsibilities of the various participants. Some will be decision makers; others will provide information, advice, or expertise; still others will evaluate and pass judgment on the final product. A well-understood organizational structure for budgeting will communicate the proper roles for each person or group to play and not create false expectations of power or influence which can lead to hostile reactions.

Types of Budgeting Organizations

Like most aspects of the budgeting process, there are alternative choices for organizational structures. They range in a continuum from a process highly centralized in the district office to a highly decentralized process where the key decisions are made at the school level or even at the instructional department level. The choice of organizational structure will depend on many things—the management behavior of district administrators, particularly the superintendent, the relationship between the superintendent and the school board, the relationship between the school district and the community, and the history of the district. This section will discuss three types of budgeting organizations which represent alternative choices along a continuum. Actual district budgeting organizations will reflect variations on these three representative structures.

Highly centralized.   In this type of structure the district office controls and directs most budgeting activities. All important decisions are made at the district level, usually by the superintendent and a relatively few other key administrators. These decisions are then turned into instructions for others in the district to carry out. This is a top-down approach with little opportunity for involvement in decision making by others. Schools and departments are given specific, and often uniform, dollar amounts for each budget category (like textbooks, instructional supplies) and required to report how the monies are spent. Permission from the district office is required to transfer funds from one budget account to another to meet particular instructional needs (such as from library books into periodicals). Schools of the same grade level within a district tend to be treated the same (that is, receive the same per pupil allocation amount for supplies regardless of the types of students or age of building). The individual schools have limited recourse for additional funds to meet special needs. Equipment and other capital outlay requests, such as building improvements, are often sent by the schools to the district office to compete with similar requests districtwide for a limited pool of funds designated for those purposes. Even though the individual school capital outlay requests may be prioritized, the choices among schools and among specific items are made at the district level. Frequently, centralization of the budgeting authority coincides with centralization of other key decisions such as curriculum, personnel selection and hiring, and evaluation.

Management teams. This organizational arrangement represents an intermediate structure between centralization and decentralization. A "management team" is formed which consists of senior central office administrators and representatives of key groups in the district, such as principals, teachers, and classified staff. The role of the team members is to participate in and make key budget decisions. This procedure provides a wider range of inputs, although it can still be dominated by central office administrators.

School site budgeting.[14] This organizational arrangement is a highly decentralized process in which the basic educational decisions, such as staffing patterns, curriculum, and personnel selection, are made at the individual school level. In school site budgeting "district funds would be allocated to each school on a lump-sum basis, and program planning, implementation, and evaluation would be carried out at the school site."[15] The school site budgeting process contains five elements:

1. The establishment of an overall district budget target.
2. The establishment of basic (nonschool site) costs.
3. The assignment of all remaining funds to individual schools on a per capita basis.
4. The development of individual school expenditure plans.
5. The assembly of individual school expenditure plans into a comprehensive district budget in accordance with Item 1.[16]

Overall spending and revenue plans are coordinated by the central office to keep the district's total expenditures within available revenues. Personnel policies are also established and monitored centrally to maintain general uniformity and compliance with negotiated employee agreements. Based on the overall district budget limit, each school is notified of its total personnel allotment and the dollars available for other expenditures. The dollars are provided to the schools in an unrestricted lump-sum amount and the decisions on how to allocate these monies are made at the school level.

There are numerous ways to organize a school site budgeting process.

One involves shifting the major instructional decision making authority down the educational hierarchy from the central office administrators to the school principal. The principal, with or without the involvement of the school staff, has the responsibility for making the budget allocation decisions.[17] Another and more radical proposal involves using school site councils or parent advisory councils elected from parents with children in the school.[18] In this approach, each school has a council which functions as a mini-board for the school and has responsibility for hiring and evaluating the principal, assisting in designing the educational programs, and approving the budget for the school. The principal serves as the site educational manager, hiring other personnel, developing the budget for the school, and negotiating the school's curriculum with the teaching staff and the parent advisory council. Decision making is pushed down to the school level and involves both school personnel and community members.

Choosing an Organization for Budgeting

There are a number of considerations when selecting an organizational structure for the budgeting process. Each district must resolve these issues appropriately. Further, the budgeting process is only part of the district's operations and its organization should be consistent with the rest of the district's structure. An attempt to impose a centralized budgeting process on top of a decentralized instructional decision making process will lead to serious organizational conflicts; curricular decisions have direct fiscal implications. For example, if an individual school having instructional decision making authority decided to implement a computer assisted instruction approach throughout the school, but the central office administration denied funds to purchase the necessary equipment and software, there would be an obvious conflict. The planning, curriculum, and fiscal organizational arrangements in a district, or in a school for that matter, must mesh smoothly to ensure coordinated and effective results.

Organizational issues.   One of the key elements in selecting a particular organizational structure for budgeting is the management style, abilities, and preferences of the superintendent and other key administrators. As the person ultimately responsible for the educational and fiscal outcomes of the school district, the superintendent must function comfortably within the organizational structure of the district. A superintendent who wishes to be fully knowledgeable about every detail of the budget and to control the process closely will need a centralized budgeting organization structure to accomplish these objectives. Conversely, a superintendent who likes to delegate responsibilities to subordinates and only monitor the outcomes will require a decentralized structure. Tied in with the choice of organizational structure is the evaluation of fiscal performance for the superintendent and other administrators. Persons can only be held responsible in areas for which they have decision making authority. A centralized structure limits authority and consequently limits the accountability of middle level administrators to following budgetary instructions. On the other hand, a decentralized structure brings more people into the process in a meaningful way and can broaden the scope of evaluation for those involved to include their fiscal activities.

The role played by the school board will also influence the budgeting organization. A board which is policy oriented (one which establishes district policies and relies on district administrators to carry them out) will work easily within a decentralized structure and rely on monitoring the activities of district personnel to stay informed and in control of district operations. However, an administrative oriented board (one which gets involved in administrative decisions and operations) is likely to want a centralized structure where they have more direct control.

The type of budgeting process which has been used in the past in the district is another important consideration. Based on past experiences, both school district personnel and community members have expectations of the role that they will play and the type of involvement that they will have. Significant changes from past procedures should be preceded by a strong effort to communicate the nature and reasons for the changes to all of those involved. Otherwise, the clash between expectations and actual involvement may cause conflict in the budgeting process.

Fiscal issues. The fiscal health of a school district may also have an influence on the appropriate organizational structure for budgeting. Districts under financial pressures may control expenditure plans tightly through a centralized structure. Budgets prepared following tight guidelines issued by the central office can limit certain expenditures (like a 10 percent reduction in the total dollars available to each school for supplies, or no capital outlay requests) and reduce the time and effort needed to cut back expenditure requests to feasible levels for the upcoming year.

Another consideration is the cost savings possible through standardization of purchases in a more centralized system which can lead to volume discounts and other purchasing efficiencies. The drawback to this approach is the potential loss of flexibility for individual schools and departments to operate their desired instructional program. This is an area where curricular considerations need to be taken into account along with fiscal ones.

Key budget organization decisions. In choosing a particular organizational structure for the budgeting process, there are a number of important decisions concerning who has responsibility for the decision or at what level in the district organizational structure the decision is made; examples of questions illustrating these decisions are listed below. If the answers to the questions tend to be central office oriented, then a centralized budgeting organization structure would be appropriate. However, if it is desired to push some of the decision making responsibility down to other levels, then a more decentralized approach is necessary. Joint determination of important budgetary decisions reflects the need for an intermediate type of structure.

1. Who has responsibility for establishing the overall dollar amount for expenditures?
2. Who has responsibility for establishing the expenditure amounts for each major program or organizational unit?
3. Who has responsibility for the selection of specific resources within the allotted dollar amounts for each program?
4. Who has responsibility for curriculum selection? Does the district prescribe the curriculum and instructional materials at each school or do individual schools or teachers make those decisions?
5. Who has responsibility for the initiation of new instructional programs and/or the elimination of existing ones?
6. Who has responsibility for establishing salaries and employee benefit amounts for various employee groups?
7. Who is responsible for hiring personnel?
8. Who decides which items and amounts are to be cut if budget reductions are required?
9. Who establishes the capital expenditure budget amount and who decides on how it is allocated?

One final point of importance is the difference between recommendations and approval in the budget process. In many instances, budget decisions are influenced by several persons or groups, although the final decision may be made by an individual. The school board, for example, even if only establishing policies to be followed by district administrators, clearly influences many of the budgetary decisions, such as expenditure amounts, salary levels, curriculum selections, program adoption or elimination. However, the specific decisions for many of these aspects may actually be made by district or school level administrators. So in reviewing the questions above, keep in mind both the decision maker and those who should be contributing to the decisions as well.

Conclusions

The purpose of this section has been to describe alternative budgeting organizations. They range from a highly centralized structure dominated by central office administrators to a highly decentralized structure where central office administrators set fiscal and programmatic parameters within which school level administrators have autonomy. In either case, or in the instances in between these two poles, the link between district office and schools is critical. Although the roles and responsibilities of all persons and groups involved will depend on the type of organization and process utilized, they must be clearly identified and communicated so that all concerned understand what is expected and what part they will play in the budgeting process. This is best done by matching the management styles of the top district administrators, the expectations of the school district personnel and community, and the financial conditions facing the district with the appropriate organizational structure for district budgeting.

PROBLEMS

2.1   What type of budgeting approach is used by your school district? Is it appropriate for planning and managing the district's operations? What would be the advantages and disadvantages of changing to another type of budgeting approach?

2.2   Obtain a copy of the budget calendar for your district. Identify the activities and critical dates for:

a.)   principals

b.)   business manager

c.)   superintendent

d.)   school board.

How could the budget calendar be improved in both content and format?

2.3   What type of organization is utilized by your school district for budgeting? Where are the key decisions made? What authority/responsibility do the principals have for:

a.)   determining the level of resources available to their schools;

b.)   determining how the available resources will be spent within the school?

2.4   Assume that you have been assigned the task of advising the school board in your district of the appropriateness of school site budgeting. What arguements would you make for school site budgeting in the district? What arguements against this organizational arrangement? What implementation problems do you forsee?

NOTES

1. For discussions of the variety of budgeting approaches, see Guilbert C. Hentschke, *School Business Administration: A Comparative Perspective* (Berkeley, CA: McCutchan, 1986), Chapter 6; Barry M. Mundt, Raymond T. Olsen, and Harold I. Steinberg, *Managing Public Resources* (New York: Peat Marwick International, 1982), Chapter 4; and I. Carl Candoli et al., *School Business Administration: A Planning Approach* 3rd edition (Boston: Allyn and Bacon, 1984), Chapter 5.

2. Mundt, Olsen, and Steinberg, *Managing Public Resources*, pp. 43-46.

3. John Greenhalgh, *School Site Budgeting: Decentralized School Management* (Lanham, MD: University Press of America, 1984).

4. John Brackett, Jay Chambers, and Thomas Parrish, "The Legacy of Rational Budgeting Models and a Proposal for the Future," Project Report No. 83-A21 (Stanford, CA: Institute for Research on Educational Finance and Governance, Stanford University, 1983).

5. Mundt, Olsen, and Steinberg, *Managing Public Resources,* p. 36.

6. Mundt, Olsen, and Steinberg, *Managing Public Resources,* p. 39.

7. This approach is also called a functional budget by Walter I. Garms, James W. Guthrie, and Lawrence C. Pierce, *School Finance: The Economics and Politics of Public Education* (Englewood Cliffs, NJ: Prentice-Hall, 1978), p. 269.

8. For descriptions of PPBS applied to education, see Harry J. Hartley, *Educational Planning-Programming-Budgeting: A Systems Approach* (Englewood Cliffs, NJ: Prentice-Hall, 1968) and William H. Curtis, *Educational Resources Management System* (Chicago, IL: Research Corporation of the Association of School Business Officials, 1971).

9. Candoli et al., *School Business Administration,* p. 148.

10. Michael W. Kirst, "The Rise and Fall of PPBS in California," *Phi Delta Kappan* vol. LVI, no. 8 (April 1975), pp. 535-38.

11. Mundt, Olsen, and Steinberg, *Managing Public Resources,* p. 46.

12. A description of this technique is provided in Guilbert C. Hentschke, *Management Operations in Education* (Berkeley, CA: McCutchan, 1975), pp. 261-75.

13. For an illustration of PERT applied to school budgeting, see Hentschke, *School Business Administration,* pp. 235-57.

14. Garms, Guthrie, and Pierce, *School Finance,* pp. 278-294 and Greenhalgh, *School Site Budgeting* provide alternative conceptions of school site management and budgeting.

15. Garms, Guthrie, and Pierce, *School Finance,* p. 292.

16. Greenhalgh, *School Site Budgeting,* p. 43.

17. Candoli et al., *School Business Administration,* p. 130.

18. Garms, Guthrie, and Pierce, *School Finance,* p. 279.

3

ACCOUNTING
The Language of
Budgeting

INTRODUCTION

To manage the fiscal aspects of a school district properly, administrators must understand the accounting system used in schools. Administrators frequently are required to take actions and make decisions with important financial implications. Further, many of these decisions are informed by or are based on financial data. Nowhere is this more true than in the budgeting process. As the title to this chapter states: *Accounting is the language of budgeting.* The fundamental relationship between budgeting and accounting was recognized in a position statement by the Association of School Business Officials.

> Each school system should adopt and record an annual budget whether required by law or not, and the financial accounting structure should provide budgetary control over the school system's revenue and expenditures.[1]

For school administrators, board members, and the public to make informed judgments about the budget amounts and the allocations proposed for the various instructional and support programs, they must have the relevant financial information in a usable format. The school accounting system provides a structure for organizing and utilizing the massive amounts of budgetary and other fiscal data present in a school district. Estimates of expenditures for the educational programs offered by the district must be aggregated and presented in an understandable and consistent form. Projections of revenues to be received during the coming year must also be organized for management decisions. Without a coherent framework for dealing with financial information, administrators and others would be rapidly overwhelmed by the magnitude of financial data present in the school district.

The accounting system provides the means for keeping track of all of the important financial transactions in the school district. Through it, all fiscal data are identified, organized, and explained. *The school accounting system is the organizing basis around which the budget is developed.* Further, during the operating year it provides information for administrators to manage their programs in a fiscally responsible manner. In sum, the accounting system controls the manner in which financial information about the district is developed, maintained, and presented. It tells: (a) where the funds come from to support the district's operation; (b) how these dollars are to be spent; and (c) what the district's financial condition is. All in all, it has a very powerful and central role in school district budgeting.

The accounting system is not independent of the operations of the school district. There is a close relationship between the organizational structure and the accounting structure. A school accounting system, based on a program budget format is designed to match administrative responsibility within the district organization.[2] Through the various dimensions of the accounting system, particularly the expenditure accounts, fiscal information is collected and presented about the financial operations of individual organizational units such as school buildings, instructional departments within schools, administrative units, and support units. As a result, the accounting system has a strong influence on financial information available to administrators and on their program operations.

ACCOUNTING FOR SCHOOL SYSTEMS

Definitions and Objectives

A general definition of accounting is: "The system of classifying, recording, and summarizing financial transactions and analyzing, verifying, and reporting the results."[3] A second and similar explanation defines an accounting system as, "A means of collecting, summarizing, analyzing, and reporting, in monetary terms, information about the business."[4] A parallel definition for *school accounting* is, that the "accounting system is the means by which financial data are captured during actual operation of the LEA, recorded in the books of account, and then analyzed to produce the various kinds of reports needed."[5]

From these definitions several key points emerge to characterize an accounting system: collection of financial data; organization of these data according to a standard classification system; aggregation of similar individual transactions to yield manageable information; review and analysis of the results; and a regular reporting of the financial results.

Another important point is that the accounting system records are kept in terms of money, that is, the dollar amounts of the transactions are recorded in the ledgers and books of accounts along with some description to identify the transactions. The complete accounting system consists not only of the books recording the transactions, but also the supporting documents and papers, the reports which are generated, and the standard procedures for operating and maintaining the accounts.

A school accounting system must serve many users with diverse needs and expectations. The primary groups which have interest in the accounting system (or, more accurately, in the information provided by the accounting system) are school administrators and other employees, school boards and other governing bodies, special interest groups such as teacher associations and advocacy organizations for handicapped children, state legislatures and the U.S. Congress, creditors of the school district, and the general public—particularly district parents and voters.[6] To meet the needs of the many potential users requires a complete and informative accounting system. As a measure of comprehensiveness, Tidwell lists seven objectives for financial accounting for school systems.

1. To provide a complete record of all financial transactions of the school system.
2. To summarize, with reasonable promptness, financial transactions of the school system in financial reports required for proper, effective, and efficient administration.
3. To provide financial information which would be helpful for budget preparation, adoption, and execution.
4. To provide financial controls or safeguards for the school system's money and property.
5. To provide a basis whereby the governing board can place administrative responsibility and minimize the possibility of waste, carelessness, inefficiency, and possible fraud.
6. To provide clear and concise financial reports to the public as a basis for judging past, present, and future financial operation of the school system.
7. To provide a historical record which, over a period of years, can be studied and analyzed critically and constructively for the purpose of aiding citizens, the governing board, and the school system's administrative officers in keeping pace with the changing concepts of education.[7]

Fund Accounting[8]

In governmental accounting, including school systems, an approach known as *fund accounting* is used.

A fund is defined as an independent fiscal and accounting entity with a self-balancing set of accounts. These accounts record all assets and financial resources together with all related liabilities, encumbrances (or commitments), reserves, and equities which are segregated for the purpose of carrying on specific activities or attaining certain objectives in accordance with special regulations, restrictions, or limitations. Every school system should establish and maintain those funds required by law and sound administration.[9]

As a result of this approach, school districts create and utilize several different types of funds; however, as a rule, the number of funds should be the least number possible for the district's operation. "Only the minimum number of funds consistent with legal and operating requirements should be established, however, since unnecessary funds result in inflexibility, undue complexity, and inefficient financial administration."[10]

The most common funds and those recommended by the Governmental Accounting Standards Board, the National Center for Education Statistics, and the Association of School Business Officials can be grouped into four major classifications with separate fund types in each. The classification scheme is shown in Table 3.1 and discussed below.

Governmental Funds. The funds through which most school district functions are typically financed. Most of the operations of the district and its programs are recorded in these funds.

1. *General Fund.* The General Fund is the most common fund and is utilized by every school district. It is used to account for all financial resources except those required to be accounted for in another fund.

TABLE 3.1 Fund Classifications

CLASSIFICATION	CODE	TYPE
GOVERNMENTAL FUNDS	1	GENERAL FUND
	2	SPECIAL REVENUE FUNDS
	3	CAPITAL PROJECTS FUNDS
	4	DEBT SERVICE FUNDS
PROPRIETARY FUNDS	5	ENTERPRISE FUNDS
	6	INTERNAL SERVICE FUNDS
FIDUCIARY FUNDS	7	TRUST AND AGENCY FUNDS
ACCOUNT GROUPS	8	GENERAL FIXED ASSETS
	9	GENERAL LONG-TERM DEBT

Source: National Center for Educational Statistics, *Financial Accounting for Local and State School Systems* (Washington, DC: National Center for Educational Statistics, 1980), pp. 77–78.

2. *Special Revenue Funds.* These funds are used to account for the proceeds of special sources of revenue which are restricted to expenditures for specified educational purposes. An example would be revenues received from the federal government for the education of handicapped children. Special revenue funds maintain separate financial records to document the proper expenditure of restricted-use funds. A district may have more than one special revenue fund if needed.

3. *Capital Projects Funds.* These funds account for the financial resources involved in acquiring or constructing major capital facilities in the school district. The revenues received for capital construction (for example, from the sale of bonds or from grants from state or federal government agencies) are recorded in the capital project fund along with expenditures the purchasing or building capital facilities, such as land, buildings, or equipment. A separate fund may be used for each capital project in the district to maintain the financial integrity of the different projects.

4. *Debt Service Funds.* These funds are used to accumulate money to repay long-term debt of the school district. Long-term debt is generally in the form of bonds which have been sold previously to finance large-scale capital expenditures. The resources in debt service funds are used to pay principal and interest amounts. The creation of a debt service fund is often required as a condition of selling bonds; it can obligate the school district to establish a systematic and regular schedule of payments into the fund so that when the interest payments and bond repayments are due, there is sufficient money available. In this manner the bondholders are protected and the school district provides for the repayment in an orderly and fiscally nondisruptive fashion. A separate debt service fund for each bond issue allows the district to control and document the proper accumulation of monies to repay their long-term obligations.

Proprietary Funds. A limited number of district activities are more similar to private enterprise operations than to those typically in the public sector. These activities are intended to be financed, at least in part, through charges for their services. To account for these activities and to keep their financial records separate from the regular school district operations, various proprietary funds are used.

5. *Enterprise Funds.* These funds are used to account for businesslike operations of the school district in which direct services are provided to consumers. These consumers, either inside or outside the school system, are charged for these services and the resulting revenues are used to help pay for the costs of the operation. Common examples include food service program, interscholastic athletics, school newspaper or yearbook, bookstore operation, and transportation program.

6. *Internal Service Funds.* As the name suggests, these funds are used to account for the operation of district functions which provide goods or services to other district programs, other school districts, or other governmental agencies on a cost reimbursement basis. To develop cost information, separate funds are established to collect, record, and document the costs of the internal service functions. Examples include central warehousing and purchasing, central data processing, and central printing operations.

Fiduciary Funds.   In some instances the school district holds certain assets as a trustee or an agent. That is, the assets (or proceeds from the assets) may be administered by the district under certain legal restraints. To account for its responsibilities for these assets, fiduciary funds are established to record both the acquisition of the assets and their disposition.

7. *Trust and Agency Funds.* Trust funds are created to account for resources (property, money, income) for which the district has accepted the responsibility to act as trustee. The district administers the fund and, depending on the conditions of the trusteeship, can expend the principal amount, the income derived from the principal, or some combination of the two. Agency funds are established when the district acts as an agent to hold resources for another group and to disperse them as instructed. Examples of agency funds include funds for teacher organizations, parent organizations associated with the school, and student body monies.

Account Groups.   These are groups of accounts to maintain the records for the district's general fixed assets and general long-term liabilities. Separate account groups are utilized to record and control the long-term assets and liabilities of the district. This is particularly helpful for budgeting because the accounting transactions for current operations (expenditures and revenues planned for the coming year) are kept separate from the long-term accounts. The only exceptions to the use of the account groups are proprietary and trust funds in which the long-term assets and liabilities are accounted for in those funds directly.

8. *General Fixed Assets.* This set of accounts is used to maintain records on the purchase cost of all property, plant, and equipment, except for those recorded in the proprietary and fiduciary funds. The general fixed assets could include land and improvements, buildings and building improvements, equipment, and machinery.

9. *General Long-Term Debt.* This set of accounts is used to maintain records of the long-term liabilities of the school district, except for those recorded in the proprietary and fiduciary funds. The types of liabilities included in the accounts are general obligation bonds, capitalized lease obligations, legal judgments, special assessments payable to other governmental units, unfunded pension liabilities, and notes and warrants which are not due within one year.

Each of the funds has a code number. If there is more than one fund of a given type then the coding system will require separate numbers for the different funds. The codes are used in classifying the financial transactions by the fund in which they belong. For example, all of the expenditure accounts in the General Fund will have a fund code number of 1, while similar expenditure accounts in a special revenue fund will have the code number 2. As we will see in later sections of this chapter, each financial transaction in the district will have several code numbers assigned to it to identify it according to the proper fund, year, and type of account.

EXPENDITURE ACCOUNTS

Expenditures are the costs of doing business of a school district. They are defined as

> the cost of goods acquired or the cost of services secured, whether paid or unpaid, and include expenses, provisions for retirement of debt not reported as a liability of the fund from which retired, and capital outlays.[11]

Budgeting consists of planning the expenditures which the district expects to make along with the revenues it anticipates receiving during the upcoming school year. Since revenue projections are usually done in the district office, expenditures are the single most important type of account that involves most administrators. Consequently, there is a need for all school administrators to become well acquainted with the conceptual structure and the specific accounts and codes used in classifying expenditures. The accounting structure for expenditures serves as a fiscal language and as the primary means of communicating financial information about the district's operations. Administrators must be fluent in this language.

Need for Expenditure Classification System

The primary purpose of the expenditure accounting system is to provide information that assists the operation of the school district. The system must be able to record initial expenditure data so that they can be aggregated and reported in useful forms. This means categorizing each expenditure according to its specific characteristics relating to future reporting requirements. The expenditure accounting system should provide for accountability for proper spending, should allow managerial control to prevent excessive spending, and should fit with the organizational structure of the school district.

The accounting system used to classify and record expenditures is the most complex of any of the financial accounts. Funds only have a single dimension—the type; revenues, as we will see shortly, have two dimensions. Systems for classifying expenditures, however, generally utilize at least four separate dimensions, and up to ten dimensions are available if desired by the school district.[12]

The reason for the many categories for expenditures is that expenditure information serves many purposes and is used by many groups with different perspectives. Principals need to be informed of the authorized expenditure levels for their schools, and know how much money they have to spend in various accounts at any given time. District administrators, on the other hand, need to have expenditure data which summarizes the entire district's operations as well as to be able to monitor individual programs or schools. The school board needs fiscal information on which to base policy decisions, but would be overwhelmed by detailed records. Special interest groups want to have expenditure information about programs that involve them. A multi-dimensional expenditure classification system allows expenditure data to be identified at the lowest level of detail appropriate, and then combined and recombined to produce the expenditure summary information required by different groups.

Expenditure Classifications

Every expenditure can be classified in a variety of ways. The most common classification dimensions are: Fund, Function, Object, and Operational Unit or Cost Center. Other dimensions which may be used include: Program, Source of Funds, Instructional Organization or Level of Instruction, Job Classification Activity, Term, and Special Cost Center.[13] The regulations and guidelines for expenditure classification are specified in individual state accounting manuals, but most are based on or similar to the system set forth in a publication issued by the National Center for Educational Statistics—*Financial Accounting: Classifications and Standard Terminology for Local and State School Systems, Handbook II, Revised.* A later publication, *Financial Accounting for Local and State School Systems,* provides a revised classification system. The *Handbook II, Revised* codes will be used throughout this book for consistency, but in actual practice administrators should use the accounting system and associated codes in their own state's school accounting manual. Definitions of all account dimensions are generally given in these documents.

To classify an expenditure, it is necessary to identify to which category it belongs for every dimension used in the expenditure accounting system. As a result, each expenditure has a separate classification for every dimension. To systematize the classification process and to keep the various classifications of each transaction distinct, a coding system for expenditures is used. Each dimension has its own account codes which identify the different categories into which it is divided. Consequently, each expenditure is recorded with a series of code numbers attached to it to identify all of the relevant classification information.

For later reporting, all expenditures with the same account codes can be summed to arrive at the total amount for a particular type of expenditure. For example, all expenditures for Edison Elementary School would have a particular code number assigned to them representing the Operational Unit. To report all of the expenditures for this school, all those items with the code number for Edison School as the Operational Unit would be summed (a relatively easy task using a computerized system). To satisfy another information need—the costs of administration in all schools in the district, for example—all of the expenditures with the code for school-level administration in the Function dimension would be aggregated. Note that this would include the administrative expenditures for Edison School along with those of the other schools in the district. With an accounting system that identifies expenditures along multiple dimensions the principal's salary can be correctly included in cost reports for both the cost of the school and for the cost of school administration, as the the occasion warrants.

Fund. Fund accounting has been discussed above. For expenditure classification, it is necessary to identify the fund in which each expenditure belongs. Table 3.1 lists the funds and their code numbers.

Function. The function represents the purpose of the expenditure. It is the reason or objective or the *why* of the expenditure.

> Function means the action a person takes or the purpose for which a thing exists or is used. Function includes the activities or actions which are performed to accomplish the objectives of an enterprise.[14]

In this accounting system, the financial activities of school districts are divided into five major functions: Instruction, Supporting Services, Community Services, Nonprogrammed Charges, and Debt Services. (The revised *Financial Accounting for Local and State School Systems* lists the five major functions as: Instruction, Support Services, Operation of Non-Instructional Services, Facilities Acquisition and Construction Services, and Other Uses.) Each of these functions is subdivided into Subfunctions, Service Areas, and Areas of Responsibility which represent further levels of specificity and detail of expenditure classification. Table 3.2 provides a listing of the expenditure functions and codes.

The two most important functions for a school system are Instruction and Supporting Services. Instruction is defined as

> Activities dealing directly with the teaching of pupils, or the interaction between teacher and pupils. Teaching may be provided for pupils in a school classroom, in another location . . . and in other learning situations. . . . It may also be provided through some other approved medium. . . . Included are the activities of aides or assistants of any type . . . which assist in the instructional process.[15]

Supporting Services, by contrast,

> are those services which provide administrative, technical, personal . . . and logistical support to facilitate and enhance Instruction. . . . Supporting Services exist to sustain and enhance Instruction, rather than as entities within themselves.[16]

The distinction is an important one and is maintained throughout the function structure. Only activities relating directly to student instruction

TABLE 3.2   Function Dimension of Expenditures

1000   Instruction
   1100   Regular Programs
      1110   Elementary Programs
      1120   Middle/Junior High Programs
      1130   High School Programs
         1131   Preparatory, Postsecondary Education Programs
         1132   Preparatory, Postsecondary Employment Programs
         1139   Other High School Programs
      1190   Other Regular Programs

   1200   Special Programs
      1210   Programs for Gifted and Talented
      1220   Programs for Mentally Retarded
      1230   Programs for Physically Handicapped
      1240   Programs for Emotionally Disturbed
      1250   Programs for Culturally Different
      1260   Programs for Pupils With Learning Disabilities
      1290   Other Special Programs

   1300   Adult/Continuing Education Programs
      1310   Adult Basic Education Programs
      1320   Advanced Adult Education Programs
      1330   Occupational Programs
      1340   Upgrading in Current Occupation Programs
      1350   Retraining for New Occupation Programs
      1360   Special Interest Programs
      1370   Life Enrichment Programs
      1390   Other Adult/Continuing Education Programs

2000   Supporting Services
   2100   Support Services–Pupils
      2110   Attendance and Social Work Services
         2111   Service Area Direction
         2112   Attendance Services
         2113   Social Work Services
         2114   Pupil Accounting Services
         2119   Other Attendance and Social Work Services
      2120   Guidance Services
         2121   Service Area Direction
         2122   Counseling Services
         2123   Appraisal Services
         2124   Information Services
         2125   Record Maintenance Services
         2126   Placement Services
         2129   Other Guidance Services
      2130   Health Services
         2131   Service Area Direction
         2132   Medical Services
         2133   Dental Services
         2134   Nurse Services
         2139   Other Health Services

TABLE 3.2 *(Continued)*

    2140   Psychological Services
        2141   Service Area Direction
        2142   Psychological Testing Services
        2143   Psychological Counseling Services
        2144   Psychotherapy Services
        2149   Other Psychological Services
    2150   Speech Pathology and Audiology Services
        2151   Service Area Direction
        2152   Speech Pathology Services
        2153   Audiology Services
        2159   Other Speech Pathology and Audiology Services
2200   Support Services–Instructional Staff
    2210   Improvement of Instruction Services
        2211   Service Area Direction
        2212   Instruction and Curriculum Development Services
        2213   Instructional Staff Training Services
        2219   Other Improvement of Instruction Services
    2220   Educational Media Services
        2221   Service Area Direction
        2222   School Library Services
        2223   Audiovisual Services
        2224   Educational Television Services
        2225   Computer-Assisted Instruction Services
        2229   Other Educational Media Services
2300   Support Services–General Administration
    2310   Board of Education Services
        2311   Service Area Direction
        2312   Board Secretary Services
        2313   Board Treasurer Services
        2314   Election Services
        2315   Legal Services
        2316   Tax Assessment and Collection Services
        2317   Audit Services
        2319   Other Board of Education Services
    2320   Executive Administration Services
        2321   Office of the Superintendent Services
        2322   Community Relations Services
        2323   Staff Relations and Negotiations Services
        2324   State and Federal Relations Services
        2329   Other Executive Administration Services
2400   Support Services–School Administration
    2410   Office of the Principal Services
    2490   Other Support Services–School Administration
2500   Support Services–Business
    2510   Direction of Business Support Services
    2520   Fiscal Services
        2521   Service Area Direction
        2522   Budgeting Services
        2523   Receiving and Disbursing Funds Services
        2524   Payroll Services

TABLE 3.2   *(Continued)*

    2525 Financial Accounting Services
    2526 Internal Auditing Services
    2527 Property Accounting Services
    2529 Other Fiscal Services
  2530 Facilities Acquisition and Construction Services
    2531 Service Area Direction
    2532 Land Acquisition and Development Services
    2533 Architecture and Engineering Service
    2534 Educational Specifications Development Services
    2535 Building Acquisition, Construction, and Improvements Services
    2539 Other Facilities Acquisition, and Construction Services
  2540 Operation and Maintenance of Plant Services
    2541 Service Area Direction
    2542 Care and Upkeep of Buildings Services
    2543 Care and Upkeep of Grounds Services
    2544 Care and Upkeep of Equipment Services
    2545 Vehicle Servicing and Maintenance Services (other than buses)
    2546 Security Services
    2549 Other Operation and Maintenance of Plant Services
  2550 Pupil Transportation Services
    2551 Service Area Direction
    2552 Vehicle Operation Service
    2553 Monitoring Services
    2554 Vehicle Servicing and Maintenance Services
    2559 Other Pupil Transportation Services
  2560 Food Services
    2561 Service Area Direction
    2562 Food Preparation and Dispensing Services
    2563 Food Delivery Services
    2569 Other Food Services
  2570 Internal Services
    2571 Service Area Direction
    2572 Purchasing Services
    2573 Warehousing and Distributing Services
    2574 Printing, Publishing, and Duplicating Services
    2579 Other Internal Services
  2590 Support Services–Business
2600 Support Services–Central
  2610 Direction of Central Support Services
  2620 Planning, Research, Development, and Evaluation Services
    2621 Service Area Direction
    2622 Development Services
    2623 Evaluation Services
    2624 Planning Services
    2625 Research Services
    2629 Other Planning, Research, Development, and Evaluation Services
  2630 Information Services
    2631 Service Area Direction
    2632 Internal Information Services
    2633 Public Information Services
    2634 Management Information Services
    2635 Other Information Services

TABLE 3.2 (Continued)

```
  2640   Staff Services
         2641   Service Area Direction
         2642   Recruitment and Placement Services
         2643   Staff Accounting Services
         2644   Inservice Training Services (for noninstructional staff)
         2645   Health Services
         2649   Other Staff Services
  2650   Statistical Services
         2651   Service Area Direction
         2652   Statistical Analysis Services
         2653   Statistical Reporting Services
         2659   Other Statistical Services
  2660   Data Processing Services
         2661   Service Area Direction
         2662   Systems Analysis Services
         2663   Programing Services
         2664   Operations Services
         2669   Other Data Processing Services
  2690   Other Support Services–Central
2900   Other Supporting Services

3000  Community Services
  3100   Direction of Community Services
  3200   Community Recreation Services
  3300   Civic Services
  3400   Public Library Services
  3500   Custody and Care of Children Services
  3600   Welfare Activities Services
  3800   Nonpublic School Pupils Services
  3900   Other Community Services

4000  Nonprogramed Charges
  4100   Payments to Other Governmental Units (within the State)
  4200   Payments to Other Governmental Units (outside the State)
  4300   Transfers of Funds

5000  Debt Services
```

Source: Charles T. Roberts and Allan R. Lichtenberger, *Financial Accounting: Classifications and Standard Terminology for Local and State School Systems*, State Educational Records and Reports Series: Handbook II, Revised (Washington, DC: U.S. Government Printing Office, 1973), pp. 24–27.

are classified under the instruction function and subfunctions; all others are classified under other functional areas. For example, at the school building level, teachers, instructional aides, instructional supplies, textbooks would all be coded as instructional expenditures, while the principal, school secretary, and other office expenditures would be recorded as school administration—a supporting service function. In this way, the costs of instruction can be kept separate and not combined irretrievably with other types of expenditures.

As the table illustrates, the functions are nested—that is, the lowest levels of activity with similar operational objectives are grouped together under the next level heading, and the activities at this level are then grouped under the next highest level, and so forth. In this manner, High School, Middle/Junior High, and Elementary program expenditures are components of Regular Program expenditures, which are themselves a part of total Instructional expenditures.

The coding system associated with the function dimension structure helps to distinguish the various functions readily. All expenditures have a four digit function code. The first digit represents the major function. So, the function code for all instructional expenditures will begin with the number 1 and the function code for all supporting services expenditures will begin with the number 2. The second digit indicates the subfunction, the third digit specifies the service area, and the fourth digit (if used) identifies the area of responsibility, which can specify the subject matter area in the instruction function sequence or a specific activity in the support services function sequence. For example, a function code of 1120 represents Middle/Junior High Programs, while a code of 2522 is used for Budgeting Services. Table 3.3 illustrates the nested arrangement of functions for these two examples. Budgeting is one element of Fiscal Services, which itself is a component of Business Services, which in turn is one of the Support Services.

Object.   The object is the item for which the expenditure is made. If the function dimension describes the why of the expenditure, the object dimension specifies the *what* of the expenditure. It is defined formally as "the service or commodity obtained as the result of a specific expenditure"[17]

Objects are divided into seven major categories: salaries, employee benefits, purchased services, supplies and materials, capital outlay, other objects, and transfers. Taken together, these categories cover all goods and services which school districts purchase. Each of the main categories has further subdivisions which provide more specific classification of object expenditures. Table 3.4 provides a listing of the object categories.

The object dimension also has its own coding system to identify the types of expenditures. It utilizes a three digit code in which the first digit represents the main category (such as, 100 for Salaries, 200 for Employee Benefits). The second and third digits allow expenditures to be coded more precisely within the object main category.

Salaries. Amounts paid to employees of the LEA {Local Education Agency or school district} who are considered to be in positions of a permanent nature or hired temporarily, including personnel substituting for those in permanent positions. This includes gross salary for personal services rendered while ON THE PAYROLL of the LEA.[18]

The object account listing for Salaries in Table 3.4 shows three subdivi-

TABLE 3.3 Function Dimension Illustrations

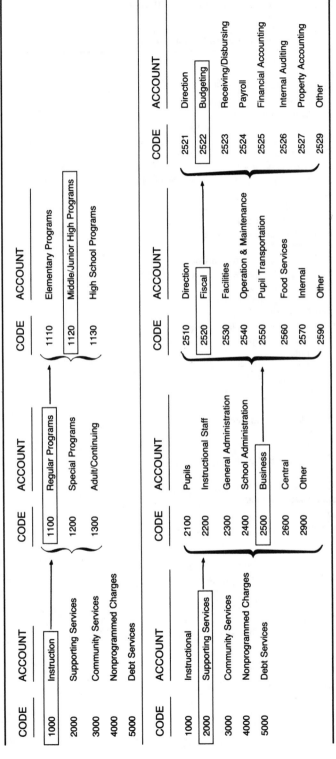

CODE	ACCOUNT
1000	Instruction
2000	Supporting Services
3000	Community Services
4000	Nonprogrammed Charges
5000	Debt Services

CODE	ACCOUNT
1100	Regular Programs
1200	Special Programs
1300	Adult/Continuing

CODE	ACCOUNT
1110	Elementary Programs
1120	Middle/Junior High Programs
1130	High School Programs

CODE	ACCOUNT
1000	Instructional
2000	Supporting Services
3000	Community Services
4000	Nonprogrammed Charges
5000	Debt Services

CODE	ACCOUNT
2100	Pupils
2200	Instructional Staff
2300	General Administration
2400	School Administration
2500	Business
2600	Central
2900	Other

CODE	ACCOUNT
2510	Direction
2520	Fiscal
2530	Facilities
2540	Operation & Maintenance
2550	Pupil Transportation
2560	Food Services
2570	Internal
2590	Other

CODE	ACCOUNT
2521	Direction
2522	Budgeting
2523	Receiving/Disbursing
2524	Payroll
2525	Financial Accounting
2526	Internal Auditing
2527	Property Accounting
2529	Other

TABLE 3.4   Object Dimension of Expenditures

100 Salaries
   110 Regular Salaries
   120 Temporary Salaries
   130 Overtime Salaries
200 Employee Benefits
300 Purchased Services
   310 Professional and Technical Services
      311 Instruction Services
      312 Instructional Programs Improvement Services
      313 Pupil Services
      314 Staff Services
      315 Management Services
      316 Data Processing Services
      317 Statistical Services
      318 Board of Education Services
      319 Other Professional and Technical Services
   320 Property Services
      321 Public Utilities Services
      322 Cleaning Services
      323 Repairs and Maintenance Services
      324 Property Insurance
      325 Rentals
      329 Other Property Services
   330 Transportation Services
      331 Pupil Transportation
      332 Travel
      339 Other Transportation Services
   340 Communication
   350 Advertising
   360 Printing and Binding
   370 Tuition
   390 Other Purchased Services
400 Supplies and Materials
   410 Supplies
   420 Textbooks
   430 Library Books
   440 Periodicals
   450 Warehouse Inventory Adjustment
   490 Other Supplies and Materials
500 Capital Outlay
   510 Land
   520 Buildings
   530 Improvements Other Than Buildings
   540 Equipment
   550 Vehicles
   560 Library Books
   590 Other Capital Outlay

TABLE 3.4 *(Continued)*

600 Other Objects
    610 Redemption of Principal
    620 Interest
    630 Housing Authority Obligations
    640 Dues and Fees
    650 Insurance and Judgments
       651 Liability Insurance
       652 Fidelity Bond Premiums
       653 Judgments Against the LEA
       659 Other Insurance and Judgments
    690 Miscellaneous Objects
700 Transfers
    710 Fund Modifications
    720 Transits
    790 Other Transfers

Source: Charles T. Roberts and Allan R. Lichtenberger, *Financial Accounting: Classifications and Standard Terminology for Local and State School Systems*, State Educational Records and Reports Series: Handbook II, Revised (Washington, DC: U.S. Government Printing Office, 1973), pp. 24–27.

sions: Regular Salaries, Temporary Salaries, and Overtime Salaries. Note that leaving the account structure at this second digit level does not allow differentiation between certificated and noncertificated employees. To accomplish this separation, both in budget planning and in reporting and management, it would be necessary to establish third level (digit) categories for Salaries. For example, one state's accounting manual has created Object 111 for Regular Certificated Salaries and Object 112 for Regular Noncertificated Salaries. Similar subdivisions are established for the other types of second level salary categories.[19]

> *Employee Benefits.* Amounts paid by the LEA in behalf of employees; these amounts are not included in the gross salary, but are over and above. Such payments are fringe benefit payments, and while not paid directly to employees, nevertheless are part of the cost of salaries and benefits.[20]

States and school districts have a wide variety of employee benefits which they provide and there is not sufficient standardization among them to make a common specification of second or third level benefits feasible. Consequently, no subdivisions of Employee Benefits were established in the Object listing in the National Center for Educational Statistics' *Financial Accounting, Handbook II, Revised* (Table 3.4). In practice, state accounting manuals may provide specific accounts and codes for some of the most common types of benefits in the state, such as employee retirement contributions, social security, health and life insurance, and Workmen's Compensation. If districts need further accounts for their particular benefit expenditures, they may be allowed to establish additional subaccounts and codes within the overall Employee Benefits object.

> *Purchased Services.* Amounts paid for personal services rendered by personnel who are not on the payroll of the LEA, and other services which the LEA may purchase.[21]

Purchased Services is the object of the expenditure category used to record the budgeted costs of personnel and nonpersonnel services to be obtained from individuals or firms outside the school district. The key aspect of purchased services is that they are performed by or purchased from individuals who are not employees of the school district or from organizations or agencies outside the district. That is, the source of the purchased services is *external,* not internal. This category covers a wide variety of items as shown in Table 3.4. The definitions below illustrate the range of expenditures included in this object.

> *Professional and Technical Services.* Services which by their nature can be performed only by persons with specialized skills and knowledge. Included are the services of architects, engineers, auditors, dentists, medical doctors, lawyers, consultants, teachers, and accountants.
>
> *Property Services.* Services purchased to operate, repair, maintain, insure, and rent property which is owned and/or used by the LEA. These services are performed by persons other than LEA employees.
>
> *Transportation Services.* Expenditures for transporting children to school and official travel of LEA employees.
>
> *Communication.* Services provided by persons or businesses to assist in transmitting and receiving messages or information.
>
> *Advertising.* Expenditures for printed announcements in professional periodicals and newspapers or announcements broadcast by radio and television networks. These expenditures include advertising for such purposes as personnel recruitment, bond sales, used equipment sales, and other objects. Costs for professional fees for advertising or public relation services are not recorded here but are charged to Professional Services.
>
> *Printing and Binding.* Expenditures for job printing and binding, usually according to the specifications of the LEA. This includes the design and printing of forms and posters as well as printing and binding of district publications. Preprinted standard forms are not charged here, but are recorded under Supplies and Materials.
>
> *Tuition.* Expenditures to reimburse other educational agencies for services rendered to students residing in the legal boundaries described for the paying LEA.
>
> *Other Purchased Services.* Expenditures for all other purchased services not included above.[22]

The chart of accounts used by many states contain similar classifications of Purchased Services and may expand this listing to include additional items in this category not specified in this standard set of accounts.

Supplies and Materials. Amounts paid for material items of an expendable nature that are consumed, worn out, or deteriorated by use; or items that lose their identity through fabrication or incorporation into different or more complex units or substances.[23]

Supplies and Materials are items purchased by the school district for current use, usually within one year. Any article or material which meets *one* or more of the criteria listed below is to be considered a supply item.

1. It is consumed in use.
2. It loses its original shape or appearance with use.
3. It is expendable, that is, if the article is damaged or some of its parts are lost or worn out, it is usually more feasible to replace it with an entirely new unit rather than repair it (which is not true of equipment).
4. It is an inexpensive item, having characteristics of equipment, whose small unit cost makes it inadvisable to capitalize the item.
5. It loses its identity through incorporation into a different or more complex unit or substance.[24]

There is sometimes confusion over whether an item should be classified as a supply or an equipment item. Many state accounting manuals contain lists of common supply items and common equipment items for reference. If the item is not found in the list, then the criteria listed above can be utilized.

Capital Outlay. Expenditures for the acquisition of fixed assets or additions to fixed assets. They are expenditures for land or existing buildings; improvements of grounds; construction of buildings; additions to buildings; remodeling of buildings; initial equipment; additional equipment; and replacement equipment.[25]

From this definition it is clear that expenditures for capital outlay are generally for more expensive items that are expected to be kept by the school district for more than one year and that are presumed to have benefits over several years.

By far the most common type of capital outlay expenditure in the district's operating budget is for equipment. *Handbook II, Revised* recommends the establishment of subaccounts for equipment to distinguish between initial and additional equipment (which increases the stock of equipment in the district) and replacement equipment (which results in no net increase in equipment for the district).

Occasionally it is difficult to differentiate between equipment and supplies when including an item in the operating budget. A material item is considered to be *equipment* when it meets *all* of the criteria listed below. Again, most state accounting manuals contain a reference list of the most commonly used supply and equipment items.

1. It retains its original shape and appearance with use.

2. It is nonexpendable, that is, if the article is damaged or some of its parts are lost or worn out, it is usually more feasible to repair it rather than replace it with an entirely new unit (which is not true of supplies).

3. It represents an investment of money which makes it feasible and advisable to capitalize the item.

4. It does not lose its identity through incorporation into a different or more complex unit or substance.[26]

Other Objects. Amounts paid for goods and services not otherwise classified. This includes expenditures for the retirement of debt, the payment of interest on debt, payments to a housing authority, and the payment of dues and fees.[27]

Transfers. This object category does not represent a purchase; rather, it is used as an accounting entity to show that funds have been handled without having goods and services rendered in return. Included here are transactions for interchanging money from one fund to the other and for transmitting flow-through funds to the recipient (person or agency).[28]

Operational Unit or Cost Center. Another useful way of classifying expenditures is by cost center. This dimension categorizes district expenditures by location. It can be used to collect and report expenditures by school building, district-level department, or other appropriate cost centers. The operational unit classification matches fiscal information with the organizational structure of the district. It allows accountability for budgeting and expenditure control to be established with administrators of operational units in the district.

The operational unit dimension is generally optional for school districts, but it can greatly enhance the capability for financial management and administration. The coding system utilized for operational units will depend on the individual district, but it will allow each unit to be identified with a separate code number.

Expenditure Accounts Summary. Each expenditure is given a multipart code to identify it along the various dimensions used in the district's expenditure accounting system. Each part of the code represents a single dimension. When this information is recorded into the books of account, or, more probably, into a computerized accounting system, it preserves all of the necessary data to summarize and report expenditure information along different dimensions for different purposes.

For example, let us assume that Evergreen School District has an expenditure accounting system that incorporates five different dimensions: Fund, Year, Function, Object, and Cost Center. To record the purchase of $100.00 of instructional supplies by Edison Elementary School, the following code would be entered along with the expenditure amount:

1 88 1110 410 105 $100.00

To those unfamiliar with the district's financial accounting system, the code numbers would be meaningless. However, those knowledgeable about the system would interpret the coded transaction as follows:

DIMENSION	CODE	EXPLANATION
Fund:	1	General Fund
Year:	88	for the school year 1987–88
Function:	1110	Elementary Programs
Object:	410	Instructional Supplies
Cost Center:	105	Edison School

The format for the complete code of an expenditure item would depend on the particular district and its accounting system. However, in the version shown above each dimension has its own field in the overall code, separated by spaces for clarity.

If the district wishes or has additional dimensions in its expenditure accounting system, then these codes would also be included in the complete code. Possibilities for other dimensions include Program (a group of activities designed to achieve a particular set of objectives), Source of Funds (useful for matching expenditures with restricted revenues), Job Classification (categories of work performed by district employees), and Term (or an instructional period less than one year).

REVENUE ACCOUNTS

Revenue is the income received by a school district. The formal definition is that revenues are "additions to assets which do not increase any liability, do not represent the recovery of an expenditure, do not represent the cancellation of certain liabilities without a corresponding decrease in other liabilities or a decrease in assets."[29] This definition distinguishes between revenues—which increase the net worth of the school district—and other forms of money which the district may receive, such as expenditure reimbursements, repayment of debts, or exchange of an asset for cash—which are exchanges that do not increase the net worth of the school district.

Budgeting for revenues consists of estimating the amount of revenue to be received by the school district during the upcoming year from each possible source. As noted before, revenues are an essential component of the district's budget. Revenues should be greater than or equal to expenditures in the budget; as a general rule, school districts are not allowed deficit spending. Consequently, accurate revenue projection is necessary in order to estimate the expenditures that can be supported, and in turn, to plan the educational program that the district will provide.

Revenue Classifications

In contrast to the expenditure classification system, revenue classification is quite simple. First revenues are classified by the *fund* to which they belong. All revenues, except those which are required to be recorded in a different fund, are classified in the General Fund. For example, districts receiving state and federal categorical monies for handicapped students are required to verify that these monies are spent only on the intended recipients; recording these revenues and their associated expenditures in a Special Revenue Fund provides an accounting record of proper usage. However, general state aid, which has no expenditure restrictions, would be recorded in the General Fund. In a similar manner, monies from sale of construction bonds are placed in a Capital Projects Fund to maintain them separately from regular district operations.

The most important means of categorizing revenues, however, is *source.* The classification system for revenues is based on the categories of possible sources for school districts. Other than by fund, this is the only classification dimension for revenues.

Revenue sources are divided into five main areas according to the level in the educational system: Local, Intermediate, State, Federal, and Other. A listing of the revenues by source and their codes is shown in Table 3.5.

Revenues have their own coding system, based on source and subdivisions within each source. A four digit code is assigned to each revenue transaction; the first digit represents the major level of the source. For ex-

TABLE 3.5 Revenue Categories

CODE	TYPE OF REVENUE

1000 REVENUE FROM LOCAL SOURCES
   1100 Taxes
      1110 Property Taxes Levied by District
      1120 Property Taxes Levied by Another Governmental Unit
      1130 Sales and Use Taxes
      1140 Income Taxes
      1180 Other Taxes
      1190 Penalties and Interest on Taxes
   1200 Revenue from Local Governmental Units Other than School Districts
   1300 Tuition
      1310 Regular Day School Tuition
      1320 Adult/Continuing Education Tuition
      1330 Summer School Tuition
   1400 Transportation Fees
   1500 Earnings on Investments
      1510 Interest on Investments
      1520 Dividends on Investments
      1530 Gain or Loss on Sale of Investments

TABLE 3.5 *(Continued)*

CODE   TYPE OF REVENUE

1600   Food Services
   1610   Sales to Pupils
   1620   Sales to Adults
1700   Pupil Activities
   1710   Admissions
   1720   Bookstore Sales
   1730   Pupil Organization Membership
   1790   Other Pupil Activity Income
1900   Other Revenue from Local Sources
   1910   Rentals
   1920   Contributions and Donations from Private Sources
   1940   Services Provided to Other School Districts
   1980   Premium on Bonds Sold
   1990   Miscellaneous

2000   REVENUE FROM INTERMEDIATE SOURCES
   2100   Grants-In-Aid
      2110   Unrestricted Grants-In-Aid
      2120   Restricted Grants-In-Aid
   2200   Revenue in Lieu of Taxes
   2300   Revenue for/on Behalf of School District

3000   REVENUE FROM STATE SOURCES
   3100   Grants-In-Aid
      3110   Unrestricted Grants-In-Aid
      3120   Restricted Grants-In-Aid
   3200   Revenue in Lieu of Taxes
   3300   Revenue for/on Behalf of School District

4000   REVENUE FROM FEDERAL SOURCES
   4100   Grants-In-Aid
      4110   Unrestricted Grants-in-Aid Received Directly from Federal Government
      4120   Unrestricted Grants-In-Aid Received from Federal Government Through the State
      4130   Restricted Grants-In-Aid Received Directly from Federal Government
      4140   Restricted Grants-In-Aid Received from Federal Government Through the State
   4200   Revenue in Lieu of Taxes
   4300   Revenue for/on Behalf of School District

5000   OTHER SOURCES
   5100   Sale of Bonds
      5110   Bond Principal
      5120   Premium
      5130   Accrued Interest
   5200   Interfund Transfers
   5300   Sale or Compensation for Loss of Fixed Assets

Source: Charles T. Roberts and Allan R. Lichtenberger, *Financial Accounting: Classifications and Standard Terminology for Local and State School Systems*, State Educational Records and Reports Series: Handbook II, Revised (Washington, DC: U.S. Government Printing Office, 1973), pp. 13–15.

ample, all local revenues are in the 1000 revenue category, while intermediate revenues have a 2000 code number, state revenues a 3000 code number, federal revenues a 4000 code number, and other revenues a 5000 code number.[30] Further subdivisions within a major source use second and third digits in the code. For example, revenue account 1110 Property Taxes Levied by the District is a component of the more general account 1100 Taxes.

Definitions of each of the major revenue sources illustrate the kinds of monies recorded under each type.

> *Local Revenues.* ". . . the amount of money produced within the boundaries of the LEA and available to the LEA for its use. Money collected in the same amount by another governmental unit as an agent of the LEA (less collection costs), is recorded as revenue from local sources. Shared revenue (revenue levied by another governmental unit, but shared in proportion to the amount collected within the LEA) is also recorded as revenue from local sources."

> *Intermediate Revenues.* ". . . revenue from funds collected by an intermediate administrative unit, or a political subdivision between the LEA and the state, and distributed to LEAs in amounts that differ in proportion to those which were collected within such systems."

> *State Revenues.* ". . . revenue from funds collected by the State and distributed to LEAs in amounts different proportionately from those which were collected within such LEAs."

> *Federal Revenues.* ". . . revenue from funds collected by the Federal Government and distributed to LEAs in amounts different proportionately from those which were collected within such LEAs. It is unimportant whether the funds are distributed directly to the LEA by the Federal Government or through some intervening agency such as the State."

> *Other Sources.* Revenues received by the school district which are not accounted for under the other four categories are listed in this category. Examples include such transactions as Sale of Bonds and Sale or Compensation for Loss of Fixed Assets.[31]

Local revenue sources are varied. As illustrated in Table 3.5, examples include taxes levied by or for the school district, tuition, transportation fees, earnings on investments made by the school district, food sales, student activities for which fees are charged, rentals, donations, and fees for services provided to others.

The bulk of funds received by school districts from outside sources fall into one of three categories: unrestricted grants-in-aid, restricted grants-in aid, and revenue in lieu of taxes. These categories comprise the subsources listed for intermediate, state, and federal revenue sources in Table 3.5.

> *Unrestricted Grants-in-Aid.* These funds are often referred to as *General Aid* monies. They are provided to the district for educational purposes from state and federal agencies without any restriction as to their use. The district can utilize these funds for any legal purpose. The bulk of state support comes to

districts in this form. These funds can be viewed as the state's share of the costs of basic education for students in the state. On the other hand, relatively few federal funds which districts receive fall into this category.

Restricted Grants-in Aid. These funds are commonly known as *Categorical Aid.* They are provided to school districts for particular purposes, such as education for handicapped children, vocational education, compensatory education. They can only be used for their designated purposes. The state and federal government provide these funds to encourage school districts to undertake certain activities or programs which they might otherwise find too expensive to operate from local funds alone, and to assist the districts in operating state mandated programs. Special accounting records are necessary to record the receipt and expenditure of these funds for the appropriate purposes. Most of the revenues received by school districts from the federal government are categorical and targeted for specific purposes or populations.

Revenue in Lieu of Taxes. State or federal property located within school district boundaries is not taxable. If the amount of property removed from the tax rolls is substantial, for example a large military installation or a national forest, then the loss of property tax revenues (if the property had been privately owned) can have a serious impact on the district. Additionally, due to actions by the state or federal governments, certain privately owned property may not be taxed on the same basis as other privately owned property. For example, in some states, timber land is not subject to a local property tax, but instead timber owners pay a severance tax to the state on the timber when it is harvested. This allows the owners to match the timing of their own revenues and taxes, but it eliminates regular property tax payments to school districts. To reduce the impact of these state and federal activities, these governments make payments to school districts which are designed to replace the lost property taxes. These payments are known as *revenue in lieu of taxes.* They come to districts without restrictions on their use and function as unrestricted funds.

When recording a revenue transaction, it is first necessary to determine the fund to which it belongs; that is, which fund is to receive the credit for the revenue. The next step is to identify the major source from which the revenue is obtained: local, intermediate, state, federal, or other. The final task is to specify the particular type of revenue within the major source. Then the revenue amount can be entered into the books of account properly, and the revenue information correctly maintained. For example, a common type of revenue is state aid received by the school district at regular intervals during the school year. The fund for these revenues would be the General Fund because they are not restricted to any special purposes. The major source would be Revenue from State Sources, and within this category the more specific source would be revenue account 3100 Unrestricted Grants-in-Aid. If there are several different types of unrestricted state revenues, the state or district accounting manual should have further detailed subsource revenue codes to distinguish among them. In this way, the different types of revenues can be kept separate for reporting and management purposes.

FINANCIAL STATEMENTS

There are many different types of financial statements which can be prepared by a school district.[32] Primarily, the statements present summaries of relevant financial information and inform various individuals and groups about the financial status of the district. For a complete district summary, the financial statement would be a combined one that includes a separate column for each of the funds used in the district's accounting system. Financial statements can also be prepared for only a single fund.

A *balance sheet* is designed to summarize the assets, liabilities, and fund balances of the district at a particular time, often the end of a fiscal year or some intermediate accounting period. A *statement of changes in financial position* identifies both the sources and uses of working capital (assets less liabilities) for a given time period.

Of more direct concern to school budgeting are the statements involving financial information about revenues and expenditures. Table 3.6 provides an example of a *Combined Statement of Revenues, Expenditures, and Fund Balances.* Notice the separate columns for each fund, and that since each one is an independent financial entity, the total amount across all funds for the same account is for information only. Since this statement is for a fiscal year, the amounts shown are the totals in each account (revenues received or expenditures made) summarized over the one year period. The excess of revenues over expenditures (or the shortfall) is added to (or subtracted from) the fund balance at the beginning of the fiscal year to calculate it at the end of the year.

Another type of financial statement and one which is of particular interest for management of budgets during the year is a *statement of revenues, expenditures, and changes in fund balance—budget and actual.* As shown in Table 3.7, this type of statement is prepared for a single fund and it compares the actual results of district operations with those budgeted for a given time period. The revenues actually received are summarized and matched against the revenue projections on an account by account basis. The overages represent more actual revenue than was originally budgeted, while the underages indicate a shortfall. The same comparison is done for expenditures, except that overages here represent actual expenditures greater than those budgeted and underages show accounts where actual expenditures were less than those budgeted. In this example, the financial statement is for the fiscal year and presents the results the the year's operations after it is over.

Similar statements can be prepared during the year to present interim results for a three or six month period. If serious deviations from the budget are indicated, there may be time to correct them. Used in this manner, a financial statement can be a management tool rather than a historical report.

TABLE 3.6 Combined Statement of Revenues, Expenditures, and Changes in Fund Balances

Example B—School district XYZ: combined statement of revenues, expenditures, and changes in fund balances; all governmental fund types and expendable trust funds, for the fiscal year ended June 30, 19XX

| | GOVERNMENTAL FUND TYPES | | | | FIDUCIARY FUND TYPE | |
	GENERAL	SPECIAL REVENUE	DEBT SERVICE	CAPITAL PROJECTS	EXPENDABLE TRUST	TOTALS (MEMORAN-DUM ONLY)
Revenues:						
Local sources:						
Taxes	$1,016,660	$238,000	$110,000			$1,364,660
Tuition	17,440					17,440
Earnings on investments	2,200	1,000	17,840	$42,050	$200	63,290
Textbook rentals	9,250					9,250
	1,045,550	239,000	127,840	42,050	200	1,454,640
State sources:						
Unrestricted grants-in-aid	413,000					413,000
Restricted grants-in-aid	30,000	2,400	14,000			46,400
	443,000	2,400	14,000			459,400
Federal sources:						
Unrestricted grants-in-aid	8,900					8,900
Restricted grants-in-aid	100,000	19,000				119,000
	108,900	19,000				127,900
Total revenues	1,597,450	260,400	141,840	42,050	200	2,041,940
Expenditures						
Instruction services						
Regular education programs	680,590	19,010				699,600
Special programs	134,200	161,230				295,430
Vocational education programs	86,270					86,270
Other instructional programs	42,090					42,090
Nonpublic school programs	1,290	4,760				6,050

TABLE 3.6 *(Continued)*

| | GOVERNMENTAL FUND TYPES | | | | FIDUCIARY FUND TYPE | |
	GENERAL	SPECIAL REVENUE	DEBT SERVICE	CAPITAL PROJECTS	EXPENDABLE TRUST	TOTALS (MEMORAN-DUM ONLY)
Adult/ continuing education programs	10,430					10,430
Community services programs	3,710					3,710
	958,580	185,000				1,143,580
Supporting services: Student	78,500	14,800				93,300
Instructional staff	51,350	9,200				60,550
General ad- ministration	52,100	18,000				70,100
School admin- istration	141,980					141,980
Business	19,970					19,970
Operation and mainte- nance of plant	169,080					169,080
Student trans- portation	17,250					17,250
Central	10,840					10,840
Other	46,820					46,820
	587,890	42,000				629,890
Operation of non-instruc- tional services					2,420	2,420
Facilities acqui- sition and construction services			813,800			813,800
Debt service			114,420			114,420
Total expendi- tures	1,546,470	227,000	114,420	813,800	2,420	2,704,110
Excess of revenues over (under) expendi- tures	50,980	33,400	27,420	(771,750)	(2,220)	(662,170)

TABLE 3.6 *(Continued)*

	GOVERNMENTAL FUND TYPES				FIDUCIARY FUND TYPE	
	GENERAL	SPECIAL REVENUE	DEBT SERVICE	CAPITAL PROJECTS	EXPENDABLE TRUST	TOTALS (MEMORAN-DUM ONLY)
Other financing sources (uses): Proceeds from the sale of bonds				950,000		950,000
Operating transfers in				18,000	2,530	20,530
Operating transfers out	(50,000)					(50,000)
Total other financing sources (uses)	(50,000)			968,000	2,530	920,530
Excess of revenues and other sources over (under) expenditures and other uses	980	33,400	27,420	196,250	310	258,360
Fund balances— July 1	201,070	85,550	142,290	139,650	26,560	595,120
Fund balances— June 30	202,050	118,950	169,710	335,900	26,870	853,480

The notes to the financial statement are an integral part of this statement.

Source: National Center for Educational Statistics, *Financial Accounting for Local and State School Systems* (Washington, DC: National Center for Educational Statistics, 1980), pp. 127–128.

TABLE 3.7   Combined Statement of Revenues, Expenditures, and Changes in Fund Balances, Budget and Actual

Example C—School district XYZ: statement of revenues, expenditures, and changes in fund balances–budget and actual; general and special revenue fund types, for the fiscal year ended June 30, 19XX

	General Fund			Special Revenue Funds		
	BUDGET	ACTUAL	OVER (UNDER) BUDGET	BUDGET	ACTUAL	OVER (UNDER) BUDGET
Revenues:						
Local sources:						
Taxes	$1,202,700	$1,146,660	($56,040)	$89,000	$109,000	$20,000
Tuition	14,000	17,440	3,440			
Earnings on investments	3,500	2,200	(1,300)			
Textbook sales and rentals	8,600	9,250	650			
	1,228,800	1,175,550	(53,250)	89,000	109,000	20,000
State sources:						
Unrestricted grants-in-aid	485,000	413,000	(72,000)			
Restricted grants-in-aid				34,000	32,400	(1,600
	485,000	413,000	(72,000)	34,000	32,400	(1,600)
Federal sources:						
Unrestricted grants-in-aid	9,200	8,900	(300)			
Restricted grants-in-aid				112,000	119,000	7,000
	9,200	8,900	(300)	112,000	119,000	7,000
Total revenues	1,723,000	1,597,450	(125,550)	235,000	260,400	25,400
Expenditures:						
Instruction services						
Regular education programs	685,000	680,590	(4,410)	20,000	19,010	(990)
Special programs	137,000	134,200	(2,800)	165,000	161,230	(3,770)
Vocational education programs	83,000	86,270	3,270			
Other instructional programs	45,000	42,090	(2,910)			
Nonpublic school programs	1,000	1,290	290	5,000	4,760	(240)
Adult-continuing education programs	10,000	10;430	430			
Community services programs	4,000	3,710	(290)			
	965,000	958,580	(6,420)	190,000	185,000	(5,000)

TABLE 3.7 *(Continued)*

	GENERAL FUND			SPECIAL REVENUE FUNDS		
	BUDGET	ACTUAL	OVER (UNDER) BUDGET	BUDGET	ACTUAL	OVER (UNDER) BUDGET
Supporting services						
Student	79,500	78,500	(1,000)	13,000	14,800	1,800
Instructional staff	50,900	51,350	450	11,500	9,200	(2,300)
General admini-stration	54,800	52,100	(2,700)	20,500	18,000	(2,500)
School admini-stration	152,000	141,980	(10,020)			
Business	18,000	19,970	1,970			
Operation and maintenance of plant	142,000	169,080	27,080			
Student transpor-tation	30,800	17,250	(13,550)			
Central	12,000	10,840	(1,160)			
Other	50,000	46,820	(3,180)			
	590,000	587,890	(2,110)	45,000	42,000	(3,000)
Total expenditures	1,555,000	1,546,470	(8,530)	235,000	227,000	(8,000)
Excess of revenues over (under) ex-pendi-tures	168,000	50,980	(117,020)		33,400	33,400
Other financing sources (uses) operating transfers out	(50,000)		(50,000)			
Excess of revenues and other sources over (under) ex-pendi-tures and other uses	118,000	980	(117,020)		33,400	33,400
Fund balances— July 1	201,070	201,070		85,550	85,550	
Fund balances— June 30	319,070	202,050	(117,020)	85,550	118,950	33,400

The notes to the financial state are an integral part of this statement.

Source: National Center for Educational Statistics, *Financial Accounting for Local and State School Systems* (Washington, DC: National Center for Educational Statistics, 1980), p. 129.

SUMMARY

For both developing budgets and managing operations, administrators need to know the school accounting system used in their state and district. Financial information is vital to successful management. Budgets are built using the accounting structure as the format. Expenditures are estimated according to function, object, and cost center dimensions. These generally correspond to the organizational structure of the school district and provide a direct fiscal accountability for administrators. Without a fluent working knowledge of the expenditure dimensions of the accounting system, school administrators cannot understand and control their operations.

Revenues accounts, on the other hand, are not regularly used by most school administrators. They are, however, very important in budget building and fiscal management. Inclusion of all feasible revenue sources and proper recording of receipts are essential aspects of financial administration. Monitoring actual collections by individual revenue sources during the year provides central- or district-level administrators with an early warning system for shortfalls, and information about which revenue sources are seriously different from projections.

A final comment concerns the consequences of information or lack information by school administrators. Information is power—particularly budget and financial information. Those administrators who have and understand the financial information about their operations are in position to control those operations. This does not mean they should reduce costs to a minimum, cut back programs to show underexpenditures on a cost report, or let the fiscal side dominate operations. Just the reverse. By knowing the budget accounts, administrators are in a position to utilize their budgets to the maximum, to manipulate the financial resources under their authority to provide the most effective educational programs, and to be in charge of and give direction to their programs. If you do not control your budget, it will control you. This is the main reason for understanding school accounting. It provides you with the language to deal with fiscal activities in the school district.

PROBLEMS

3.1 Specify the proper expenditure codes for the items listed below. Use the listings of funds (Table 3.1), functions (Table 3.2), and objects (Table 3.4) as a reference source. For each item identify the fund, function, and object code to the lowest level given the available information. For example:

	FUND	FUNCTION	OBJECT
Salary of School Nurse	1 (General)	2134 (Nurse Services)	110 (Regular Salaries)

a) Employee benefits for district Guidance Supervisor.

b) Cost of an outside consultant to assist in the development and implementation of a new budgeting system for the district.

c) Salary of a high school French teacher.

d) Rental of a typewriter for a school principal's office

e) Standardized testing materials to use for psychological testing of district students.

f) New instruments for a junior high school band program.

g) Tuition paid to a neighboring school district for a student from this district attending classes in that high school.

h) Salary of a temporary instructional aide (noncertificated) in a class for emotionally disturbed students.

i) Reimbursement of travel expenses for a school librarian to attend the National American Librarian's Association convention in another state.

j) Annual interest due on school construction bonds.

k) Overtime to the secretary of the district superintendent.

l) Maintenance agreement for the mini-computer used in the district's data processing office.

m) New typewriter to replace worn-out model in elementary school. Typewriter is used by teachers to prepare instructional materials.

n) Honorarium for out-of-state expert's workshop provided to district teachers on improving teaching effectiveness.

o) District payment of professional association membership dues for the director of the community services program.

p) Textbooks for the district's introductory adult education classes.

q) Invoice from county elections office for school district's allocated share of costs for recent elections.

r) An additional pure tone audiometer for testing children with suspected hearing deficiencies.

s) Purchase of new school buses with seat belts for general district use.

t) Separate telephone line for the district school social worker to use to contact parents.

3.2 Specify the proper revenue codes for the items listed below. Use the revenue listings in Table 3.5 as a reference source. For each item identify the fund and revenue code. For example:

	FUND	REVENUE
Tuition from individuals attending adult education classes	1 (General)	1320 (Tuition from Individuals)

a) General aid for basic school support from the state.

b) Sales of meals to students in a school lunchroom.

c) District levy for property taxes.

d) State funds for vocational education.

e) Annual tuition payment from another school district for four of their students attending regular day classes in this district.

f) Monies for inservice training from the intermediate education unit in which this district is situated.

g) Admission receipts collected from the high school football games.

h) P.L. 94-142 funds (Education of All Handicapped Children Act) from the U.S. Department of Education.

i) Penalties paid on overdue taxes.

j) Monies from the bilingual educational appropriation provided by the state.

k) Sale of seven excess school buses at book value.

l) Interest on funds invested in short-term money market accounts.

m) Receipts from rental of district property.

n) Payments from parents for transportation of their children during summer school.

o) Receipts from sale of construction bonds.

NOTES

1. Association of School Business Officials, *Resolution No. 12, Financial Accounting Standards and Procedures for School Systems* (Reston, VA: Association of School Business Officials, October 27, 1977).

2. These are termed the program structure and the responsibility structure in Robert N. Anthony and Regina Herslinger, *Management Control in Nonprofit Organizations* (Homewood, IL: Richard D. Irwin, Inc., 1975), p. 21.

3. *Webster's New Collegiate Dictionary* (Springfield, MA: G. & C. Merriam Company, 1974), p. 8.

4. Robert Anthony, *Management Accounting Principles* (Homewood, IL: Richard D. Irwin, Inc., 1965), p. 1.

5. *Financial Accounting for Local and State School Systems* (Washington, DC: National Center for Educational Statistics, 1980), p. 9.

6. Ibid., pp. 7-8.

7. Sam B. Tidwell, *Financial and Managerial Accounting for Elementary and Secondary School Systems* (Reston, VA: The Research Corporation, Association of School Business Officials, 1985), p. 8.

8. This section is based on *Financial Accounting for Local and State School Systems*, pp. 17, 77-78; Tidwell, *Financial and Managerial Accounting*, Chapter 2; and Association of School Business Officials, *Resolution No. 12, Financial Accounting Standards.*

9. Tidwell, *Financial and Managerial Accounting*, p. 18.

10. Governmental Accounting Standards Board, *Statement 1, Governmental Accounting and Financial Reporting Principles* (Chicago, IL: Governmental Finance Officers Association of the United States and Canada, March, 1979).

11. Tidwell, *Financial and Managerial Accounting*, p. 40.

12. *Financial Accounting for Local and State School Systems*, p. 9.

13. Charles T. Roberts and Allan R. Lichtenberger, "Financial Accounting: Classifications and Standard Terminology for Local and State School Systems," *State Educational Records and Reports Series: Handbook II, Revised* (Washington, DC: U.S. Government Printing Office, 1973), Chapter 4. *Financial Accounting for Local and State School Systems*, Chapter Three

provides an updated account classification system, but one which has not yet gained widespread implementation in the states.

14. *Financial Accounting, Handbook II,* Revised, p. 35.

15. Ibid., p. 36.

16. Ibid., p. 39.

17. Ibid., p. 30.

18. Ibid., p. 30.

19. Oregon Department of Education, *Program Budgeting and Accounting Manual* (Salem, OR: Oregon Department of Education, 1980), pp. 80-81.

20. *Financial Accounting, Handbook II, Revised,* p. 31.

21. Ibid., p. 31.

22. Ibid., pp. 31-33.

23. Ibid., p. 33.

24. Ibid., p. 93.

25. Ibid., p. 33.

26. Ibid., p. 108.

27. Ibid., p. 34.

28. Ibid., p. 35.

29. Ibid., p. 138.

30. *Handbook II, Revised* lists only Local, Intermediate, State, and Federal revenue categories. However, the 1980 update, *Financial Accounting for Local and State School Systems* and individual state accounting manuals offer an Other Revenue category to account for revenues not classified elsewhere.

31. *Financial Accounting for Local and State School Systems,* pp. 78-83.

32. Ibid., pp. 123-131 provides example of financial statements used by school districts.

4

BUILDING THE BUDGET

INTRODUCTION

The principal task of the budget process is to develop the budget document itself. While the Budget Message (with its explanation and rationale for the budget request) is important for communicating with the public and justifying the need for funds, the bulk of the document is devoted to developing estimates for expenditures and revenues.

It should be emphasized that the numbers in the budget are *estimates*. They represent the best estimates of how much money the district will spend and how much it will collect. The budget cycle requires that districts make these estimates well in advance of when they actually occur. Districts which prepare their budget document in January or February are estimating expenditures and revenues which will occur up to eighteen months in the future—June of the following year. This is well before the number of students for the next year is known, sometimes before the salary levels have been established, perhaps before the State Legislature has determined the level of state aid, or before new prices for supplies and equipment are provided by vendors. Further, some of the expenditures, such as utility bills, insurance premiums, and interest payments, will be largely out of the control of school personnel.

Despite these difficulties the anticipated expenditures and revenues must be estimated. While every effort should be made to make them acccurate, administrators should not be discouraged if the actual expenditure and revenue results are not precisely what were estimated; they were never intended to be. The original estimates are just that—the best guesses at the time. They can be updated later in the process if better information becomes available, and adjustments can be made during the operating year to accommodate differences between the estimates and the actual circumstances.

This does not mean that significant deviations are not a cause for concern; they are and should be examined carefully, as they could indicate errors in the estimation process or problems in the spending control procedures used by the district. Further, since the adopted budget sets spending limits for the district, it is important that the estimates be substantially correct, at least in total. For example, if revenues are estimated too high and there is a revenue shortfall or if certain expenditures are significantly greater than estimated, the district may have to reduce spending precipitously in the final few months of the school year to avoid overspending available revenues. Conversely, underestimating revenues or overestimating important expenditure categories could leave the district with an overly large cash balance at year end, leading to questions about excessive taxation and/or complaints about the missed educational opportunities for expanded or improved programs.

ROADMAP FOR BUDGET DEVELOPMENT

In this chapter an overview of the sequence and relationships among the steps for making appropriate budget estimates is provided—a roadmap through the budget development process. Within each step a variety of techniques used in preparing a budget will be presented. The purpose is to place each technique in a context that will illustrate why it is needed, what information is developed, and how it contributes to the development of the complete budget estimates.

The major estimation steps in budget development are: (1) projecting the number of students; (2) determining personnel requirements; (3) estimating expenditures; (4) estimating revenues; and (5) balancing the budget. The general order and content of each step is illustrated in Table 4.1. Each of these estimation steps is examined in detail in subsequent sections of this chapter.

Student enrollment.   The first step is to estimate the number of students expected for the upcoming year. This establishes the basic informa-

TABLE 4.1   Steps in Building Budget Estimates

STUDENTS

Project the number of students to be enrolled next year.
  Total number of students in district
  Number by major program area

PERSONNEL

Estimate the number of personnel required next year.
  Instructional staff by major instructional area
  Instructional support staff
  School level administrative, clerical, and custodial staff
  District level administrative, supervisory, and clerical staff

EXPENDITURES

Estimate amount of expenditures for each district program
  Resources needed to operate programs
  Prices for resources
  Quantity of resources

REVENUES

Estimate the revenues anticipated from each revenue source.
  Local sources
  Intermediate sources
  State sources
  Federal sources

BALANCING EXPENDITURES AND REVENUES

Revise estimates until expenditures balance revenues.
  Reduce expenditures
  Increase revenues

tion on the anticipated level of operation within the school district. The projections are done for the total number of students in the district and also by the number of students in each major program area (such as school building, grade level, and special categories receiving earmarked funding such as handicapped, gifted, and bilingual students).

Personnel.   Once the enrollment projections are completed, the number of personnel needed to operate the district's programs can be estimated. The number of instructional and support personnel is based on the projected numbers of students; while the administrative, supervisory, and classified personnel requirements are determined by the size of the district and the workload in each operation.

Expenditures.   Following personnel projections, expenditures needed to operate each of the district's instructional, support, and administrative programs are calculated. This is accomplished by establishing the types and quantities of resources needed for each program, the prices for each resource, and a capacity measure for each program (such as student/teacher ratios, specialists' caseloads, staffing patterns and policies).

Revenues.   On a parallel track, estimates of the revenues to be received from local, intermediate, state, and federal sources are developed. Particular emphasis is given to the amount of local property taxes required and the district's tax rate.

Balancing the budget.   The last major step is to balance the planned expenditure level with the revenues expected to be received. Total planned expenditures are compared with total available revenues. If expenditures are greater, then planned expenditures must be reduced or revenues must be increased (or both) until expenditures equal revenues.

STUDENT ENROLLMENT PROJECTIONS

Student enrollments are a key factor in budget development. They determine or influence many of financial estimates that go into the budget, particularly in the instructional area. Most types of personnel requirements are derived directly or indirectly from estimates of the number of students to be served. Allocations of funds for instructional supplies and materials and for equipment are frequently made on the basis of projected student enrollments. The needs for facilities, such as number of schools or classrooms, are calculated using the projected enrollments, as are the level of support services. In addition to expenditure estimates, certain revenue projections may also be directly related to the number of students in the school district. State or federal aid which is distributed to districts on a dollar per student basis is determined by multiplying the number of students by the dollar per student aid amount.

There are several different approaches to counting the number of students in a school district, and the approach utilized will probably be determined by the student accounting definitions established by the state department of education. The two principal approaches are average daily membership (ADM) and average daily attendance (ADA). ADM counts all students who are enrolled in school (that is, on the membership list) whether or not they are actually attending school at the time the student count is taken. ADA, on the other hand, counts only those students actually attending school at the time the count is made. The difference between the two approaches is how they treat absences; ADM counts will always be higher than ADA counts, a situation which disadvantages school districts with high absentee rates. Modifications to the basic approaches are possible—counting excused absences as part of ADA counts, for example.

Another differentiation that may be made in student counts is enrollment versus full-time equivalent (FTE) counts. Enrollment generally corresponds to head counts of students, where every student enrolled in a program counts as one whether full-time or part-time. FTE counts adjust the number of students for the actual amount of time in a program; a student who participates part-time in a particular program is counted only for that fraction of time. For example, in a student accounting system requiring this differentiation, a mildly handicapped student receiving special education in a resource room for one period (out of five periods in the school day) would have an FTE count of 0.20 in special education and 0.80 in regular education.

ADA or FTE student counts do not necessarily correspond to how school districts must plan and budget for programs. The special education student in the previous example will probably require a full complement of services in regular education even though the FTE enrollment is only 0.80. For the period per day spent outside of the regular classroom in the resource room very little of budgetary significance changes in the regular classroom—the teacher is paid the same, the student's desk remains and takes up the same space, heat and light consumption are not reduced; perhaps some instructional materials are not required, but these are usually quite minor. As a result, school districts operating under an ADA or FTE approach may have to maintain two separate, but related student accounting procedures—one for state reporting and one for local planning and budgeting.

Enrollment projections are usually done centrally for the school district, either by district office personnel or through a contract arrangement with an outside vendor. To build the budget for the next budget year, enrollment projections are needed which provide detailed estimates of the number of students to be served in the school district during the upcoming year. These projections are generally made along several dimensions—district total, school building, grade level, type of student (regular, handicapped, bilingual, vocational, compensatory). The enrollment projections answer the questions of "How many students are we going to have in that program next year?" Consequently, the dimensions used by the school district to project next year's student enrollments should correspond to the instructional and instructional support programs which the district is planning to provide for its students.

Once the projections are completed, the relevant results are provided to district personnel who are developing budget requests for each program or organizational area. For example, estimates of individual school enrollments, both in total and by grade level, are frequently given to building principals to use in their budget preparation activities; likewise, the special education director could receive estimates of the number of handicapped students (by type of handicap, age, and severity of condition) to establish a baseline for developing a budget request in that area. The enrollment projections would then be used to estimate total personnel requirements and allocation of positions among different grades or types of handicapped students, as well as to determine the amount of money available for instructional supplies and equipment.

Enrollment Projection Techniques

There are several different methods for estimating student enrollments for the upcoming year. They range from simple to sophisticated, and vary in their reliability. At the simplest end is an educated guess by the district superintendent and/or others based on the current enrollments and their projections about what may occur next year. This approach is fast, inexpensive, and understandable. It can also incorporate relevant information about district economic, social, or political conditions into the enrollment estimates. On the other hand, it is also subject to considerable error or bias since the estimates are derived from subjective assessments.

Other more formalized projection approaches have been successful in estimating student enrollments. They utilize various mathematical forecasting techniques for projecting future enrollments based on past trends. However, the basic rationale underlying these extrapolative techniques is the assumption that the same conditions affecting enrollment in the past will continue to prevail in the future.[1] This may not be the case in districts undergoing demographic and economic changes. These assumptions and conditions should be examined to see if they make sense in light of what administrators know or believe about the district's condition in the upcoming year. Adjustments can and should be made to the projections calculated by the forecasting techniques to accurately reflect changes in the district's future. For example, a district which has been economically depressed and losing population for the past several years may not want to project a decreasing enrollment trend into the next year if several manufacturing firms have opened up new plants in the community and the economy is showing signs of recovering.

Trend line analysis.[2]   Trend line analysis is a form of linear regression which uses the year as the predictor variable and the district enrollment as the dependent or predicted variable. With a simple statistical program on a computer or even a statistical hand calculator it is possible to calculate future enrollments easily. The data needed are the enrollments of the pertinent populations for each of the past several (approximately five or six) years. Future years' enrollments are estimated by projecting the trend line from the past years' data. The statistical methodology of linear regression is utilized to calculate the line of "best fit" for the previous enrollments. The result is an equation of a straight line.

Future Enrollment = Constant + (Coefficient × Future Year)

A future year is substituted into this equation and the estimated enrollment for that future year is calculated. This procedure is illustrated in Figure 4.1. As seen in Figure 4.1, the enrollments of the school district have been fluctuating up and down over the past several years, with two years showing increases and two years showing declines. The problem is to project the enrollments for the next three years. Using the past five years' enrollments, a trend line is calculated to estimate future years' enrollments. The trend line equation is

FORECAST ENROLLMENT = 5559 + 38.2 × YEAR NUMBER

Note that the number of the year (1 for 1981, 2 for 1982) is substituted for the actual year date. This does not change the results of the trend line equation at all, but only makes the calculations easier and clearer. To obtain the projected enrollment for the next year, 1986 (Year 6), the number of the year (6) is substituted into the equation and an estimate of 5,788 students is obtained. This procedure assumes that the student enrollments will be growing as shown by the trend line in Figure 4.1 and that any past or future differences from the line are relatively minor deviations from the prevailing long-term trend.

Cohort survival.   Another forecasting technique, termed cohort survival, uses a different methodology to project future student enrollments. In this technique, each grade level is treated as a cohort and the passage of students from one grade level to the next is followed through the school system from year to year. This is illustrated in Table 4.2.

The 920 students who were in kindergarten in 1981-82 became the 915 students in first grade in 1982-83 and then the 905 students in second grade in 1983-84, and so forth. For each year in the past several years (usually five or six), the number of students enrolled in each grade level is listed. Then a *survival rate* is calculated for each transition of one grade of students into the next grade in the following year. For example, the survival rate of kindergartners to first graders from 1981-82 to 1982-83 was 0.995 (915/920). Similar rates are calculated for each grade/year cell in the

FIGURE 4.1 Trend Line Analysis Projection Example

	PAST YEARS' DATA			FUTURE YEARS' DATA	
YEAR	YEAR NUMBER	STUDENT ENROLLMENT	YEAR	YEAR NUMBER	STUDENT ENROLLMENT
1981	1	5,642	1986	6	?
1982	2	5,529	1987	7	?
1983	3	5,695	1988	8	?
1984	4	5,809			
1985	5	5,693			

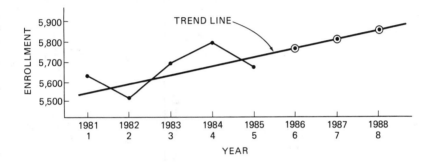

TREND LINE PROJECTIONS FOR NEXT THREE YEARS

TREND LINE EQUATION IS CALCULATED USING A LINEAR REGRESSION EQUATION

FORECAST ENROLLMENT			=	5,559	+	38.2	×	YEAR NUMBER
1986	(YEAR 6)	5,788	=	5,559	+	38.2	×	6
1987	(YEAR 7)	5,826	=	5,559	+	38.2	×	7
1988	(YEAR 8)	5,865	=	5,559	+	38.2	×	8

enrollment data matrix. Using the various years' rates, an average for each grade to grade transition is calculated over the given time period. In the example the five year average survival rate for kindergarten to first grade was 0.987, which is the average of the individual survival rates of kindergarten to first grade from 1981-82 through 1986-87.

This method does not trace individual children; it only is concerned with the aggregate numbers in each grade in each year. All of the children in the following grade were not necessarily in the prior grade; transfers into the next grade from outside the school system are common. When more students transfer into than leave the school system, the survival rate will be greater than 1.0. This was the case in several grades in the example.

TABLE 4.2 Cohort Survival Enrollment Projection Example

ELEMENTARY ENROLLMENTS

GRADE	1981–82	1982–83	1983–84	1984–85	1985–86	1986–87
K	920	941	977	855	868	843
1	856	915	938	826	836	888
2	813	845	905	887	804	824
3	847	805	843	879	934	819
4	828	830	803	799	913	923
5	842	799	838	789	832	923
K–5	5,106	5,135	5,204	5,035	5,187	5,220

SURVIVAL RATES

GRADE	1981–82	1982–83	1983–84	1984–85	1985–86	1986–87	5 YEAR AVERAGE
K							
1		0.995	0.997	0.942	0.978	1.023	0.987
2		0.987	0.989	0.946	0.973	0.986	0.976
3		0.990	0.998	0.971	1.053	1.019	1.006
4		0.980	0.998	0.948	1.039	0.988	0.990
5		0.965	1.010	0.983	1.041	1.011	1.002

ENROLLMENT PROJECTIONS

GRADE	AVG. SURVIVAL RATE	ACTUAL 1986–87	1987–88	1988–89	1989–90
K*		843	865	884	897
1	0.987	888	832	854	872
2	0.976	824	867	812	833
3	1.006	819	829	872	817
4	0.990	923	811	872	864
5	1.002	923	925	813	823
K–5		5,220	5,129	5,056	5,106

*Kindergarten enrollments estimated independently from census data.

The average survival rates are then used to project future enrollments on a grade by grade basis. The actual enrollments in each grade during the latest year are multiplied by their respective average survival rates and the results are the projected enrollments in each grade for the next year. For example, the five year average survival rate for kindergarten to first grade (0.987) is multiplied by the students in kindergarten in 1986-87 (843) to obtain a projected enrollment of 832 in first grade for 1987-88.

If additional years' projections are desired, the same procedure is followed. The same survival rates are used, but the enrollments for the latest projected year are substituted for the actual enrollments of the prior year. To continue the example, the 832 students projected in the first grade in 1987-88 would be multiplied by the first to second grade average survival rate (0.976) to obtain the estimate of 812 students in second grade in 1988-89.

As with all extrapolation techniques, the cohort survival estimates become less secure the further out they are made. While the 1987-88 projections in the example are based on the actual enrollments in the prior year, the projections in later years are based on projected rather than actual enrollments. Further, it also assumes that the same conditions which prevailed in past years will continue into the future.

There is one hole in the set of grade level projections for the next year—kindergarten. The projection for a given grade level is based on the students in the previous grade. The entry grade into the school—kindergarten in this example—has no prior grade or students from which to derive its projected enrollment. Therefore, it is necessary to estimate the enrollment in the entry grade separately. This is normally done by looking at past trends, reviewing county birth records for five years previously, obtaining enrollment information from preschool programs in the district, estimating either the in- or out-migration of families, and then translating these into an estimate of entering students for the following year.

Cautions. The results from any enrollment projection methodology—the cohort survival method, trend line analysis, or others—should not be automatically accepted as perfectly correct or accurate.[3] The past conditions (such as, annual survival rates, enrollment levels, or changes in enrollment levels) should be reviewed for deviations from the general pattern for the grade level. For example, in Table 4.2, the third to fourth grade survival rate in 1985-86 was the only rate in that group greater than 1.0; in every other year in the past five years there was a loss of students from the third to fourth grades.

An annual rate or enrollment level that seems out of line is not necessarily wrong, but it should be identified and possibly investigated to see if it was an aberrant condition or a normal difference. Since the average of the annual survival rates is used as the multiplier in making the projections, one year which is abnormal will distort the average rate and hence the pro-jected enrollments. The same is true for enrollment levels in calculating the trend line equation.

A final aspect to observe is enrollment pattern trends. A steadily in-creasing or decreasing rate of a grade level may indicate that the last year's survival rate would be a more accurate indicator of next year's transition than the five year average rate which includes information different from expected future conditions. Where appropriate, the projection results can be modified to reflect the expected future situation more accurately. This may be necessary when districts are facing significant changes such as the end of declining enrollments and the beginning of increasing enrollments.[4]

PERSONNEL PROJECTIONS

The single most important and expensive resource utilized by schools is personnel. Consequently, it is crucial that the estimates of personnel re-quired to operate the school district are as accurate as possible.

Personnel requirements are generally derived from enrollment esti-mates, since the number of students determines the need for personnel; this is particularly true in the instructional area. The general procedure is for the district to establish student/personnel ratios for various instruc-tional and support programs and to use these ratios to calculate the num-bers of positions required in the upcoming years.

The ratios are very important for both the quality and costs of the educational programs. In some states, student/teacher ratios are estab-lished by state law or department of education guidelines. In districts which are not completely constrained by outside requirements, they are most fre-quently established by the school board as a policy decision. However, even in these cases the board usually does not act without information and ad-vice from school district administrators, instructional personnel, and even the public about the programmatic implications and estimated costs of their decisions.

Staffing ratios can be established for all types of programs in the school district, although some lend themselves to this approach more read-ily than others. For example, staffing ratios in the instruction area may be established for each major type of program (such as, elementary, middle, and high school) and type of student served (regular, handicapped, bilin-gual). The number of students can also be used to specify support service personnel caseloads and classified positions as well. Table 4.3 gives some examples of district staffing ratios for instructional, support services, and classified personnel.

It is important to make clear which personnel are included in the staffing positions calculated by the ratios. For example, a single instruc-

TABLE 4.3 Examples of District Staffing Ratios

TYPE OF PERSONNEL	STUDENT/PERSONNEL RATIO
Certified Staff[a]	
Elementary	20.4:1
Middle School	19.5:1
High School	18.5:1
Clerical Staff for Schools[b]	83.0:1
Health Services	
Nurses	1,700:1
Classified (6 hour aide)	0.5 Aide per Nurse
Handicapped Program	
Certified	23.5:1 (Yearly load)
Classified (8 hour aide)	50.0:1

[a]Includes staffing for regular classrooms; support areas of music, media, counseling, and physical education; and remedial services in reading and math
[b]Includes secretaries, library aides, lunch aides, and classroom aides

tional staffing ratio could cover the total number of certified instructional and support personnel in the school buildings (such as, classroom teachers, reading specialists, mathematics specialists, physical educational teachers, librarians, media specialists, music teachers, and counselors). Alternatively, separate ratios could be established for classroom teachers and for each type of instructional support personnel needed by the district. The single ratio which combines all teaching and instructional support staff would be smaller (that is, fewer students per staff member) than a separate classroom teacher ratio. A single ratio for all instructional personnel gives the principal more flexibility in allocating positions within a school and allows schools to adapt to individual needs; although, it makes it harder to explain to district patrons why the district has an average of twenty-four students per classroom when the instructional personnel ratio is 19:1.

Staffing ratios determine by type of position the number of personnel required in the upcoming year. A district which has projected the number of next year's students can use this information (along with district staffing ratios) to determine its instructional staff needs. Table 4.4 illustrates some of these calculations for a hypothetical school district. The district has a projected elementary school enrollment of 3,470 students and a staffing ratio of 20.4 students per instructional staff at the elementary school level. Dividing the number of students by the staffing ratio yields 170 instructional staff positions that will be required next year in the district's elementary schools. Similar calculations are shown for other types of positions.

The district ratios can be used to set the overall limit on district staffing and also to determine the number of personnel to be assigned to an individual school. In the example shown in Table 4.4, the total building staff for all elementary students in the district was calculated to be 170

TABLE 4.4   Sample Staffing Needs Calculations

POSITION	ENROLLMENT	STAFFING RATIO	STAFF POSITIONS
CERTIFIED			
Elementary	3,470	20.4	170
Middle	2,040	19.5	105
High School	2,220	18.5	120
Total	7,730		395
CLERICAL			
Elementary	3,470	83.0	42
Middle	2,040	83.0	25
High School	2,220	83.0	27
Total	7,730		94
HEALTH SERVICES			
Nurses	7,730	1,700	5
Aides	7,730	3,400	2
HANDICAPPED PROGRAM			
Certified	680	23.5	29
Aides	680	50.0	14

teachers and 42 clerical positions. This establishes the total number of instructional and clerical staff to be allocated among all of the elementary schools in the district.

Assume, for example, that one of the elementary schools in this district had 350 students as its expected enrollment. Using the district staffing ratios, it would be assigned 17 certified instructional positions (350 divided by 20.4) and 4 clerical positions (350 divided by 83). Depending on district policy, the principal could decide how to allocate these positions among various classroom and support personnel in the school. These decisions would have to be within certain district constraints, such as one full-time teacher assigned to every classroom, a maximum of 27 students per classroom, and at least a half-time librarian and a half-time physical education teacher in every elementary school. However, within this hypothetical allocation, it would be possible to have a full-time physical education teacher, a half-time music teacher, one librarian, and a half-time reading specialist to complement the 14 classroom teachers with an average of 25 students per classroom. Another school might select a different combination of instructional personnel which would meet its needs better (such as, two additional classroom teachers to lower class sizes in crowded classrooms, but only a half-time physical education teacher and librarian, and no music teacher or reading specialist).

Allocations of classified and custodial personnel to schools sometimes are calculated on different bases than those of certified personnel. For example, some districts use the number of students in a school to determine the classified personnel allocations, but they are calculated in terms of hours-per-day of classified personnel time rather than in numbers of people. This allows school administration flexibility in terms of the types of personnel to hire and their working hours (for example, an eight hours-per-day secretary, six hours-per-day instructional aides, or two hours-per-day lunchroom aides). Custodial positions are frequently allocated to schools based on engineering standards, such as one custodian per so many square feet of building space to maintain. Adjustments to these standards may be made for special types of spaces—cafeterias, gyms, locker rooms, or auditoriums.

Sometimes the staffing calculations yield poor results. This usually happens in either very small or very large schools because the staffing ratios are generally established for average sized schools in the district. A small enrollment school will not generate sufficient staff to operate its programs adequately. This may be a rationale for considering closing the school and consolidating its students into larger schools where additional services can be provided. However, for geographical, logistical, or political reasons it may be necessary to continue operating the school. A common practice in this situation is to establish certain building or program minimum staffing levels which will be utilized regardless of the staffing ratio calculations. Examples of these minimums would be: a full-time teacher in every elementary classroom; a half-time vice principal per middle school; or one full-time counselor per high school.

Large schools present the opposite problem—more staff positions are generated than would be necessary. This is primarily due to economies of scale which are possible in some areas. The correction is the reverse of the small school situation: a maximum number of positions for the building is established which is less than would be provided through a straight application of the staffing ratios.

Both the minimum and maximum levels are arrived at through professional judgment and educational and fiscal considerations. If a district has both small and large schools of the same type, it has the opportunity to balance the additional staff for small schools with the staff savings from the large schools. Otherwise, the extra personnel in the small schools must be provided in addition to the overall positions calculated for the district. Otherwise, the allocations to larger schools will have to be reduced in order to provide the minimum staff to the small schools.

Another way of allocating certain staff positions to schools is based on ranges of students rather than specific enrollment numbers and fixed staffing ratios. For example, librarian positions could be allocated to schools in 0.5 full-time equivalent (FTE) increments which increase with the size of the school. A hypothetical staffing arrangement is shown in Table 4.5. Here the minimum staffing for the smallest schools is a half-time (0.5 FTE) librarian. As the school gets bigger, it qualifies for additional li-

TABLE 4.5 Allocation of Librarian Positions by School Size

SCHOOL ENROLLMENTS	LIBRARIAN POSITIONS ALLOCATED
FROM TO	
250 – 400	0.5
400 – 800	1.0
800 – 1,400	1.5
1,400 – 2,000	2.0
More than 2,000	2.5

brarian positions according the specified enrollment ranges. Note that in Table 4.5 expected economies of scale are built into the staffing schedule. Other examples of positions which might use this allocation procedure include vice principals, counselors, and reading specialists.

Determining central office positions—both certified and classified—is generally less standardized than those at the building level. The type and number of positions depend on the size of the district, the organizational structure of the central office, the scope of the work expected, and the volume of work for which the district office is responsible. For certain positions—administrators, supervisors, secretaries—it may be possible to compare their numbers with national ratios. However, to achieve a comprehensive estimation of the numbers and types of positions needed, one must study the tasks and activities required from the district office. This is best done on a department by department basis since the work is usually organized this way.

Several interconnected steps can be used to obtain the appropriate staffing patterns in the district office. First, reviewing the positions historically will provide information about the number and types of positions filled in each of the district level departments. Reviewing the adequacy of the current staffing is a useful second step; this can be done through formal and informal observations by district administrators, and through discussions with district staff at all levels. Ultimately, the decision involves management judgment based on the benefits and costs of maintaining or increasing the number of positions, versus the cost savings and potential problems caused by a reduction in available staff.

EXPENDITURE ESTIMATES

Expenditure Estimation Approach

Different sections of the budget are developed by different parts of the district organization. The personnel office and the business office develop a great deal of budget-related information used by others in the district; they also make personnel and cost projections for activities and operations related to the total district. Individual schools or district level departments are responsible for budget estimates for certain parts of their activities. All of the pieces need to be compatible so that everyone is using the same planning assumptions and budgeting rules throughout the district, and to ensure that, when combined, they all fit together. This requires a consistent set of procedures within an overall approach which directs the expenditure estimation efforts. The objective is to prepare complete, appropriate, and understandable expenditure estimates for the school district's budget.

The state accounting system is the vehicle for establishing and maintaining a consistent and complete budgeting format. Budget estimates are made in accordance with the program structure built into the school accounting system. The general approach is to work within the lowest level function utilized by the district, to identify the objects of expenditure required by the activities of that function, and then to estimate the costs for each of the objects of expenditure.

The overall procedures for estimating expenditures are shown in the three steps below. The steps are general ones, but provide a structure for understanding the purpose and context of the specific expenditure estimations.

1. *Identify the functions to be used in the budget.* This step specifies the particular programs or functions around which the budget will be built. The school accounting system provides the framework to designate the functions.

2. *Determine the resources needed to carry out the tasks in each program or function.* These are the items which will be employed or purchased by the school district. Specification of the resources is determined by the objects of expenditure listed in the district's accounting system. Not every type of object of expenditure will be utilized in every program, so only those items actually needed should be specified. The actual determination of resources is done in a variety of ways, including policies, standards, formulas, and historical relationships.

3. *Estimate costs of each program or function.* This last step involves putting prices on the resources and summing up the total costs for each program first within schools and district level departments, and then for the entire district.

Format for Estimating Expenditures

The building block of school district budgets is the *Cost Center.* That is, the organizational unit where the expenditures will take place. Common cost centers are each school building and district level department. This allows (or requires) each cost center, such as a school, to develop its own budget request. These budget requests are collated by major function to arrive at a budget for the entire district.

The format for estimating expenditures within a cost center follows the same classification structure used by the school district. Budget requests

TABLE 4.6 Examples of Function and Object Levels for Expenditure Estimates

COST CENTER (DISTRICT OPTIONAL)		FUNCTION (STATE REQUIRED)		DEPARTMENT (DISTRICT OPTIONAL)		OBJECT OF EXPENDITURE (STATE REQUIRED)		COSTS
CODE	DESCRIPTION	CODE	DESCRIPTION	CODE	DESCRIPTION	CODE	DESCRIPTION	
061	Lincoln High School	1130	High School Instruction	10	Language Arts	110	Regular Salaries	$186,300
						210	Employee Benefits	69,700
						350	Communication	1,400
						410	Supplies	2,400
						420	Textbooks	8,800
						440	Periodicals	200
						540	Equipment	1,500
							Department Total	$270,300
				11	Social Studies		(Each instructional department and support and administrative function would have its Objects of Expenditure specified, similar to Language Arts above)	
				12	Science			
				18	Mathematics etc.			
		2120	Guidance Services	2122	Counseling Services			
		2220	Educational Media Services	2222	Audiovisual Services			
				2223	School Library Services			
		2410	Office of Principal					

are established for each major program or function by estimating expenditures for the actual objects which will be purchased.

The function and object levels at which the estimates are made are often established by state regulations, but districts may develop estimates at greater levels of detail and aggregate them up to the required levels. This permits districts to generate additional information for internal planning and control. An example illustrating the levels of expenditure estimates in a high school budget is given in Table 4.6.

The hypothetical cost center in this illustration is Lincoln High School, whose budget estimates contain several different functions, such as High School Instruction, Guidance, Educational Media, and Office of the Principal. These third level functions are the assumed level to which state regulations mandate expenditure estimates. For districtwide planning and reporting purposes, all of the instructional costs for high schools can be aggregated together into the High School Instruction category. Within Lincoln High School, the instructional expenditures are estimated for each major department or instructional area, such as Language Arts, Social Studies, Science, and Mathematics. In this example, the department is the lowest function level utilized in the budget. Within each department the budget identifies anticipated objects of expenditure and gives the estimated costs for each category. Similar estimates are made for departments within all high school support services and administrative functions.

Estimating Salary Expenditures

Salaries for personnel are the most important cost object in the school district's budget. Typically, 60 to 70 percent of the total budget is for salaries. The levels of salaries for teachers, other certified personnel, and classified personnel are generally established through collective bargaining negotiations between the district and representative associations or unions. These negotiated agreements act as constraints on the budget and provide the information to develop salary cost estimates.

There are many different kinds of salary costs to be considered in the budget. These are illustrated by the account listing for salary objects of expenditure in Table 4.7. Salaries are categorized as: regular, temporary, overtime, or for sick pay. Within each of these categories, the expenditures are shown separately for certified and noncertified (or classified) personnel. Separate expenditure estimates are made for each object subcategory for which program expenditures are anticipated during the upcoming year.

Teacher salaries.   Most school districts use a *single salary schedule* for determining teacher and other certified salaries. An example of such a salary schedule is shown in Table 4.8.

TABLE 4.7 Salary Categories

CODE	TITLE	DESCRIPTION
100	Salaries	Amounts paid to employees of the school district. This is the summary category which is used to aggregate all salary subcategories.
110	Regular Salaries	Amounts paid to employees of the district who are in permanent positions.
111	Certified Salaries	
112	Noncertified Salaries	
120	Temporary Salaries	Amounts paid to employees of the district who are hired on a temporary or substitute basis.
121	Certified Salaries	
122	Noncertified Salaries	
130	Overtime Salaries	Amounts paid to regular or temporary employees of the district for work performed in addition to the normal work period.
131	Certified Salaries	
132	Noncertified Salaries	
140	Sick Pay	Amount paid to a district employee for sick leave due to sickness or injury which prevents the employee from performing normal work duties.
141	Certified Salaries	
142	Noncertified Salaries	

This salary schedule is a matrix with years of experience as one axis and educational level as the other. The figure in each cell in the matrix specifies the salary for an individual with a specific amount of experience and education. For example, a teacher with eight years of experience and a Master's degree would receive $22,900 under the schedule in Table 4.8.

Salary schedules are constructed to provide incentives for teachers to remain with the district for a number of years and to continue their professional development through additional education. As teachers gain experience they move down the salary schedule, one level for each additional year. Each step downward up to a maximum number of years brings a higher salary level as experience increments are added to the base salary. Similarly, as teachers obtain additional educational credits or degrees, they move to the right in the matrix, and each further educational level reached brings an additional salary increment.

Most salary schedules are designed with an approximate 2:1 ratio between the highest and lowest salaries. In the example shown in Table 4.8, teachers who have worked for the district for fifteen years and have a doctorate would earn twice as much as a beginning teacher with a Bachelor's degree. In between these two extremes, it is possible for an individual teacher to get a triple salary increase in one year if: 1) the district negotiates

TABLE 4.8 Salary Schedule for Certified Professional Employees

EXPERIENCE LEVEL	BACHELOR'S	BACHELOR'S + 23 HOURS	BACHELOR'S + 45 HOURS	MASTER'S	MASTER'S + 45 HOURS	MASTER'S + 90 OR DOCTORATE
1	$16,014	$16,494	$16,975	$17,455		
2	$16,655	$17,135	$17,615	$18,176		
3	$17,295	$17,776	$18,256	$18,897		
4	$18,016	$18,496	$18,977	$19,697	$20,818	$21,459
5	$18,736	$19,217	$19,697	$20,498	$21,619	$22,420
6	$19,457	$19,937	$20,418	$21,299	$22,420	$23,380
7	$20,178	$20,658	$21,138	$22,099	$23,220	$24,341
8	$20,898	$21,379	$21,859	$22,900	$24,021	$25,302
9	$21,619	$22,099	$22,580	$23,701	$24,822	$26,263
10	$22,340	$22,820	$23,300	$24,501	$25,622	$27,224
11	$23,060	$23,541	$24,021	$25,302	$26,423	$28,185
12	$23,781	$24,261	$24,742	$26,103	$27,224	$29,145
13	$24,501	$24,982	$25,462	$26,904	$28,025	$30,106
14				$27,704	$28,825	$31,067
15				$28,505	$29,626	$32,028

an overall increase in the salary schedule; 2) the teacher stays with the district for an additional year; and 3) the teacher completes another educational level.

A practice sometimes used in developing salary schedules to express the differences between experience and educational levels in terms of a percentage of the base salary (beginning salary for beginning teacher with lowest education level—upper left hand corner of the salary matrix) in the schedule. So there would be said to be a 5.0% difference or increment between the eighth and ninth year salaries for Master's degree teachers in Table 4.8. ($23,701 − $22,900 = $801; $801 / $16,014 = 5.0%)

Two other features of this salary schedule are interesting because they illustrate important district personnel policies. This district has no provision for hiring inexperienced teachers with more education than a Master's degree. The minimum experience level for those with forty-five or more hours beyond a Master's degree or a Doctorate is four years. This requires teachers to have teaching experience either in the district or transferred in from another district to go along with their advanced educational training. At the other end of the schedule, the district has placed a limit of thirteen years on the experience increases for those teachers with only a Bachelors degree. This feature, coupled with the educational level increments, provides an incentive for teachers to continue their education.

Salary expenditure projections are developed by the district office since they maintain the necessary personnel records and are generally responsible for contract negotiations. Estimates for teacher and other certified personnel salary cost begin with an update of the salary amounts in the salary schedule. The procedure used will vary with the conditions and timing of the contract with the teachers' association or union. If the district is in an interim year of a multi-year contract, then the annual increase will probably be specified in the contract, perhaps tied to an economic indicator, such as a regional or state consumer price index (CPI). Once the indicator is determined or estimated, it is used to update the salary schedule for the upcoming year.

In years when the district is scheduled to negotiate a new contract which will not be signed prior to the budget process, one must estimate the increase and incorporate that into the salary schedule. Unfortunately, this has serious overtones in collective bargaining negotiations since budget documents are generally available to the public (including union negotiators), and knowledge of what the district has budgeted for salary increases can strengthen the union's bargaining position. Consequently, some districts exclude salary increases from this portion of the budget, use the current year's salary schedule as a preliminary estimate of next year's salaries, and place the estimated settlement amount for salary increases into an unspecified contingency account (or accounts) to conceal their negotiation strategy. In any event, a first step in developing salary expenditure estimates is to update the salary schedule for the upcoming year.

The next step is to project the number of personnel at each salary level in the schedule for the next year. The format of the salary schedule can be used as a matrix with years of experience and educational level as the dimensions, and the number of people at each particular experience/education combination in the respective cells of the matrix. Using this format, the number of people currently in each cell of the matrix is determined—the present location matrix. These numbers are then adjusted by: (1) eliminating any persons who will be retiring, moving, resigning, or going on leave; (2) adding any persons expected to be returning to the district payroll next year; (3) advancing those remaining in the matrix by one year in experience; (4) estimating the number of those who will qualify for a higher educational level next year, usually based on historical records; and (5) estimating who will be entering the district next year and their placement in the matrix, at the initial cell or elsewhere. The resultant matrix provides an estimate of the numbers of persons to be employed according to their salary category.

A shortcut to this procedure for districts with fairly stable enrollments and personnel requirements is to take the persons in the existing teaching positions and advance all those eligible one year in experience (taking care not to advance those already at the maximum experience level). Educational level increases can be budgeted for by estimating a lump sum amount (usually based on historical experience) to cover the cost of these increments, rather than trying to estimate them more precisely.

The projected number of teachers at each point on the salary schedule is multiplied by the corresponding amounts in the updated salary schedule. Overall salary expenditure estimates for instructional personnel are then obtained by summing the results of each calculation. These salary expenditure estimates can be developed for the total number of teachers in the district or for any subgroup. For example, to obtain separate salary estimates for elementary, middle, and high school instructional personnel, the district would simply use the number of teachers in each of the desired groups and carry out the calculations for each using the same salary schedule. An illustration of the general procedure using the shortcut method of advancing present personnel is provided in Table 4.9.

Administrative salaries.   Salary costs must also be estimated for administrators. Examples of such positions are school principals and assistant principals, curriculum coordinators, central office directors, administrators, and coordinators. Although they occupy professional positions and are frequently certified, they are noninstructional personnel and their salaries are usually not determined by the teachers' single salary schedule.

Instead, for most administrative positions salary amounts are established by a separate schedule. Each administrative position is located within one category or salary range which contains similar positions. Within each

TABLE 4.9 Sample Calculation of Teacher Salary Expenditures Advanced in Salary Schedule by One Experience Level

		MASTER'S DEGREE		
EXPERIENCE LEVEL		NUMBER OF	SALARY AMOUNT	SALARY
CURRENT	NEXT YEAR	TEACHERS	NEXT YEAR	EXPENDITURES
	1	0	$17,455	$0
1	2	0	$18,176	$0
2	3	4	$18,897	$75,588
3	4	6	$19,697	$118,182
4	5	9	$20,498	$184,482
5	6	18	$21,299	$383,382
6	7	16	$22,099	$353,584
7	8	14	$22,900	$320,600
8	9	13	$23,701	$308,113
9	10	22	$24,501	$539,022
10	11	25	$25,302	$632,550
11	12	17	$26,103	$443,751
12	13	27	$26,904	$726,408
13	14	21	$27,704	$581,784
14	15	27	$28,505	$769,635
15	15	215	$28,505	$6,128,575
	TOTAL	434		$11,565,656

range there are usually several levels corresponding to years of experience in the position. Higher levels receive higher salaries. The number of experience levels are generally much less than for teachers, which limits the salary growth possible for administrators within a given position range. Unlike the teachers' salary schedule, the administrators' schedule generally contains no salary increments for educational level. An example of an administrative salary schedule is given in Table 4.10.

The administrative salary schedule is also updated annually, usually on a percentage basis, and the new amounts are used in estimating administrative costs for the upcoming year. To calculate the projected administrative costs for a given function, the number of administrative positions at each range and level are specified. These position counts are multiplied by the corresponding salary amounts from the administrative salary schedule and the results are summed.

For a few upper level administrative positions, such as superintendent, the salary amount may be established on an individual basis outside of the administrative salary schedule. In these cases the salary projections are determined directly from the employment contracts for those positions, adjusted for any annual increases.

Supervisor salaries. Supervisors of classified personnel comprise another category for whom a separate salary schedule is sometimes estab-

TABLE 4.10   Administrative Salary Schedule

	LEVEL 1	LEVEL 2	LEVEL 3	LEVEL 4	LEVEL 5
RANGE I	Directors				
	$43,570	$45,300	$46,960	$48,760	
RANGE II	Senior High Principals, Personnel Administrator, Business Services Administrator, Educational Services Administrator				
	$41,742	$43,046	$44,350	$45,655	$46,959
RANGE III	Middle School Principals				
	$36,523	$37,828	$39,132	$40,437	$41,742
RANGE IV	Media Services Coordinator, Curriculum Coordinators, Senior High Assistant Principals, Maintenance & Operations Manager				
	$35,219	$36,523	$37,828	$39,132	$40,437
RANGE V	Senior High Assistant Principals & Athletic Coordinators				
	$33,263	$34,567	$35,872	$37,136	$38,480
RANGE VI	Elementary School Principals, Chapter 1 Coordinator, Middle School Assistant Principals				
	$31,306	$32,611	$33,915	$35,219	$36,523
RANGE VII	Elementary School Assistant Principal				
	$28,698	$30,002	$31,306	$32,611	$33,915

lished. This group would include personnel who manage such functions as maintenance and plant operations, buildings, grounds, district shops, painting, printing, electronics, mechanical services, transportation, and custodial services. These positions do not usually require an administrative certificate or other educational qualification. Persons in these positions generally supervise the activities of skilled and semi-skilled classified employees.

The salary schedule for supervisors is similar to that of administrators. Positions that are believed to be equivalent are grouped together in a single range. Within each such range there are several levels representing years of service in that position. The salary amount increases as a person moves to a higher range or moves to a higher level within a given range. Typically there are more levels in the supervisors' salary schedule than in the administrative schedule; this allows for more salary growth for supervisors within a particular position.

Salary expenditures for supervisory personnel are estimated very much like those for administrators. First, it is necessary to identify that a position is a supervisory one and then to find the range on the schedule containing the position. Next, the person who holds that position (or is expected to hold it next year) is specified so that their level or years of service can be determined. This then locates the exact placement for the person on the salary schedule and gives the salary expenditure amount to be budgeted for next year.

Classified salaries. Salary expenditures must also be estimated for classified personnel. Examples of classified positions include clerical and secretarial workers; custodians; food service workers; maintenance craftsmen, technicians, and specialists; instructional aides; bus drivers; transportation technicians, mechanics, and specialists; and a variety of specialized positions which do not require a certificate for employment.

These classified positions represent a wide variety of skills and abilities needed by the school district. They also represent a wide range in salaries and wages which the school district must pay to compete for these persons in the labor market. To accommodate the various levels and types of compensation for this diverse group of employees, districts establish separate salary schedules for similar groups of classified employees. Salary schedules for classified personnel reflect the manner in which those positions are paid—hourly, monthly, or an annual contract based on days, months, or years. The schedules also incorporate experience increases into the salary amounts for employees who continue employment with the district. Generally, the experience increments for classified positions reach a maximum sooner than for teachers. As an example, a Custodial Services Salary Schedule is shown in Table 4.11.

For this schedule, all custodian positions were identified and classified according to the ranking of the position; similar ranking positions were grouped together. The schedule contains the wage or salary amounts for each position classification and appropriate experience step. The amounts correspond to the type of payment for the position and are noted on the schedule. For example, a Custodial Sweeper (C.S.T.-1) is paid on an hourly basis, while the remainder of the positions are paid on a monthly or annual basis.

The same approach is used to estimate salary costs for classified positions as described for other types of personnel. The number of persons expected in each level of the classified salary schedule is estimated. These numbers are multiplied by the appropriate salary or wage amounts to arrive at an overall salary cost estimate for this group. Determining classified salary costs for individual cost centers is accomplished by calculating actual salaries of individuals assigned to each center.

Position counts versus salary amounts. In working with their cost center budgets, school administrators and district level department heads generally deal only in position counts, usually expressed in *full-time equivalent* positions (FTE). They allocate the available positions among the instructional and support areas in accord with district policies, but do not have to be concerned with the salary costs of individual teachers, other professionals, ad-

TABLE 4.11 Custodial Services Salary Schedule

CLASSIFICATION.	POSITION
C.S.T.-1	Custodial Sweeper
	Laundry Worker
C.S.T.-2	School Custodian
C.S.T.-3	Assistant Custodial Supervisor—High School
	Custodial Supervisor—Small Elementary School
	Custodial Specialist
C.S.T.-4	Custodial Supervisor—Large Elementary School
C.S.T.-5	Custodial Supervisor—Middle School
C.S.T.-6	Custodial Supervisor—High School

SALARY SCHEDULE AMOUNTS

CLASS.	1	2	3	4	5	6	7	8	9
C.S.T.-1									
$/hr	4.61	4.73	4.85	4.96	5.06				
C.S.T.-2									
$/mo	1,075	1,104	1,132	1,164	1,195	1,228	1,260	1,294	1,329
$/12 mo	12,900	13,284	13,584	13,968	14,340	14,736	15,120	15,528	15,948
C.S.T.-3									
$/mo	1,132	1,164	1,195	1,228	1,260	1,294	1,329	1,362	1,393
$/12 mo	13,584	13,968	14,340	14,736	15,120	15,528	15,948	16,344	16,716
C.S.T.-4									
$/mo	1,164	1,205	1,244	1,269	1,292	1,324	1,355	1,393	1,432
$/12 mo	13,968	14,340	14,736	15,120	15,528	15,948	16,344	16,716	17,184
C.S.T.-5									
$/mo	1,260	1,294	1,329	1,362	1,393	1,430	1,467		
$/12 mo	15,120	15,528	15,948	16,344	16,716	17,160	17,604		
C.S.T.-6									
$/mo	1,329	1,362	1,393	1,430	1,467	1,505	1,542		
$/12 mo	15,948	16,344	16,716	17,160	17,604	18,060	18,504		

ministrators, supervisors, or classified personnel. The salary cost figures are put into each cost center's budget by the district office based on the actual salaries of the particular personnel working in that center. If desired, salary costs can also be identified for each instructional department within a school through the same procedure.

At the school level, working with only position counts eliminates the cost disparities among different school programs caused by seniority of staff assigned the programs. This procedure permits the principal to allocate staff based on instructional skills and expertise rather than on cost considerations. The same is true for assignments for administrative, supervisory, and classified personnel.

Additional salary expenditures.   All of the salary expenditures discussed above have been for *regular* salaries. As shown previously in Table 4.7, there are other types of salary expenditures which need to be considered in constructing a school district budget. The most common of these are *temporary salaries* and *overtime salaries*. Within each of these classifications, there are a number of different possible types of salary expenditures which a district may wish or need to include in the budget. Further, different rules, procedures, and contract provisions frequently govern the amounts to be budgeted for certified and classified personnel.

Examples and illustrations of some of the more common types of other salary expenditures for each of the certified and classified staffs are shown in Table 4.12 (pp. 410-11). For certified personnel, the two types of temporary salaries most commonly included in school district budgets are: (1) pay for substitutes for instructional staff; and (2) salaries for hiring instructional personnel on a short-term basis. The purpose of the substitute costs is to replace a teacher who is not in the classroom, either for a planned or an unplanned reason. Examples would include substitutes for teachers who are sick, released for other duties, given professional leave, or otherwise absent from the classroom. The purpose of the second type of temporary expenditure is to increase the professional staff for a brief period of time to take care of a need. An example of this type of temporary salary expenditure would be hiring a teacher on a short-term contract to teach one semester of an advanced French class for a limited number of students. (This last type of salary expenditure could be included in the regular salary expenditures as a fractional FTE instead of in temporary salaries.)

Two different methods of estimating the amounts for temporary certified salaries in the budget are illustrated in Table 4.12—current amount and number of days calculation. Both are based on historical trends and patterns, but adjusted for changes in pay scales and operating patterns in the budget year. Of the two, use of the current expenditure amount as the calculation basis is the simplest as it utilizes existing data. Alternatively, the district personnel office can determine the average number of substitute days required per classroom teacher over the past several years and multiply this number by the projected daily substitute rate to reach the budget estimate. This procedure requires the additional step of reviewing and extracting the necessary data from relevant personnel records.

The need for certified personnel hired on a short-term basis (such as for one semester) can be estimated from the instructional plans of the individual schools or operating plans of district level departments. Cost projections are developed from information specifying the number of temporary positions for teachers or other professionals which are planned and the amounts in the short-term contracts.

Overtime expenditures for certified personnel include a variety of additional assignments given to the professional staff. Examples of such activities are extended contracts for teachers to work in the summer on curriculum development, salary increments for school department heads or curriculum coordinators, and extra duty pay for coaching or supervising other after school activities. Estimation of the amounts to include in the budget for these items will vary with the type of activity, but generally involve an established contract amount, either as a dollar amount, a percentage of salary, or an hourly rate.

Similar to the certified personnel, the other salary costs for classified personnel include both temporary and overtime expenditures. The temporary salary costs are to purchase substitute personnel for those classified positions which must be filled daily even if the regular staff member is absent. Examples include teacher aides, cooks, or bus drivers. Overtime salaries are to pay for additional work done by regular district classified employees. Estimates for these costs are generally developed by school and district level department administrators and are based on the type and amount of work which is required.

In Table 4.12, two calculation methods are shown for these salary costs. In the first method, the current dollar amount in the budget is adjusted for historical patterns or trends and for salary and wage changes anticipated next year. The second approach utilizes an estimate of the time to be required, adjusted for any differences expected in the workload or pattern in the upcoming year and for changes in daily or hourly rates for classified personnel. These other salary expenditures are frequently viewed as additional costs, beyond the basic operating costs, and often receive a closer scrutiny from the district office for their consistency.

Employee Benefits

Employee benefits are additional employee related costs which have to be paid by the school district on behalf of their employees. They are not salaries, although they are a personnel-related expenditure. Estimation of these expenditures requires separate calculations from salary expenditures. Further, expenditures for employee benefits are shown in a separate object of expenditure category in the budget.

TABLE 4.12 Other Salary Expenditures

PERSONNEL	TYPE OF SALARY EXPENDITURE	EXAMPLES	ALTERNATIVE CALCULATION PROCEDURES FOR DEVELOPING BUDGET ESTIMATES
CERTIFIED	TEMPORARY	Substitutes for teachers for absences due to sickness, release time, personal and professional leave	1. Current dollar amount adjusted for historical trends and inflation 2. Number of days of substitute time per teacher (from historical records) × daily substitute rate ($/day) adjusted to next year's rate
		Additional professional personnel for short term assignments	1. Contract amounts
	OVERTIME	Extended contracts for teaching personnel	1. Contract amounts
		Department head increment	1. Contract amount 2. Percent of actual salaries for department heads

	Extra duty compensation for duties outside normal teaching day such as coaching, club advisor, band or drama supervisor	1. Contract amount 2. Hourly rate (in contract) × estimated hours to be worked (judged from past experience)
	Nonprofessional duty pay for activities such as being a chaperone	1. Hourly rate × estimated hours to be worked
CLASSIFIED	TEMPORARY Substitutes for teacher aides, cooks, bus drivers	1. Current dollar amount adjusted for historical trends and inflation 2. Number of days of substitute time per position (from historical records) × daily substitute rate ($/day) for each position adjusted to next year's rate
	OVERTIME Additional time for custodians, bus drivers, aides for handicapped students	1. Current dollar amount adjusted for historical patterns and wage increases 2. Number of hours of overtime estimated per position (from historical records) × hourly overtime rate ($/hour) for each position adjusted to next year's rate

For the most part, these benefits are not paid directly to employees, but are paid to other agencies or organizations which then provide certain services, benefits, or compensation to the employees. Some of these expenditures, such as Social Security and Workmen's Compensation, are mandated by state or federal statutes or regulations. Other employee benefit expenditures for the district, such as contributions to employee retirement or health and life insurance premiums, are agreed upon as part of an individual or union employment contract. In the accounting structure used by the district, each required employee benefit should be identified as a subcategory of the main employee benefits object of expenditure. The benefits are shown individually in the budget within the function and cost center where the related salary expenditure is incurred.

Generally, the employee benefit amounts for which the district needs to budget are related to the salaries of the employees. However, the relationship will change depending on the type of benefit, the type of employee, the area in which a person is working, and the amount of time a person works.

The two principal means of estimating employee benefits are: (1) as a percentage of gross salary; or (2) as a fixed dollar amount. The method used depends upon the particular benefit being estimated. For example, benefits such as Social Security, Unemployment Insurance, Workmen's Compensation, and retirement contributions are usually based on a percentage of an employee's salary, sometimes limited by a maximum contribution amount. Medical, dental, disability, and life insurance expenditures are frequently estimated as dollar amounts per employee. Both the percentages and the dollar amounts may change with different groups of employees. An illustration of the types of employee benefits paid by a school district along with the percentages and amounts used to calculate them is shown in Table 4.13 (see p. 114).

For the percentage-based expenditures, estimation of the amounts depends on which benefits apply to which types of salaries. For example, retirement contributions may be made for only regular and overtime salaries; persons employed on a temporary basis may not be eligible to receive retirement contributions. The second step is to establish the rate to use for each of the types of benefits. The percentage amounts for the same type of benefit may vary among different groups of personnel (as is the case with Workmen's Compensation). Some of the percentages will be known in advance, such as Social Security or retirement contributions. Others may have to be estimated from past experience adjusted for expected future conditions, or from estimates obtained from the outside agencies. The final step is to apply the percentages to the appropriate salary amounts. These calculations have to be done for each individual employed by the school district and the results summed to obtain the total for the district. While tedious to do by hand, they are easily done on a computer programmed with the appropriate personnel, salary, and rate information.

For those employee benefits which are calculated on a dollar amount per person, the steps are similar, but the information is modified to account for the different calculation basis. The types of benefits are identified along with their applicable positions. Next, the dollar amount per person for each benefit is estimated. For the same type of benefit the dollar amount per person may vary depending on the type of position involved (such as, medical and vision insurance). It is also necessary to determine the number of individuals for whom each benefit applies. This number is frequently different from the FTE counts used in salary calculations because the benefits can apply to each individual working over a specified amount of time, often half-time (0.50 FTE) or more. This means that four teachers working at three-quarter's time each (0.75 FTE) would be counted as four individuals in calculating some employee benefit amounts, not as the 3.0 FTE which they represent. The last step is to multiply the number of persons eligible for a given benefit by the estimated dollar amount per person to obtain the projected expenditure.

Purchased Services

Purchased Services are expenditures for personnel services or other items obtained from individuals or organizations which are *not* employed by the school district. They are for services purchased from outsiders not on the district payroll. Examples of the major types of purchased services in district budgets include: professional and technical services; property services; transportation service; communication, advertising, printing and binding; and tuition.

There are many ways of estimating the expenditures to be budgeted for purchased services items. In some cases, there are district guidelines for the amounts to be budgeted. In other instances, the most appropriate method may be the recent historical expenditure pattern adjusted for any anticipated inflation. For items without a stable expenditure pattern or for which significantly different levels of activity are expected, other approaches are necessary. These could include obtaining price quotations from possible suppliers or costing out an item by estimating the expected level of activity, the resources required, and the cost of those resources.

Supplies and Materials

Another important expenditure category is supplies and materials. Due to the wide range of items classified in this category, it is useful to subcategorize supply and material items in the budget. The most common of these groupings include: *supplies* (a general account for all supplies for the

TABLE 4.13   Employee Benefits

	TEACHERS	ADMINIS-TRATORS	CLERICAL	CUSTODIAL & FOOD SERVICE	BUS DRIVERS
For Regular, Overtime, andExtra Duty Salary Amounts (% of Salary Amount)					
District Retirement Contribution	10.92%	10.92%	10.92%	10.92%	10.92%
Employee Retirement Contribution (Paid by District)	6.00%	6.00%	6.00%	6.00%	6.00%
Social Security	7.10%	7.10%	7.10%	7.10%	7.10%
Unemployment Compensation	0.55%	0.55%	0.55%	0.55%	0.55%
Workmen's Compensation	0.43%	0.43%	0.43%	3.63%	4.45%
For Temporary Salary Amounts (% of Salary Amount)					
Social Security	7.10%		7.10%	7.10%	7.10%
Unemployment Compensation	0.55%		0.55%	0.55%	0.55%
Workmen's Compensation	0.43%		0.43%	3.63%	4.45%
For Every Regular Salaried Person Who Works Half Time or More (0.5 FTE for Certified and 3 Hours/Day for Classified) ($ per Person)					
Medical & Vision	$1,479	$1,346	$1,265	$1,265	$1,265
Employee Dental	$569	$546	$546	$546	$546
Long-Term Disability Insurance	$71	$71	$71	$71	$71
Life Insurance	$61	$433			
Professional Dues		$250			
Physical Examinations		$200			
Tax Sheltered Annuities		$2,466			

operation of the district which are not otherwise specified); *textbooks; library books;* and *periodicals*. Within each of these areas, it is possible to detail the type of supplies by further subdivisions (such as, audio-visual supplies) or by cross-classifying with the area of responsibility in which the supplies are to be used (such as, library, music, or science supplies). This is particularly useful when allocating supply amounts within schools or district cost centers.

A common approach to the budgeting of supplies for instruction is to use a lump sum amount, usually a dollar per pupil amount, to estimate the necessary expenditures in the upcoming year for the various schools in the district. In this system, the district office establishes an appropriate dollar per pupil amount to be allocated to each school. This is an important step, as it determines the amount of money which teachers will have available for purchasing needed instructional supply items. Setting this dollar per pupil amount is not a scientific process, although it can be helpful to maintain and analyze supply expenditure records. The final amount is often a compromise between educational desires and fiscal reality and both aspects should be considered. The easiest beginning point is the per pupil amount for the current year. This can be reviewed with instructional personnel to evaluate the adequacy of the amount; supply expenditure records for the last several years can be examined to identify areas of inadequate funds or underspending. If there appear to be serious problems with the allocation amounts, then adjustments in the per pupil amounts can be considered. A common adjustment is an inflationary increase from one year to the next to reflect the rising cost of supplies. The amount available for supplies is calculated by multiplying the dollar per pupil amount by the number of students projected for next year.

The supplies and materials amount per pupil can be the same for all pupils in the district or it can vary with the type of school. Usually high schools qualify for the greatest amount per pupil followed by middle schools and then elementary schools. An example of such amounts is shown below.

Elementary Schools (K–Grade 5)	$64.16/pupil
Middle Schools (Grades 6–8)	$82.47/pupil
High Schools (Grades 9–12)	$91.66/pupil

A variation on the single lump sum per pupil allocation is an allocation to schools based on separate amounts per pupil for specific supply categories. In this approach dollar per pupil amounts are established for each of the supply subcategories which are utilized by the schools. The school then receives a series of allocations which are based on the various supply subcategories. If the school also has authority to shift money from one subcategory to another then this approach functions much like the single lump sum allocation. It does, however, provide a more detailed record of where supply expenditures were incurred. An illustration of this approach is shown in Table 4.14.

The amount of money for supplies available to an individual school under this system is the dollar per pupil amount times the number of students estimated to be enrolled next year. In the example of the dollar per pupil supply allocation in Table 4.14, a high school with an estimated enrollment of 2,100 students for next year would receive a budget allocation of $192,486 for supplies and materials for the upcoming year ($91.66 per student x 2,100 students).

TABLE 4.14   Supply and Material Allocation Amounts Per Pupil

CODE	ACCOUNT	ELEMENTARY SCHOOLS	MIDDLE SCHOOLS	HIGH SCHOOLS
410	General Supplies	$29.39	$18.55	$18.84
410	Library Supplies	$0.36	$0.58	$0.64
410	Audiovisual Supplies	$2.82	$2.87	$3.09
410	Testing Supplies	$0.69	$0.66	$0.66
410	Arts & Crafts Supplies	—	$4.50	$4.50
410	Home Ec. Supplies	—	$5.83	$5.83
410	Industrial Arts Supplies	—	$5.83	$5.83
410	Music Supplies	$0.97	$2.64	$2.74
410	Physical Ed. Supplies	$0.97	$4.61	$4.61
410	Science Supplies	$1.44	$3.32	$4.02
410	Vocational Ed. Supplies	—	$1.58	$4.34
421	Textbooks	$18.90	$18.73	$23.04
431	Library Books	$5.27	$7.82	$8.04
432	Reference Books	$1.93	$2.34	$2.52
440	Periodicals	$1.42	$2.07	$2.42
494	Handbooks	—	$0.54	$0.54
	TOTAL	$64.16	$82.47	$91.66

Another approach which can be used is to establish a minimum dollar amount per school for certain supply and material items required for the basic operations of a school regardless of its size. These amounts can be determined by multiplying the standard dollar per pupil amount for the basic items by a minimum enrollment figure for the type of school. Examples of basic items for elementary schools could be library supplies, audiovisual supplies, principal's office supplies, library books, reference books, and periodicals. Schools with low enrollments would receive the base dollar allocation for these items even though their enrollments are below minimum levels and they otherwise would not generate the base funding level using dollar per pupil amounts. Larger schools would generate more than the minimum funding level since the standard dollar per pupil amount is multiplied by the number of pupils in the school. Table 4.15 illustrates these calculations.

Once the supply and materials allocations have been made to the schools, it is then the responsibility of the principal and staff to decide on the amounts to be allocated to each instructional department, support area, and administrative activity within the school. Their flexibility in this process is constrained by the district guidelines on transferring money among different allocation accounts. The internal school procedures for doing this range from an assignment of dollar amounts by the principal to a participatory decision making process involving faculty, administrators, and classified staff.[5] Once these internal allocations are decided upon, the

TABLE 4.15   Calculations for Minimum Allocation for Supplies and Materials

SCHOOL	PROJECTED ENROLLMENT	MINIMUM ENROLLMENT	SUPPLY $ ALLOCATION (1)	MINIMUM $ ALLOCATION (2)	ADDITIONAL ALLOCATION
Small Creek	205	250	$13,153	$16,040[a]	$2,887
Large Pond	400	250	$25,664[a]	$16,040	$0

(1) Supply $ Allocation equals the Projected Enrollment × $64.16.
(2) Minimum $ Allocation equals 250 students × $64.16.
[a]The actual allocation to each school. It is the larger of the Supply $ or Minimum $ Allocation amounts.

school reports them to the district office for incorporation into the district budget document.

Capital Outlay

Capital outlays are expenditures for generally more costly items such as land, buildings (including acquisitions, additions, and alterations), other capital improvements, equipment, and vehicles. There is a wide range in the types of capital outlay items which a school district might consider. Some of the items purchased represent a continuation of commitments to existing programs and activities, while others are required for the addition of new programs or approaches. Consequently, while the number of capital outlay items in a district's budget may be relatively small, it is not uncommon for these items to receive a great deal of attention from the school and district level administration, the school board, and even the public.

Purchases of land or building construction are very large dollar expenditures, but occur relatively infrequently for a school district. These items may require special financing arrangements, a more detailed examination and justification of their purchase, and a different approval process. Due to their special nature, districts frequently establish a separate capital budget to plan for these large, and sometimes multi-year, expenditures.

Items with lower costs, such as equipment or some alterations to buildings, are more often a part of the annual operations of the district. The relatively smaller dollar amounts involved mean that they can be a part of the annual operating budget.

Equipment. By far the most common type of capital outlay expenditure in the district's operating budget is for equipment. A variety of approaches to budgeting for equipment purchases is available. As a first step, these approaches generally establish a total dollar amount to be spent for equipment purchases for the entire district. The available funds are then distributed to schools and district level departments. A straightforward way to determine the total equipment dollars to be budgeted for the district for next year is to adjust the current equipment dollar amount for inflation and anticipated changes in needs. In some instances, the district administration or school board will establish a total equipment dollar amount to stay within an overall district budget.

Another procedure is to use a percentage replacement amount for the value of the capital equipment owned by the district. For example, if the district had equipment on the books valued at $10,000,000 and established a replacement percentage of 2 percent each year, then it would have a total equipment budget for the district of $200,000. This equates to a fifty year average replacement cycle. A 4 percent replacement would yield an equipment budget of $400,000 and a twenty-five year average replacement cycle. An advantage of this last approach is in communicating with the school board and public. Rather than have to justify each equipment item, the district receives approval to spend a fixed sum based on an agreed upon replacement cycle which, in effect, may sound very conservative.

There are also a number of options for districts to distribute the total equipment dollars available, once that amount has been determined. A district can follow the same general allocation procedures as described for supplies and materials. A dollar per student amount is established for equipment and this amount is used to calculate a lump sum allocation to each school based on enrollment. The determination of what equipment items to purchase is left to the principal and staff at each school. It is also possible to combine the dollar per student amounts for supplies, materials, and equipment into one single amount to cover all of these items for a school. This allows the school the flexibility to allocate the total available dollars generated between supplies and equipment as they see fit.

A variation of this approach is to provide a lump sum amount for each school (for example, each high school will be allocated $90,000 to spend for equipment, each middle school $75,000, and each elementary school $40,000). If schools at each level are approximately the same size, an equal allocation of the total available funds is the most easily understood procedure; however, it does not account for differences in age and condition of the facilities, types of students, or types of instructional program among schools.

Another approach is to require the schools and district level departments to submit their equipment requests to the district office. The lists contain the description, quantity, price, and justification of every piece of equipment requested. Often the list items are prioritized so that if the requests exceed the available dollars (the usual state of affairs), there will be a guide to cutting back. For unified districts the total available dollars are sometimes divided into amounts for elementary, middle, and high schools prior to allocating funds to individual schools to avoid having the different types of schools compete with each other for limited funds.

To gain further control over these high expenditure items, some districts also require that all equipment requests over a specified dollar amount be approved by the school board. This extra step, even if the request is within the total district or school allocation, provides an additional check of spending practices by the body charged with fiscal oversight responsibility for the district.

At times, districts will wish to make special equipment purchases or allocations outside the normal procedures. This situation can occur when the district wants to implement a new program or activity which has high equipment needs, but does not wish to shift money from the existing programs to pay for the new program. An example would be the introduction of microcomputers into the curriculum. It is possible for the district to earmark certain funds for particular uses and allocate them to schools or departments in addition to the regular equipment allocation. These special equipment funds are usually one time arrangements to cover a particular purpose. For example, a district may provide each high school and middle school with a grant of $40,000 to equip a microcomputer laboratory. This is an expensive venture which would otherwise seriously deplete the instructional equipment funds for existing instructional programs. The one time special grant allows the schools to institute a new program desired by the district while maintaining existing programs' operations.

Other Capital Outlay.   School districts face other types of capital outlay needs besides equipment. Two common areas which appear in district budgets are care and upkeep of buildings, and improvements of sites. The capital outlay expenditures related to these areas are generally not regular, but rather sporadic with some being emergencies (such as, replacing a leaking roof) and some part of a long range improvement plan (like, landscaping one school in the district every year). For emergencies, which by their nature cannot be foreseen, a contingency amount can be set aside. The amount can be established by review of historical records for expenditures of this type.

Other capital outlay expenditures are needed during the year for improvements to both buildings and grounds. Once a dollar amount which the district expects to spend for these items has been established (and perhaps divided among elementary, middle, and high schools and central office departments), schools and departments submit requests ranked by priority to utilize the funds. As there is inevitably more money requested than available, the highest priority expenditure requests are approved in order until the funds are exhausted. Within these requests, an item to improve the safety of students or to remove a safety hazard is usually given highest priority; these are followed by those requests affecting the largest number of students, those critical to instructional programs, and those which have been on the request list for the longest time.

Other Objects of Expenditure

There are other expenditures which the school district incurs and must budget for, but which do not fit into any of the previous categories. It is for these expenditures that this *other* category is used.

The most common types of Other expenditures include payments for the retirement of debts, interest on the district's debts, housing authority obligations, dues and fees for the district and its employees, and insurance premiums and judgments paid by the district as a result of court decisions. Due to the nature of these expenditures, budgeting for Other expenditures is usually done at the district level by the business manager or other fiscal officer. Information to develop the budget estimates for debt and interest payments, and for housing authority obligations comes from district financial data (like a debt repayment schedule, or interest due in upcoming year).

Expenditures for memberships, associations, or other organizations or services for the district or its employees can be budgeted by identifying the particular items and their costs, by projecting a similar cost from prior years' data, or by estimating a cost per employee for which the district has agreed to pay a lump sum. Insurance expenditures estimates can be obtained through quotations from the companies writing the district's insurance. Expenditures to cover judgments rendered against the district are much more difficult to estimate. If the district is not involved in a lawsuit at the time of budget preparation and has not had such a history, then it may not be necessary to budget anything for this item. However, if there is an active lawsuit, or the district expects one, or the district wishes to self-insure against the possibility of losing a suit, then an expenditure amount can be included in the budget. It is usually put in a contingency fund or a reserve account until it is actually required, if at all. The amount set aside is based on the size of the expected judgment against the district.

REVENUE ESTIMATES

Revenues are the monies coming into the school district. They come from a variety of sources—local property taxes, state government, and federal agencies. They are used to pay for the expenditures incurred to operate the instructional, support, administrative, and other operations of the district.

As noted in several times before, in almost all states revenues and expenditures *must* balance; state statutes require that districts' planned expenditures cannot exceed their revenues. If on initial estimates, the anticipated revenues of a school district are less than the projected expenditures, then the district must reduce the expenditures, find other revenues, or utilize some combination of both actions to reach a balance. If, however, the initial estimates indicate that the revenues in the upcoming year will be greater than the planned expenditures, the district can reduce the taxes on its patrons, expand existing or begin new programs, and/or establish a contingency fund to achieve a balance between revenues and expenditures.

Proper revenue estimation is important. It allows the district to plan for and provide the best possible educational program. It assists in maintaining the financial credibility of the school district with the school board and community. Large sums which are "found" during the school year (as a result of underestimating revenues) can cause suspicion among district voters and have on occasion caused superintendents to lose their jobs. On the other hand, overestimating revenues can cause program cutbacks during midyear as the expected revenues do not materialize to cover expenditures.

Revenue estimation is not necessarily easy. School districts have much less control over revenues than expenditures. They are dependent upon state and federal legislatures for decisions on amounts to be appropriated for education; they rely on state and federal departments of education for receiving the amounts actually allocated to them; and they may need approval from the local voters for a property tax levy. All of these processes can be influenced to some degree by school district efforts, but unlike the expenditure side of the budget, the school district does not have the final authority to determine many of its revenues.

Nevertheless, revenue estimates must be made, and they should be as accurate as possible. All available information should be used; the district can and should obtain the latest projections of revenue levels from its various sources. These projections should be updated as new information becomes available, so that when the final budget for the district is established the revenue estimates will be the most accurate possible.

Estimating revenues is a much more centralized process than is estimating expenditures. Revenue estimation is usually done by the business office. The process consists of collecting information about anticipated revenues from the agencies providing those funds, organizing and analyzing this information, and developing revenue estimates for the upcoming year. In comparison with estimating expenditures, revenue estimation involves only a few people since the number of revenue sources are relatively few. This allows the district administration to maintain a close control over the process.

Estimating Revenues

There are two primary dimensions to estimating revenues. First, revenues are estimated by *fund*; that is, projections are developed separately of revenues for the General Fund, Special Revenue Funds, Capital Projects Funds, Debt Service Funds, Enterprise Funds, and any other funds utilized by the school district. Second, within each fund, estimates are made of the revenues to be received from each individual *source* of revenue. The sources are categorized by organizational level within the educational system and include local, intermediate, state, federal, and other sources. For each level, the amount of money anticipated from each particular revenue item or agency is projected. A revenue classification scheme for organizing, developing, and presenting estimated revenues is shown in Chapter Three.

The procedures for developing revenue estimates are fairly straightfoward, although it may be difficult at times to obtain reliable information on certain revenue items. Generally, the steps involve: (1) identifying the specific items or agencies from which the district is anticipating revenues in the upcoming year; and (2) estimating or calculating the dollar amount which is expected from each item or agency.

Local Revenues.   Local revenues come from a variety of places. The largest single item is the current property tax which is levied by the local school district. However, there are a number of other important local revenue elements. These include: other types of taxes; revenues from other local government units, such as cities or counties; tuition; transportation fees; earnings on investments; food service operations; pupil activities, such as admissions to school sponsored activities, membership fees, and participation fees; and other local sources, such as rentals of district facilities or equipment, contributions from private sources, sale of fixed assets owned by the district, and revenues for services provided to other school districts.

Since property taxes are so important to the district, they are treated separately in the revenue estimation process; these procedures are discussed below. The other local revenue items are projected on an item-by-item basis. Using the revenue classification system and the district's historical revenue records as guides, the responsible district personnel develop estimates of money to be received from each local revenue source. As the sources are quite different, the particular estimation procedure will vary. For example, tuition revenues can be estimated from data projecting estimated numbers of tuition-paying students and the tuition amounts to be charged, while earnings on investments can be estimated from projected interest rates, the dollar amounts, and length of time which the district will have its funds invested over the next year.

The procedures for estimating current property taxes which the district will receive next year depends on state regulations. In states that limit the amount of local property tax a district can raise, districts can calculate the maximum property tax allowable. This becomes the estimated revenue amount to go into the budget. When summed with the other revenue amounts, the total revenue amount establishes a limit on expenditures, since total expenditures cannot exceed total revenues. This is, in effect, a revenue-driven budgeting process. The available revenues establish the level of expenditures, which in turn determine the programs and services offered by the school district.

In other states, where the only limits on a district's local property tax levy are political (that is, what the school board or voters will approve), a different procedure is used. The total expenditure requests determine the total amount of revenues needed. From this total amount, the revenues from all other sources (state, federal, intermediate, and local revenues, except the current property tax) are subtracted. The balance remaining is the amount needed from local property taxes. This budgeting process is primarily expenditure-driven. The desired level of expenditures is the fixed element which determines the level of local property tax levy needed to finance the programs and services to be provided by the school district. The two different processes are contrasted in Table 4.16.

After the local property tax amount is established, it is possible to calculate the district's tax rate. Tax rates are usually expressed in one of two ways: millage or property tax dollars per thousand dollars of assessed value. Both approaches are identical even though different terminology is used. One mill is equal to $1.00 per $1,000 of assessed value. To calculate the tax rate, the total property tax amount levied by the district is divided by the assessed valuation of the taxable property in the district, divided by 1,000. A sample tax rate calculation is shown in Table 4.17. The assessed value amount should be available from the tax assessor's office, which, since it has the assessment data, may even do the calculation for the district.

The tax rate is only one component of the property tax levy. It works in conjunction with the assessed value of the property in the district. The assessed value of the district multiplied by the tax rate yields the property tax to be collected. Unfortunately, this is not always clearly understood by the public or the media. If the district's assessed valuation is rising, it may still be able to raise more local property tax dollars even though the tax rate may be lower than in prior years. This relationship also works in reverse; a reduced assessed valuation in the district can lead to higher tax rates, but no more actual property tax dollars for the district. The greatest opportu-

TABLE 4.16 Types of Budget Processes

REVENUE DRIVEN PROCESS	EXPENDITURE DRIVEN PROCESS
Available revenues determine expenditure levels	Desired expenditures less all other revenues determine amount of property taxes needed
Total revenues, except current property taxes	Total Expenditures
+ Current Property Taxes	− All other revenues, except current property taxes
= Total Expenditures	= Current Property Taxes

TABLE 4.17   Tax Rate Calculation

$$\text{Tax Rate} = \frac{\text{Current Property Tax Levied by District}}{\text{Assessed Value of Property in District/1,000}}$$

EXAMPLE:

If the district levies $13,000,000 in property taxes and the total assessed value of the district is $1,000,000,000 then its tax rate is:

$$\text{Tax Rate} = \frac{\$13,000,000}{\$1,000,000,000} = \$13.00/\$1,000 \text{ AV}$$
$$\text{or}$$
$$13 \text{ Mills}$$

nity for property tax increases (or decreases) occurs when changes in both factors work in the same direction—a rising assessed valuation in the district coupled with a higher (lower) tax rate.

Funding from Intermediate Sources.   Intermediate sources are those agencies which are located between the local district and the state in the educational system; examples include county units, multi-county units, multi-district cooperatives, and regional programs. If the district receives revenues from any intermediate sources, these must be included in the district's budget.

In some instances an intermediate unit may have its own taxing authority and distribute some of the revenues it raises itself to districts inside its boundaries. In other cases, a district may receive funds from an intermediate unit for operating a program which also serves students from several other districts. An example would be revenues received by a large district from a county educational unit for operating a special education program for the whole county which enrolls handicapped students from surrounding smaller districts.

To develop estimates of revenues from intermediate sources, district officials need to contact the intermediate educational agency personnel who will have information about the funding they expect to provide to the district. These estimates can be refined and updated during the budget process with regular contact through the intermediate educational agency.

State Revenues.   While there are wide variations across states, nationally almost half of the money spent on elementary and secondary education is provided by state governments; local funds are a close second; and federal funds rank a distant third. The primary types of state revenues for school districts are general aid, categorical aid, and in some states, revenues in lieu of taxes. Of these three, by far the most important in terms of total revenue dollars are the general aid monies. State aid is appropriated by the state legislature and distributed to school districts by the state department of education or other state agency. The best source of information about the expected level of state aid will usually be the department of education. School finance personnel in the department may provide districts with departmental estimates of the amount of general fund revenues they can expect in the upcoming year. Similar estimates can be obtained for categorical revenues. Estimates of the level of revenues in lieu of taxes may come from the department of education, or perhaps from the state department of revenue, if they are the agency distributing these funds.

The timing of state revenue estimates may be awkward for district budget planning if the legislature is slow in reaching educational appropriation decisions or if it changes the amounts to respond to changing state fiscal conditions. If the legislature has not determined the state funding support for education before the district has to compile its budget document, then the state revenue estimates will be uncertain. This uncertainty cannot be allowed to paralyze the budget process, however. Districts must use the best estimates available. A conservative estimate is usually made in such situations to protect the district against overspending revenues it will not receive. Throughout the district's budgeting process, district officials responsible for revenue estimates should keep in contact with the appropriate state contacts to obtain the latest estimates for state aid.

Federal Aid.   Money for federal aid is appropriated by the U. S. Congress and distributed by the U. S. Department of Education. The federal funds are largely directed to categorical programs (as in Chapter One [compensatory education] and Chapter Two [block grants] of the Educational Consolidation and Improvement Act, handicapped programs, vocational programs, bilingual programs); operationally, most of these funds are channeled through the state to be distributed as grants to local school districts. In addition, large dollar amounts are distributed in the form of revenues in lieu of taxes through such programs as Impact Aid to school districts for operation (P.L. 874) or Federal Forest Fees.

Federal sources usually represent less than 10 percent of the total district revenues and generally an even smaller proportion of the General Fund revenues. However, in some programs the operations are largely supported by federal monies. Without federal funds, some districts would find it difficult to maintain certain categorical programs at their present levels of service and would face either reducing or eliminating programs or supporting them with funds from other sources.

The federal funding process is much farther away from the district, both in geographic distance and in the information which may be available to the district. Since most federal monies come to the district via the state department of education, the personnel responsible for federal programs are often the best contacts for funding information. From these state contacts, districts should be able to obtain the most reliable information on expected funding levels, timing of receipt of funds, and associated regulations with which to comply.

BALANCING EXPENDITURES AND REVENUES

The final phase of budget building is to balance the expenditure requests with the projected revenues. Contrary to what might be implied above, there is generally not an automatic balancing of expenditures and revenues. With either a revenue-driven or an expenditure-driven process, estimated expenditures may exceed the anticipated revenues. (The other situation is possible, of course. Projected revenues could be greater than estimated expenditures, but usually this is not the case as there is rarely a shortage of legitimate expenditures.) It is necessary to revise expenditure estimates and revenue projections to reach a balance. This is an iterative process that may take several attempts to complete.

There are two basic methods of balancing the budget when expenditure requests are greater than projected revenues. The first is to reduce expenditures and the second is to increase revenues. If the expenditure reductions needed are relatively small, it may be possible for the central office administrators to make them in consultation with the school administrators and district department heads. Larger cuts can also be made this way, particularly if the expenditure requests have been prioritized when they were developed. However, if the required cuts are significant, it may be useful and necessary to have the school administrators and district department heads resubmit their expenditure requests after having decided on where cuts could be best made (or where they will do the least damage).

Revenue increases are more difficult for the district to obtain. One place to start is with updated revenue estimates from state and federal department of education officials and with the latest assessed valuation and property tax collection projections from the tax collector's office. The latest estimates should be more accurate, but there is no guarantee that they will show an increase. Nevertheless, it is essential to be working with the most reliable information available.

Other possibilities for revenue increases are from local sources. A tactic which can work for one year is for the district to reduce its cash carryover (the amount of money carried over from the end of one fiscal year to fund the expenditures during the beginning of the next year before state aid and property tax revenues are received) and to reduce the amounts held for contingencies. This may provide additional revenues for the upcoming year, but it reduces the district's financial flexibility and increases the risk of not being able to respond to emergencies. The district may also undertake such strategies as: writing grant proposals for funds from public agencies or private foundations; seeking community and business contributions of money, equipment, or personnel; improving its cash management procedures to increase investment earnings; or leasing vacant facilities. While the income received from these ventures may be helpful, it is usually marginal to the overall budget. If the gap between expenditures and revenues is large, it will not usually be closed by attempts to increase other local revenue.

The most significant revenue source to balance revenues and expenditures is the local property tax. If the district is legally limited on the amount which it can levy, then this avenue is also closed. However, in those situations where an increase in the property tax levy is permissible, this offers an opportunity to balance the budget. The analysis and the ultimate answer is political rather than economic. The district administrators and the school board must decide if the property tax levy increase necessary to balance the budget is politically acceptable. Will it be accepted by the taxpayers, and, if necessary, supported by the voters? If they believe so, then the proposed tax levy (or tax rate or school budget, depending on the form of the election) can be approved by the board and submitted to the voters, if required. If property tax increases are not politically feasible or if the voters reject the increase, then expenditures must be reduced until they equal available revenues.

SUMMARY

Developing accurate expenditure and revenue estimates is the key element in budget preparation. It is an activity that involves many people in the district. Establishing the level of expenditures is the aspect of the budget that is under the greatest control of administrators. In contrast, the school district is dependent upon the decisions of state and federal legislatures and agencies for much of its revenue.

The accounting structure is used to organize the detailed expenditure and revenue estimates in the budget. While sometimes a bit tedious, the accounting codes do provide an indispensable means of categorizing and planning district expenditures and revenues in a uniform and manageable way.

Expenditure estimates begin by projecting the number of students expected by the district in the next year. Using the student projections, the numbers and types of personnel which will be required can be calculated. Then the anticipated expenditures are estimated for each cost center (such as, school, or district-level department); by function and subfunction (like High School Instruction and, within that, by Language Arts, Social Studies, Office of Principal, Audio-visual Services, Library Services); and by the type of expenditure within each cost center and function (such as, salaries, employee benefits, purchased services, supplies and materials, capital outlay, and other objects).

The budget in its completed form can be a massive document with an overwhelming amount of detail. However, it is built up from individual school and department budget requests and separate revenue projections which are less complex. Revenue estimates are developed for each anticipated source from which the school district will receive funds. The expenditure estimates are generally developed by: (1) the cost center where they will occur; (2) the program or function being carried out in the cost center; and (3) the particular item to be purchased. These steps are reflected in the general approach to developing expenditure estimates, which is shown below.

1. Identify the programs and activities in the organizational unit or subunit for which the expenditure budget is being developed.
2. Specify the resources needed to carry out the tasks for the program at the expected level of activity.
3. Put prices on the resources and sum up to reach a total cost for the program.

The budget is an important management tool for planning and implementing educational programs. The projected expenditures reflect the priorities of the district as determined by the educational philosophy and beliefs of the school board members, district administrators and instructional staff, parents, students, and the community, by the regulations and requirements from state and federal agencies, and, at times by mandates from the courts. The revenue estimates determine the expected availability of funds to support those desired and required programs. In developing expenditure estimates for next year's operations, districts have to work within fiscal constraints, as expressed in the revenue projections. The objective is to provide the best and most effective educational programs with the available dollars. The budgeting process should help districts to achieve this goal.

PROBLEMS

4.1 North City Elementary School District has had the student enrollments listed below over the last five years.

GRADE	4 YRS. AGO	3 YRS. AGO	2 YRS. AGO	1 YR. AGO	THIS YR.
K	532	507	517	528	535
1	521	526	523	525	537
2	505	502	492	481	498
3	510	495	484	477	491
4	486	479	482	476	457
5	475	488	488	465	486
6	495	467	459	456	441

Using the cohort survival method, calculate the survival rates in each of the grades 1 through 6 for the past five years.

If outside data indicated that the number of incoming kindergarten students for the next two years were 545 and 550 respectively, project the district's total enrollment for the next two years.

4.2 Develop a teacher salary schedule having the following characteristics:

   a. Twelve experience level steps.

   b. Five education level steps. (Title them appropriately).

   c. An experience level increment of 5.0 percent for the first two educational levels and a 6.0 percent increase for the last three education levels.

   d. An educational level increment of 4, 6, 9, and 14 percent beginning with the lowest to the next lowest level increment.

   e. A beginning salary level of $18,000 for the first experience level and first educational level cell.

   f. An experience level maximum of the ninth step for the first two educational levels.

   g. An experience level minimum of the fourth step for the last two educational levels.

4.3 STUDENT SUPPORT SERVICES BUDGET FOR ALDER SCHOOL DISTRICT.

   Dr. Chancy has recently been appointed Associate Superintendent for Student Services for Alder School District. In a recent meeting, the district superintendent has asked Dr. Chancy to prepare a budget for the costs of the student support services for the next year.

   According to established district policy, student support services consist of five main activities: attendance and social work; guidance; health; psychological services; and speech pathology and audiology. The student support services activities are managed centrally by Dr. Chancy assisted by a speech therapist serving as assistant director and one secretary.

   Some services are provided to all students, while others are differentiated academically or vocationally. Additionally, specialized services are offered to handicapped students by specially trained personnel. District personnel guidelines have been established for student services personnel; they are given in Table 1.

   In addition to the personnel requirements, other activities undertaken in the program require consideration in the budget. The Guidance program does career aptitude testing for all eleventh graders; the usual procedure is to purchase a package from an outside firm which includes the tests (which are administered by the homeroom teachers) and their scoring for a fee of $6.00 per pupil. Historically, about 10 percent of the emotionally disturbed students annually have required psychotherapy services by an outside mental health professional; the cost has averaged about $3,600 per student treated.

   In a visit to the Planning Office, Dr. Chancy obtained estimates of student enrollments for next year. They are shown in Table 2.

   From the Business Manager, Dr. Chancy collected cost information relevant to the student services programs. The average salary and the salary range for various positions in the district are also shown in Table 1. Benefits in the district averaged 28 percent of salary plus $1,700 per person for medical insurance. The Business Manager told Dr. Chancy that the recently concluded salary ne-

TABLE 1

POSITION	STAFFING PATTERN	TYPE	AVERAGE SALARY	SALARY RANGE
Attendance Officer	1.0 per district	Noncertificated	$12,600	
School Social Worker	1.0 per High School 1.0 per Middle School 0.2 per Elementary School	Certificated	$18,900	$16,065 to $20,790
Guidance Counselor	1 per 800 high school students 1 per 1500 middle school students 1 per 150 handicapped students	Certificated	$17,800	$15,130 to $19,580
Secretary I	1 per 5 Guidance Counselors	Noncertificated	$12,100	$10,285 to $13,310
School Nurse	0.5 per High School 0.3 per Middle School 0.5 per Elementary School	Certificated	$16,700	$14,195 to $18,370
Health Aide	0.5 per school	Noncertificated	$9,600	$8,160 to $10,560
Speech Therapist	1 per 50 speech handicapped	Certificated	$19,100	$16,235 to $21,010
Audiologist	1 per 100 hearing impaired	Certificated	$17,400	$14,790 to $19,140
Secretary III	1 for Director	Noncertificated	$18,300	$17,500 to $19,100

Dr. Darcy's current salary is $35,600.
Assistant Directors receive a 20% salary increment over their normal salary.

gotiations would increase salaries by 4 percent in the coming year. The Business Manager also provided a list of cost estimation standards for other budget items. They included: $150 per position (certificated and noncertificated) for office supplies; $80 per position for telephone charges; $750 per position for local travel for all positions except clerical; $40 per certificated position for periodicals; and $50 per certificated position for postage. Equipment costs for new and replacement equipment are estimated at $1,000 per certificated position and $500 per noncertificated position.

Prepare a budget covering the costs associated with the district's student support services activities for next year. In presenting the budget, follow the instructions below.

1. The budget should be prepared in a standard format by third level FUNCTION code where possible, and by OBJECT of expenditure code within each function. Use different function codes as needed to separate costs by their purposes. In addition to other functions, use a separate function (2101

TABLE 2

ELEMENTARY		MIDDLE		HIGH SCHOOL	
Number of Schools	13		5		3
Total number of Students in District*					
Kindergarden	890	Grade 6	920	Grade 9	860
Grade 1	900	Grade 7	900	Grade 10	820
Grade 2	930	Grade 8	880	Grade 11	760
Grade 3	920		————	Grade 12	710
Grade 4	910		2700		————
Grade 5	910				3150
	————				
	5460				
Number of Handicapped Students in District					
Mentally Retarded				240	
Learning Disabled				310	
Hearing Impaired				31	
Visually Impaired				12	
Physically Handicapped				42	
Speech Impaired				366	
Emotionally Disturbed				92	
				————	
				1093	

*Includes both handicapped and nonhandicapped students

Service Area Direction) to account for the overall administration of Student Support Services. Give the object codes to the lowest level for which you have information (for example, 111 Certificated Salaries).

2. Present your results in a neat, easy to follow format.

3. Show your calculations separately and include them as an explanation for your budget.

4. Round all positions to the nearest one-tenth (0.10) full-time equivalent (FTE) and show position counts in the budget.

5. Include personnel costs in your budget.

6. Round all cost calculations to the nearest $10.

4.4 SPECIAL EDUCATION IN DUNN SCHOOL DISTRICT

As the recently appointed Assistant Superintendent for Special Education in Dunn School District, Dr. Kirk was developing the budgets for the upcoming school year for the three district programs for handicapped children: physically handicapped (PH); emotionally disturbed (ED); and learning disabilities (LD). To begin this task, she gathered the information described below.

CURRENT ENROLLMENT BY PROGRAM	
Physically handicapped	61
Emotionally disturbed	22
Learning disabilities	193

The physically handicapped students are served in one of two instructional settings—self-contained classrooms or with instructional aide assistance in regular classrooms. There are presently forty-eight physically handicapped students in special classrooms and this number is projected to grow by 20 percent next year. The other PH students receive aide assistance and a 25 percent growth in students in this placement is expected next year. (Note: The aide assistance component is considered the only element of special education instruction for these students and all of its associated costs are part of the special education budget. The costs of their regular classroom instruction are included in the regular programs budget.)

All of the emotionally disturbed students are placed in a special program operated by a neighboring school district. The same number of students are expected in this program next year. Dunn School District pays a tuition of $2,750 for each of these students to the neighboring district. Tuition will increase to $3,000 per student next year.

Eighteen of the learning disabled students are now placed in special classes and an approximate 10 percent growth in this placement is expected next year. (Note: The special classes for each handicapping condition contain only students with that handicap, that is, learning disabled and physically handicapped students are not mixed in the same special class.) The remainder of the learning disabled students are served in resource rooms involving part-time special education instruction for these students; a 12 percent growth in students served in this placement next year is anticipated.

The district follows the state guidelines for class size and staffing for each of their special education placements. These are outlined below.

PRO-GRAM	PLACEMENT	STATE GUIDELINES	DISTRICT CLASS SIZE	STAFF/UNIT
PH	Special Class	10–12	11	1 Teacher and 2 Aides
	Aide Assistance	2–4	3	1 Aide
LD	Special Class	10–12	11	1 Teacher and 1 Aide
	Resource Room	25–35	30	1 Teacher and 1 Aide

In determining the number of staff needed, the district policy is to round to the nearest whole number for teachers and to the nearest half position for aides. For example, 2.3 teachers would be rounded to 2 teachers and 2.2 aides would be rounded to 2 aides, while 2.4 aides would be rounded to 2.5 aides. However, in program units involving both teachers and aides, the teacher rounding rule is used for both types of positions to maintain the proper staffing patterns.

Special education teachers are given three days per year of release time to assist in developing formal instructional plans for their students and to confer with parents. Substitute teachers are hired to replace the teachers during release time. Aides are sometimes required to work extra hours to deal with specific student problems. They average five hours per month in overtime duties for which they are paid additionally.

Some of the physically handicapped students also require additional services. Thirty-five students receive two individual ½ hour physical therapy sessions per week from private physical therapists. These services are provided for the entire school year (thirty-six weeks) and cost $20.00 per hour. Also, twenty-two PH students require special transportation to transport them from home to school; this cost averages $850 per student annually. No change is expected in the numbers of students receiving either of these services or their costs next year.

Both the PH and LD programs have program supervisors who work to direct and improve the instructional programs by assisting teachers, developing and evaluating curriculum, and monitoring student progress and teacher performance. They are considèred supervisory, not instructional, personnel. Half of one supervisor's time is assigned to the PH program, while the LD program has a full-time supervisor. They share a single secretary.

The district's business manager, Mr. Martin, provided information on salaries and cost standards for budgeting. The average special education teacher has a Master's degree and ten years of experience. Use Table 4.8 as the district's salary schedule for teachers. The average salary for instructional aides is $12,600 for a nine month contract. The recently concluded collective bargaining negotiations provide for a 5 percent increase in salaries for all instructional personnel next year (teachers and aides) and a total employee benefit package costing the district 30 percent of base salaries. Aides will receive $16.00 per hour for any overtime work. Substitute teacher costs are projected at $110 per day for each substitute teacher used. Additionally, the district will pay professional dues of all certified staff; these average $70.00 per staff member in special education.

Supervisors' salaries are based upon 125 percent of average teacher salary. Secretaries currently average $14,800 per year and will receive the same percentage salary increase and benefits as the instructional personnel. Supervisory personnel have a budgeted allotment of $1,400 per full-time position for traveling among the schools, $300 per full-time position for supplies, and $80.00 per full-time position for communication expenses. These allotments are based on certified supervisory positions only.

The table below gives the district cost standards for other items in the special education programs.

ITEMS	SPECIAL CLASS	RESOURCE ROOM	AIDE ASSIST.
Supplies	$150/student	$105/student	$85/student
Textbooks	$ 60/student	$ 45/student	$25/student
Replace. Equip.	$900/classroom	$400/res. rm.	$250/aide

The special classrooms for both the PH and LD programs are all housed in a single building which is rented by the school district for $1,600 per month. The district utilizes the building during the school year (nine months) only for these classes and utilizes the building for other activities during the summer. The terms of the rental agreement call for the school district to pay for property insurance (annual twelve month premium of $2,400) and for electricity ($240 per month average). Resource rooms and aide assistance are carried out in regular school buildings and are not charged with any of the building operation costs.

The revenues to fund these special education programs come from three sources. Federal monies from the Education for All Handicapped Children Act are received by the district in the amount of $200 per handicapped child. The state contributes 30 percent of the total district special education expenditures from its categorical funding program for handicapped students. Any additional revenues needed to support the program are provided by the district from its available resources.

Prepare a budget for all of the relevant expenditures and revenues for these three special education programs in Dunn School District next year. In developing and presenting the budget, assume that a separate FUND has been established to account for all expenditures and revenues for these programs. In presenting the budget, follow the instructions below.

1. The budget should be prepared in a standard format with expenditures presented by third level FUNCTION and by OBJECT of expenditure codes within each function. Use different function codes as needed to separate expenditures by their different purposes. Give the object codes to the lowest level for which you have information (for example, 111 Certified Salaries).

2. Revenues should be presented by appropriate source code.

3. Present the results in a neat, easy to follow format.

4. Show the calculations separately and include them as an explanation for the budget.

5. Include personnel costs in the budget.

6. Round all cost calculations to the nearest $10.

4.5 BILINGUAL EDUCATION BUDGET FOR LA ESPERANZA SCHOOL DISTRICT.

Dr. Cabeza has recently been appointed head of Bilingual Education for La Esperanza School District. The district has been selected to receive a large grant from the U.S. Department of Education to develop a model bilingual elementary school. The district expects that the grant will cover all of the costs of operating the model school. Bolivar Elementary School has been designated as the site for the model bilingual school that will teach some courses in English and others in Spanish. The bilingual elementary school will provide students with an opportunity to learn Spanish through "partial immersion" in the language. Authorization for the establishment of the bilingual elementary school was based on research findings which suggest that children have a superior capacity for learning a second language at an early age and that children in bilingual programs meet or surpass their peers in English reading tests and in their mastery of subject content by the end of the fifth grade. The program would also serve to broaden the students' awareness of other cultures and encourage better relations among ethnic groups.

The district superintendent has asked Dr. Cabeza to prepare a budget for the new bilingual school for the next year. The school board has requested that both the costs and revenues associated with the new school be included.

The program is scheduled to begin next September and will include all six grades in the school. Bolivar will operate on a nine month schedule, corresponding to that of the other schools within the district. Projected enrollments for next year are:

grade 1	51 students	grade 4	52 students
grade 2	46 students	grade 5	48 students
grade 3	45 students	grade 6	46 students

Bolivar School will be directed by Dr. Cabeza as the principal with the assistance of an assistant principal (nonteaching) plus one full-time and one half-time secretary.

Personnel guidelines have been established for the upcoming school year for Bolivar Elementary. They are:

Two teachers for every grade

One full-time aide for every 10 students in grades 1-3

One full-time aide for every 25 students in grades 4-6

The equivalent of six FTE aides will be upper-level Spanish students from the nearby Montezuma High School. Each of the high school students aides will work at no cost, but will receive scholastic credit based on job performance. These aides will be evaluated and supervised by the individual classroom teachers, as well as the assistant principal. All other aides will be employed by the school district.

In determining the number of staff positions needed, the district policy is to round to the nearest whole position for teachers and to the nearest half position for aides.

A workshop and week-long orientation to prepare the program staff is scheduled for late August. Dr. Cabeza has arranged for faculty from a local university to provide the training at a cost of $6,000.

Transportation from home to school will be provided by the district for students who live more than one mile from the school. This will involve about 60 percent of the students. The district contracts with SchoolTrans Bus Co. for its transportation services. Next year's contract specifies an annual cost of $650 per student for every student utilizing the bus services regularly.

The district's business manager, Mr. Negocios, provided the following information on salaries and cost standards for budgeting purposes. For a nine month contract, the average teacher salary in the district is projected to be $21,200, beginning teacher salaries are projected at $14,400, and the full-time instructional aide salary is projected to be $9,600. Teachers and aides are also paid on a nine month basis. However, due to the shortage of qualified bilingual teachers, Dr. Cabeza estimates that an additional salary increment of 5 percent will be necessary to attract and keep the bilingual teachers needed at the new school. The district has agreed to pay professional dues of all certified staff; these average $120 per certified position. Bilingual teachers are encouraged to attend one-day statewide bilingual education conferences which occur twice yearly, and $200 in travel expenses are allotted to each teacher annually for this purpose. Substitute teachers are hired to replace them during these conferences. Bilingual substitutes are also in high demand and are projected to cost $130 per day.

Principals and assistant principals have eleven month contracts in La Esperanza School District. Their monthly salaries are based respectively upon 140 and 120 percent, of the average district teacher monthly salary. Secretaries also have eleven month contracts. During the nine months that school is in session, full-time secretaries normally average about ten hours of overtime per month and half-time secretaries average five hours per month. The district pays them $10.00 per hour for overtime. Secretaries will average $13,000 per year and will receive the same benefits as the instructional and administrative staff, which is 32 percent of their contract salary amount. In addition, the district will pay for the Public Employees Retirement System (PERS) benefits for each position after a six month waiting period for new employees; the cost of this benefit is 6 percent of total eligible salary. Five new first-year teachers and the full-time secretary are planned to be hired for the school next year. All other teachers, aides, administrators, and clerical staff are already employed by the district and PERS members and have no waiting period.

District guidelines allow $50 for general instructional supplies and $30 for textbooks per student. Each instructional certified position qualifies for $60 for Hispanic periodicals, $300 for equipment, and $20 for postage. A one-time start-up expenditure of $16,000 for special instructional equipment for the school is also planned. The school office will have a copying machine which costs $120 per month on an annual lease arrangement. Three telephones in the principal's office are expected to cost $30 each per month. Additionally, the district allocates $1.00 per student to each elementary school principal for postage and $5.00 per student for office supplies.

1. Prepare a budget for the district's bilingual education program for the next year. In developing and presenting the budget, assume that the activities at Bolivar Elementary represent the bilingual program for the district and that a separate FUND has been established to account for all expenditures and revenues associated with the program. Include both expenditures and revenues in your budget.

    a. The budget should be prepared in a standard format with expenditures presented by third level FUNCTION code and by OBJECT of expenditure codes within each function. Use different function codes as needed to separate expenditures by their different purposes. Give the object codes to the lowest level for which information is available (for example, 111 Certificated Salaries).

    b. Revenues should be presented by source with appropriate codes.

    c. Present the results in a neat, easy to follow format.

    d. Show the calculations separately and include them as an explanation for the budget.

    e. Include personnel and employee benefit costs in the budget.

    f. Round all cost calculations to the nearest $10.00.

2. After the budget was prepared, the district received notification from the U.S. Department of Education that the model bilingual school grant had been awarded to them in the amount of $675,000 to support next year's

operation. Assume that the La Esperanza school board wishes to implement the model bilingual school at Bolivar Elementary as described above with no reductions in planned expenditures, and is willing to fund any shortfall in grant revenue from the district's General Fund. Prepare a new revenue section for the budget to account for this change.

3. If the school board had not been willing to make up the shortfall from grant revenue, what items would you suggest modifying to reduce the budget to match the available revenue from the grant? Identify the particular items to be reduced, the dollar reduction and method of calculation of the reduction, and the potential effect on the district's bilingual program.

NOTES

1. Guilbert C. Hentschke, *Management Operations in Education* (Berkeley, CA: McCutchan, 1975), pp. 364-65.

2. Trend line analysis is one example of a curve fitting technique to match historical data. For others see Hentschke, *Management Operations in Education*, pp. 368-72.

3. For a review of weaknesses of forecasts, see David Hoaglin, et al., *Data for Decisions: Information Strategies for Policymakers* (Lanham, MD: University Press of America, 1982), pp. 229-232.

4. For a different approach to enrollment forecasting based on census data to project geographic changes of students within a school district see Hentschke, *Management Operations in Education*, pp. 372-77.

5. William T. Hartman, "Resource Allocation in High Schools" (Eugene, OR: Center for Educational Policy and Management, University of Oregon, 1985).

5

BUDGET ANALYSIS

INTRODUCTION

District budget figures change from one year to the next. Mostly they increase, but sometimes they decrease. Inevitably, comparisons are made between the current amounts and those proposed in the budget for the
upcoming year. The school board, the superintendent, school district personnel, the media, and the district patrons all are interested in how much
more or less is being spent in the upcoming year. This is a natural comparison, one made by school administrators and others interested in the district
budget.

Many budget document formats encourage these comparisons by
having one or more past years' budget figures included with the proposed
budget figures. Some states, for example, require school district budget
documents to be prepared with separate columns for the proposed budget,
the current budget, and the prior two years' budgets—four years of data.
Other similar formats are also used. District budget documents may even
include columns for showing the amounts and percentages of increases
and decreases. Rather than view the presentation of past years' data as inappropriate and potentially troublesome, school administrators should
look on this practice as helpful in explaining to their publics what directions the district is taking and where their monies are being spent. Having

the past years' data in the budget document ensures that budget information is in a consistent format; it also saves time later because requests for the past years' budget amounts will certainly be made if this information is not available.

However, differences in spending from one year to the next—since some programs show spending increases while others remain constant or even shrink—soon raise the question of *why*. Many things can cause changes in the budget amounts of different programs between two years. The district or individual programs may enroll more or less students. A different number of teachers or other personnel may be employed. Existing school buildings may be closed or new buildings opened. Salaries and wages may have changed due to a new contract. The prices of goods and services purchased by the district may have changed. The district may have changed some of its policies which affected expenditures.

The comparison of the total budgeted expenditures for the current school year with those proposed in the budget for the upcoming year gives the aggregate results of all of the changes. Some of the changes may have resulted from decisions which the school board or school district personnel made, while others may have been caused by circumstances out of the control of the district. It is instructive from an administrative standpoint and may be useful politically to show what caused the changes.

How can this be done?

BASELINE BUDGET ANALYSIS

The procedure for making the comparisons to explain the causes of the changes is known as *baseline budget analysis*. This technique uses the current year budget as a benchmark or baseline against which to measure, explain, and evaluate changes in the budget proposed for the next year. It is a procedure which has been successful in higher education budget analysis, but has had relatively little application in elementary and secondary school budgeting. To make the comparisons meaningful and administratively manageable, it is helpful to conduct separate analyses for specific programs or functions within the overall budget (such as, high school instruction, a particular school, or the personnel section of the district office). Not all programs need be analyzed as this would be too time consuming. Rather, the initial analytic effort should be concentrated on those programs which are experiencing relatively large budget changes from one year to the next. In this way, the important budget changes which are likely to require explanation are examined. The explanations are easier to communicate when the analyses are associated with identifiable operations or programs. This allows unique measures for those programs to be utilized and administrative responsibility to be pinpointed.

Conceptually, all changes between the baseline budget and the proposed budget can be categorized by changes due to *WORKLOAD, PRICE,* and *PROGRAM STANDARDS.*

What do these changes mean? In general, they mean *the dollar change in the budget caused by a change in one factor with the other two factors held constant.* With this approach, one can determine the cost change in the budget associated specifically with the change in either workload, price, or program standards. Each of these changes has an independent effect on the budget and each effect can be calculated if the changes in the factors can be quantified. The separate calculations for each factor are theoretical in the sense that they only consider changes in one factor at a time whereas, in reality, changes in all three factors occur simultaneously. However, the simultaneous changes of all three factors make a determination of the impact of each individual factor difficult. Consequently, it is necessary to separate the workload, price, and program standard effects mathematically. With this technique it is possible to calculate and to present the individual causes of overall budget changes.

Workload

Workload is the measure of the *level of activity* of a program. It indicates the volume of business done by that budget unit. Workload changes represent an increase or decrease in the measure of the level of activity for a program from one year to the next. The type of measure varies with the program being analyzed. For example, the workload measure for high school instruction or an individual school may be the number of students enrolled, while the workload measure for custodial services could be the square feet to be maintained, and for the personnel section could be the number of district staff. In each case, the workload measure should represent the best available indication of the level of activity of an operation.

The budget change due to workload is caused by the increase or decrease in the measure of workload of a program from the current year to the budget year, with no change in either price or program standard measures. These are the changes attributed solely to workload. As the calculation procedures (see p. 143) indicate, it is as if nothing else had happened in the program except the workload change. The workload change analyses answer questions such as: How much did the budget change because we added fifty-five students in the upcoming year? How much less would we be spending for custodial services if the only thing that happened was that one less school had to be maintained? Did adding twenty-two more district staff have a significant impact on the costs of the personnel section?

Price

Price is the *unit price* paid for an item, the cost per item. Price changes represent the increase or decrease in the unit price of the budget item analyzed. For example, the most important prices in the school district are the salaries of personnel. Changes in salary or wage contracts from one year to the next will certainly affect the budget expenditures for the district's programs. Likewise, changes in the prices of textbooks, paper, electricity, insurance, and other items or services will also impact on the district budget.

The budget change due to price is caused by the increase or decrease in the unit price of an item from the current year to the budget year, with no change in either workload or program standard measures. These are the changes attributed solely to price. It is as if nothing else had happened in the program except the price change. The price change analyses answer questions such as: How much did the instructional budget for middle schools change because of the negotiated salary increases for next year? What is the cost impact of the new textbook prices for next year? How much of the increased cost of operating the school buildings can be attributed to an increase in electrical power rates?

Program Standards

Program standards are the *district policies or operating procedures* which guide the implementation of programs. They can be either educational standards or guidelines, established operating procedures, or engineering standards applied to school district operations. Examples of program standards include student/teacher ratios, classified staffing patterns in elementary schools, maintenance standards (such as one custodian per 40,000 square feet of building space), and microcomputers per student in computer science classes.

District actions can change program standards from one year to the next. These changes in program standards can cause changes in the budget as well. Board action which modifies an existing district policy, such as the student/teacher ratio for high schools, will have a direct and identifiable impact on the budget. Adding a new program, such as computer literacy, is another type of program standard change. Similarly, reducing an existing district service, such as increasing the walking distance before providing transportation, will also have specific budget implications.

To determine the change in program standard, a proper measure of that standard must be identified. The type of measure will vary with the particular budget unit analyzed, but it should relate both to the resources utilized by or the activities of the unit and to the workload measure. For example, instructional programs typically have the number of students as a workload measure. The major resource in such programs is usually teachers; consequently an appropriate program standard measure for these programs would be the student/teacher ratio. In every case, the measure should reflect the principal activity or operation of the unit.

The budget change due to program standards is caused by the increase or decrease of the relevant program standard of the budget unit analyzed with no change in either workload or price measures. These are the changes attributed solely to program standards. The program standard change analyses answer questions such as: What would it cost the district to lower its overall student/teacher ratio in elementary schools from 20:1 to 19:1? What would the financial impact be of increasing the frequency of home visits by school social workers? How much does it cost to provide each middle school student with a daily session on a microcomputer rather than only two sessions per week?

Uses of Baseline Budget Analysis

There are many uses for the data developed in the baseline budget analyses. They generally revolve around having better and more relevant information on which to make decisions.

The baseline calculations can be used to show the dollar amounts of budget changes under the district's control or influence, and the amounts which are not. Workload changes reflect more or less work to do for the budget unit—a situation which may be out of the district's control. For example, if more students enroll next year, the school district will have to increase its budget to provide them with the same level of services available to existing students. Other items which are also out of the district's control include prices for items purchased from outside vendors. For example school districts have little or no influence in the price charged by textbook publishers, for energy rates, or for liability insurance.

There are items in the budget over which the district does have control or at least influence. Primary among these are salaries for certificated and classified personnel which are generally set through some type of negotiation process. Large concessions at the bargaining table will show up as large price increases for personnel in the baseline budget analysis. School board or administrator actions, which are often under district control, also have budget implications. Revising existing program standards—student/teacher ratios in particular—will frequently cause a budget change, as will adding or reducing programs.

Communicating to the public the causes of changes, especially increases, can assist administrators in gaining support for the proposed budget. Objections may be raised to overall budget increases. Cost increases due to enrollment increases or rapid rises in energy or insurance costs are readily understandable if explained convincingly. If additional budget increases are required for new programs, improved program standards, or salary increases, the baseline budget analyses can illustrate the costs of these improvements. If the district patrons wish the quality of their educational programs improved, they can be informed what the cost implications of the program improvements are.

Understanding the baseline budget analysis can help the school board members to recognize the impact of board decisions, particularly those involving policy changes which have budgetary implications. The analyses can provide important information on the financial impact of educational decisions. With this information the board will be better able to balance educational priorities and fiscal constraints.

Procedures for Calculations

In order to determine the differences between the current and proposed budgets which are due to workload, price, and program standard changes, it is necessary to perform a set of calculations. The calculations are straightfoward and utilize budget data and measures of each of the three factors.

1. Identify budget item for analysis.   The first step is to specify which budget item is to be analyzed. The identification includes the program or function in the budget and the particular expenditure items within that program which are of interest. Selection of the programs and expenditures for analysis should be based on the educational and/or political importance of the program and the magnitude of the dollars involved in the expenditure item balanced against the time and effort required for the analyses. Not all program units need or deserve a baseline budget analysis each year. Administrative judgment should be used to select those programs or budget units most appropriate for analysis.

Budget data for the programs selected for analysis must be assembled. Usually the necessary data can be taken directly from the budget document. What are needed are the current year's expenditures for each object of expenditure item to be analyzed, the proposed expenditures for the upcoming year, and the difference between the two expenditure amounts. This difference between the expenditures of the current and the proposed budgets is the amount to be explained in the baseline budget analysis. The remainder of the steps are devoted to determining how much of the total difference in each expenditure item is due to changes in workload, price, and program standards associated with the program.

2. Specify cost equation.   The cost equation is the calculation which is used to determine the total expenditure for a given budget item. The equation should be constructed to calculate the object of expenditure item required for the given program. The equation will vary with the budget item being investigated, but should contain workload, price, and program standard measures. These are combined to yield an estimate of expenditure for the budget item. For example, total certified salaries for a particular program can be calculated by dividing the students to be served (workload factor) by the district's student/teacher ratio (program standard factor) and multiplying this number by an average salary amount (price factor). Consequently, the cost equation for certified salaries would be:

$$\frac{\text{Number of Students}}{\text{Student/Teacher Ratio}} \times \text{Average Salary} = \begin{array}{c}\text{Salary} \\ \text{Expenditures}\end{array}$$

3. Identify measures for each factor.   Specific measures for workload, price, and program standard need to be established for the expenditure items analyzed. For workload, the measure should indicate the level or volume of activity in the budget unit. Examples of workload measures would include number of students, number of personnel supervised, number of records to be processed, and square footage. The particular measure will depend on the nature of the activities of the program.

The price measure is the unit price of the resource for which the expenditure is made. Examples of price measures include average salaries, cost per textbook, and cost per equipment item. The program standard measure is the educational standard or district policy which affects the expenditure level for the budget item. It usually sets the guidelines for estimating how many of the resource items are needed or how many of the workload numbers are eligible for some service. Examples of program standards are student/teacher ratios, quantities of supplies or equipment per student, and proportion of students eligible for subsidized school lunch program.

There is a close connection between the cost equation specified in the previous step and the identification of measures for each of the factors. The measures of the factors are used in the cost equation and in practice these two steps are carried out jointly. It may be necessary to try several cost equation formulations before a correct one is established which contains proper measures of all three factors.

One common mistake is to combine two of the individual factors into one measure. For example, a cost equation for salary expenditures which included only the number of personnel and the average salary would be incorrect, although it would calculate the same expenditure amount as the one illustrated above. The problem is that the number of personnel required is not an individual factor; it is the combination of two other factors—workload and program standard. That is because the number of personnel is determined by how many students are enrolled in the program (workload) *and* by the standard student/teacher ratio established by the district (program standard). Combining these separate factors into one measure prevents the determination of the effects of changes in the individual factors. Similarly, an average textbook cost per student is not a proper measure; it combines the average cost per textbook (price) and the number of textbooks per student (program standard) measures into a single number.

4. Specify values for each measure.   For each measure in the previous step, two specific values must be established—one for the baseline year and one for the upcoming year. These data can be obtained from budget estimates, student or personnel data, district policies or guidelines, cost records, and calculations from other information. They should represent the actual or estimated value for workload, price, and program standard factors for the expenditures of the program unit being analyzed. Differences between the values from year to year indicate that there have been changes which will have budget implications.

It is often useful to organize the data into a table in which the values of the three factors in each year can be entered. The format shown below will prove helpful and efficient in the upcoming calculation steps.

	BASELINE YEAR VALUES	BUDGET YEAR VALUES
Workload	aa	xx
Price	bb	yy
Program Standard	cc	zz

As a check for the procedures so far, substitute the baseline year values into the cost equation. The result should equal the current expenditures for the program. Next, substitute the budget year values into the cost equation. The result of this calculation should equal the proposed expenditures for the program. If the calculations do not match the current and proposed expenditures, then there is an error somewhere and the first four steps should repeated and the error eliminated.

5. Calculate single factor expenditure changes. For each factor in turn, calculate the expenditures which would result from changing only the value of that factor from the baseline year value to the budget year value. This is done by using the cost equation and substituting the budget year value into it for one factor, while keeping the baseline year values for the other two factors. The result is the expenditure which would have resulted if the only change between the two years was the change in the single factor. Three calculations should be carried out—one for each factor. The values to substitute into the cost equation to calculate the expenditures due to the change in each factor are shown below.

Workload change expenditures	
Workload value:	Budget year
Price value:	Baseline year
Program standard value:	Baseline year
Price change expenditures	
Workload value:	Baseline year
Price value:	Budget year
Program standard value:	Baseline year
Program standard change expenditures	
Workload value:	Baseline year
Price value:	Baseline year
Program standard value:	Budget year

6. Calculate budget impact of each factor.   To determine the cost impact of the change in each single factor, subtract the baseline expenditures from the single factor change expenditures which were calculated in the previous step. The difference is the amount of budget change due to the change in each single factor. That is, the change in the budget due solely to the change in workload is the workload change expenditures less the baseline expenditures. Similarly, the change in the budget due solely to the change in price is the price change expenditures less the baseline expenditures; and the change in the budget due solely to the change in program standards is the program standard change expenditures less the baseline expenditures.

7. Calculate interaction effect.   Usually when the budget changes due to the three factors are added together they do not equal the total budget change between the baseline and the budget year expenditures. This is because of the interaction among the changes in each of the three factors. The individual changes interact with one another to yield changes which are beyond the independent effects of each factor alone. For example, the expected additional students for next year will also have the new student/ teacher ratio applied to them in the total expenditure calculation, whereas in the workload change expenditures which were calculated in Step 5, the old (baseline) student/teacher ratio would be applied to the additional students. To reflect the complete budget changes which will occur, it is necessary to account for the interaction of the three factors. The interaction effect is calculated by summing the individual factor effects and subtracting this sum from the total budget change. The difference, which can be either positive or negative, is the interaction effect.

This is illustrated most easily in two dimensions as shown in Figure 5.1, but the principle is readily extended to three dimensions (or factors). In this illustration the budget item is the total dollar amount of out-of-district tuition paid by the district for students receiving educational services from other districts. The two factors which determine the total budget amount are the number of students (workload) and the out-of-district tuition per student (price) paid by the district. For this illustration it is assumed that from the baseline year to the budget year the number of students increases from fifty to sixty and the tuition per student increases from $2,000 to $3,000.

The total cost amount increases from $100,000 to $180,000 between the two years. Of this total increase, the amount due solely to the increase in number of students is $20,000; this represents the cost of the workload increase—ten students at the baseline price of $2,000 per student. Similarly, the tuition increase alone would cause an increase of $50,000: this represents the cost of the price increase—$1,000 per student for the baseline number of fifty students. Together, the workload and price

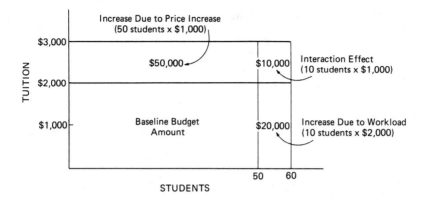

		CURRENT YEAR AMOUNT	BUDGET YEAR AMOUNT	BUDGET CHANGE
Total		$100,000	$180,000	$80,000
Workload	(Number of Students)	50	60	$20,000
Price	(Tuition)	2,000	3,000	$50,000
Interaction				$10,000

FIGURE 5.1 Interaction Effect

changes account for $70,000 of the total budget change. The remaining $10,000 is an interaction effect between the increases in workload measure and the price measure; that is the ten additional students and the price increase of $1,000 per student. In the individual workload and price change calculations the new changed value (budget year) of the factor was used along with the old (baseline) value of the other factor. As a result, the changes in the factor values never had an opportunity to interact jointly. Hence the need for the interaction term.

The interaction effect is the most difficult to explain to board members, school personnel, or school district patrons, but it is a necessary component to present a complete picture of the budget changes from one year to the next.

Baseline Budget Analysis Example

The example is for high school instruction (function 1130), and three object of expenditure items have been singled out for analysis—certificated salaries, student transportation, and textbooks. The current or baseline year and budget year amounts for each of these expenditures are given in Table 5.1 as they would be in a budget document, and the difference between the amounts for the two years is calculated for each of the expendi-

TABLE 5.1 Baseline Budget Analysis Example

BUDGET DATA	CURRENT YEAR	BUDGET YEAR	DIFFERENCE
BASIC DISTRICT INFORMATION			
1130 High School Instruction			
111 Certificated Salaries	$7,094,970	$8,063,400	$968,430
.			
.			
331 Student Transportation	$1,134,000	$945,000	($189,000)
.			
.			
420 Textbooks	$171,520	$145,950	($25,570)
OTHER INFORMATION			
Students	6,700	6,950	250
Student/Teacher Ratio	24	23	−1
Average Salary per Teacher	$25,430	$26,700	$1,270
Average Annual Cost per Bus	$42,000	$45,000	$3,000
% Students Eligible for Trans	20.0%	15.0%	−5.0%
Students per Bus	50	50	0
Textbooks Purchased	10,720	8,340	(2,380)
BUDGET ANALYSIS CALCULATIONS			
Teachers[a]	279	302	23
Buses[a]	27	21	−6
Average Cost per Textbook	$16.00	$17.50	$1.50
Textbooks per Student	1.60	1.20	−0.40

[a]Rounded to the nearest whole number

ture items. In certificated salaries, it is proposed to spend almost one million dollars more in the upcoming year than in the current year, while the budget for student transportation is decreased by almost $190,000 and textbook expenditures are reduced by approximately $26,000. It is these differences which the baseline budget analysis will explain.

In order to carry out the analysis, additional data are required to provide information about the workload, price, and program standards measures in each expenditure area. These are also shown in Table 5.1.

Certificated Salaries. The baseline budget analysis of certificated salaries is shown in Table 5.2. As a first step, a cost equation for this expenditure item must be established. The equation must contain separate measures for workload, price, and program standards. The cost equation used is:

$$\frac{\text{Number of Students}}{\text{Student/Teacher Ratio}} \times \frac{\text{Average Teacher}}{\text{Salary}} = \frac{\text{Salary}}{\text{Expenditures}}$$

From the available data, all of the necessary elements are present. The number of students reflects the instructional workload in the high schools, the average salary measures the price factor, and the student/teacher ratio represents the program standard. As a check, substituting the current year or baseline values into the equation yields the current year total expenditure amount and substituting the budget year values into the

TABLE 5.2 Baseline Budget Analysis of Certificated Salaries

COST EQUATION

$$\frac{\text{Number of Students}}{\text{Student/Teacher Ratio}} \times \text{Average Teacher Salary} = \text{Salary Expenditures}$$

Current Year Values Yield Current Year Expenditures

$$\frac{6,700 \text{ students}}{24 \text{ students/teacher}} \times \$25,430 = \$7,094,970$$

Budget Year Values Yield Budget Year Expenditures

$$\frac{6,950 \text{ students}}{23 \text{ students/teacher}} \times \$26,700 = \$8,063,400$$

	CALCULATED SALARY EXPENDITURES	FACTOR BUDGET CHANGE
WORKLOAD FACTOR		
Budget year students with baseline salary and ratio		
$\frac{6,950 \text{ students}}{24 \text{ students/teacher}} \times \$25,430 =$	$7,374,700	$279,730
PRICE FACTOR		
Budget year salary with baseline students and ratio		
$\frac{6,700 \text{ students}}{24 \text{ students/teacher}} \times \$26,700 =$	$7,449,300	$354,330
PROGRAM STANDARD FACTOR		
Budget year ratio with baseline students and salary		
$\frac{6,700 \text{ students}}{23 \text{ students/teacher}} \times \$25,430 =$	$7,400,130	$305,160
TOTAL FROM 3 INDEPENDENT FACTORS		$939,220
INTERACTION AMONG ALL 3 FACTORS		$29,210
TOTAL BUDGET CHANGE		$968,430

equation yields the budget year total expenditure amount. Note that the first term in the cost equation (number of students divided by the student/teacher ratio) calculates the number of teachers required; in this analysis, the number of teachers has been rounded to the nearest whole position.

To calculate the change in the total budget due to a change in workload, the *budget year value for the workload measure* (6,950 students) is substituted into the cost equation along with the *current year values for the price and program standard measures*. This yields a calculated salary expenditure amount of $7,374,700 or an increase due to workload alone of $279,730 (assuming the other two factors remained constant). Similar calculations are made for the price factor. The *budget year value for the price measure* ($26,700 per teacher) is substituted into the cost equation while keeping the *workload and program standard factors at their current year values*. This results in a calculated salary expenditure amount of $7,449,300 or an increase due to price alone of $354,330 (assuming the other two factors remained constant). For the calculations for the program standard change, the *budget year value for the program standard measure* (23 students/teacher) is substituted into the cost equation along with the *current year values for the workload and price factors*. This yields a calculated salary expenditure amount of $7,400,130 or an increase due to program standard alone of $305,160 (assuming the other two factors remained constant). In this example, each of the three factors contributes approximately equally to the relatively large increase in total salaries.

The independent changes from the three factors sum to $939,220, which is $29,210 less than total difference between the baseline and budget years. This difference is the interaction amount. It represents the budgetary effect of the increase in number of students, salaries, and reduced student/teacher ratio working together.

Student Transportation. The baseline budget analysis for student transportation is provided in Table 5.3. A different cost equation is needed to calculate the expenditures for student transportation. The equation utilizes the number of students (workload), the average annual operating cost for a school bus (price), and the percentage of students eligible for transportation services (program standard) to calculate the expenditures for student transportation. In the equation shown below another term is necessary (students/bus) to determine the number of buses needed during the year. This term represents the current equipment or technology used by the school district in this area (school buses of a certain capacity) and remains constant for the two years being analyzed; as a result, it has no effect on the budget changes.

$$\frac{\text{Students} \times \% \text{ Eligible}}{\text{Students per Bus}} \times \text{Cost per Bus} = \frac{\text{Transportation}}{\text{Expenditures}}$$

Once again, all of the data needed for each of the measures are in the basic information provided for the example. Putting the current year values and the budget year values for each of the measures into the equation yields, respectively, the current year and budget year expenditure for student transportation. Note that the first term in the cost equation (number of students times the percentage eligible for student transportation divided by the student/bus capacity) calculates the number of buses required;

TABLE 5.3   Baseline Budget Analysis of Student Transportation

COST EQUATION

$$\frac{\text{Students} \times \text{\% Eligible}}{\text{Students/Bus}} \times \text{Average Cost Per Bus} = \text{Transportation Expenditures}$$

Current Year Values Yield Current Year Expenditures

$$\frac{6{,}700 \text{ students} \times 0.20}{50 \text{ students/bus}} \times \$42{,}000 = \$1{,}134{,}000$$

Budget Year Values Yield Budget Year Expenditures

$$\frac{6{,}950 \text{ students} \times 0.15}{50 \text{ students/bus}} \times \$45{,}000 = \$945{,}000$$

	CALCULATED TRANSPORTATION EXPENDITURES	FACTOR BUDGET CHANGE
WORKLOAD FACTOR		
Budget year students with baseline cost and % eligible		
$\dfrac{6{,}950 \text{ students} \times 0.20}{50 \text{ students/bus}} \times \$42{,}000 =$ $1,176,000	$42,000
PRICE FACTOR		
Budget year cost with baseline students and % eligible		
$\dfrac{6{,}700 \text{ students} \times 0.20}{50 \text{ students/bus}} \times \$45{,}000 =$ $1,215,000	$81,000
PROGRAM STANDARD FACTOR		
Budget year % eligible with baseline students and cost		
$\dfrac{6{,}700 \text{ students} \times 0.15}{50 \text{ students/bus}} \times \$42{,}000 =$ $840,000	($294,000)
TOTAL FROM 3 INDEPENDENT FACTORS		($171,000)
INTERACTION AMONG ALL 3 FACTORS		($18,000)
TOTAL BUDGET CHANGE		($189,000)

in this analysis, the number of buses has been rounded to the nearest whole number.

The calculations to determine how much of the overall change in the student transportation expenditures are due to workload, price, and program standard measures follow the same pattern as before. First, the *budget year value for the workload factor* is substituted into the cost equation along with the *current year values for the price and program standard factors*. This yields a calculated salary expenditure amount of $1,176,000, which would be the student transportation amount if the only thing that changed between the two years was an increase in the number of students. The difference from the baseline amount is $42,000, which is the cost increase due to workload alone. In a similar fashion, the budget change due to the change in price is calculated at $81,000, while the budget change due to the change in program standard (reducing the percentage eligible for transportation) is a negative $294,000. This illustrates that a large overall decrease in the student transportation expenditures was funded by reducing transportation services. In fact, the budget reduction due to program standards was even larger than the total budget reduction, reflecting the fact that the increases in workload and price as well as the overall reduction in student transportation expenditures were funded by a reduction in service. It is this type of tradeoff which is illustrated by the baseline budget analysis; this procedure can provide useful decision-making information for a school board trying to make budget allocation choices.

The interaction amount is calculated at a negative $18,000. It is negative due to the large effect of the negative program standard change which dominates the results.

Textbooks.   The baseline budget analysis for textbook expenditures is shown in Table 5.4. The cost equation shown below is specific to this object of expenditure. It contains a workload measure (number of students), a price measure (cost per textbook), and a program standard measure (textbooks per student). Combining the price and program standard measures into a combined textbook cost per student measure—while it would calculate the overall textbook expenditures correctly—would not allow the separate analysis of cost changes for these two factors. Likewise, combining the number of students and the textbooks per student into a single measure of the number of textbooks would obliterate the separate changes due to workload and program standard. Substituting the current year and budget year values for each factor into the cost equation results in the current year expenditure amount and budget year expenditure amount for textbooks.

$$\begin{array}{c}\text{Number of}\\\text{Students}\end{array} \times \begin{array}{c}\text{Cost per}\\\text{Student}\end{array} \times \begin{array}{c}\text{Textbooks}\\\text{per Student}\end{array} = \begin{array}{c}\text{Textbook}\\\text{Expenditure}\end{array}$$

In this case, not all of the values for the workload, price, and program standard factors are given in the basis problem data. The average cost per textbook and the number of textbooks per student must be calculated from other information. For both the current year and the budget year, the average cost per textbook is found by dividing the total expenditure amount by the number of textbooks purchased and the number of textbooks per student is determined by dividing the number of textbooks by the number of students. The results of these calculations are shown in Table 5.1.

   The same type of calculations are performed to determine amount of the total budget change which is due to each of the workload, price, and

TABLE 5.4 Baseline Budget Analysis of Textbooks

COST EQUATION

   Students × Cost Per Textbook × Textbooks Per Student = Textbook Expenditure

Current Year Values Yield Current Year Expenditures
   6,700 students × $16.00 × 1.60 books per st. = $171,520

Budget Year Values Yield Budget Year Expenditures
   6,950 students × $17.50 × 1.20 books per st. = $145,950

	CALCULATED TEXTBOOK EXPENDITURES	FACTOR BUDGET CHANGE
WORKLOAD FACTOR		
Budget year students with baseline cost and books/student		
6,950 students × $16.00 × 1.60 books per st. =	$177,920	$6,400
PRICE FACTOR		
Budget year cost with baseline students and books/student		
6,700 students × $17.50 × 1.60 books per st. =	$187,600	$16,080
PROGRAM STANDARD FACTOR		
Budget year books/student with baseline students and cost		
6,700 students × $16.00 × 1.20 books per st. =	$128,640	($42,880)
TOTAL FROM 3 INDEPENDENT FACTORS		($20,400)
INTERACTION AMONG ALL 3 FACTORS		($5,170)
TOTAL BUDGET CHANGE		($25,570)

program standard changes. For the change due to workload, the *budget year value for the workload measure* (6,950 students) is substituted into the cost equation along with the *current year values for the price and program standard measures*. This yields a calculated expenditure amount of $177,920 and a budget change due to workload of $6,400. Successive substitutions of the budget year values for the price and program standard measures result in budget changes due to price of $16,080 and due to program standard of a negative $42,880. In this example, once again there is a reduction of a program standard in order to reduce the overall budget expenditures and to allow increases for workload and price. The baseline budget analysis clearly points out these results of budget decisions.

Summary

Baseline budget analysis is a powerful technique for identifying and explaining the causes of changes in school district budgets from one year to the next. Isolating the reasons for budget changes can assist school personnel, school board members, and the public to understand why district budgets are increasing or decreasing. Certain elements are out of the control of the district, such as the number of students enrolled or the prices charged by outside vendors. Other types of cost elements (such as personnel salaries, staffing ratios, and levels of supplies and equipment furnished to students) are under the control or influence of the district. Distinguishing between these types of cost changes will improve the understanding of the district's budget and focus attention on those elements which can be modified.

Another important feature of baseline budget analysis is the improved decision-making information which is developed. The additional costs needed to maintain the same level of service in the face of increases in district enrollments and prices from outside vendors are readily determined and this information can be made available to district personnel and school board members (and even to district voters if an election is needed to raise additional funds). The information can also be used to make tradeoff decisions among competing uses of district funds or to show the costs of upgrading district program standards to more desirable levels.

A caution is in order, however. Most school board members and district patrons are not familiar with this type of analysis and the information which is generated. Presentation of the results may need to be simplified in order to convey the relevant information without confusing and overwhelming the audience, and ultimately having them reject the results through lack of understanding. A summary of the results without the calculations may be an appropriate level of information to present, with the analytical calculations available to those who wish to investigate the matter more thoroughly.

COST ANALYSIS

This section reviews important cost concepts which are useful both in developing a new budget and in analyzing expenditures within a given budget. Its purpose is to familiarize you with the most common cost concepts. These concepts are originally derived from economic theory and provide useful tools of analysis for administrators. In particular, an understanding of how the different types of costs vary with expected programmatic changes in the school district allows administrators to project expenditures more accurately. Such knowledge is also helpful in cost control and reduction actions by focusing attention on areas where the impact can be greatest.

The various cost categories discussed below—total and unit costs, fixed and variable costs, direct and indirect costs, and average and marginal costs—are not necessarily mutually exclusive. One expenditure item can be described using several different concepts to represent different cost dimensions. For example, a teacher's salary could be a unit cost, a variable cost, a direct cost, and a marginal cost all at the same time. Each of these categories differentiates specific characteristics of that expenditure item.

Administrators should recognize the various dimensions which costs can have. This allows them to utilize these concepts to analyze an existing or proposed budget, to improve the validity of future cost projections, and to manage the cost and budget implications of program changes.

Total and Unit Costs

Possibly the simplest differentiation of types of costs is that of total and unit costs. The total cost is the *total dollar amount* of a given program or unit of operation. It is an aggregate figure summarizing all aspects of the particular operation. For example, the total cost of operating an elementary school may be $720,000. This would include all of the expenditures for school administration, instruction, and support services located in the school.

The unit cost is the *cost per unit* of a particular program or operation. To determine the unit cost it is first necessary to define the program or unit of analysis. For example, if we wished to analyze the unit costs of an elementary school program in the district, then the individual elementary school would be the unit of analysis. Next a measure of activity for that unit must be specified. The measure of activity selected will depend on the unit cost which is desired. In the elementary school example, two different measures of activity or volume are possible—teachers and students. If we wished to determine the unit cost per teacher in the school, then the number of teachers would be the appropriate measure of activity. Similarly, to determine the unit cost per student in the school, the appropriate measure of activity would be the number of students.

To calculate the unit cost, first determine the total cost of the program being analyzed. This is divided by the number of units (measure of activity) to yield the unit cost of the program. Table 5.5 illustrates both total and unit costs for two elementary schools.

$$\text{Unit Cost} = \frac{\text{Total Costs}}{\text{Number of Units}}$$

Unit costs provide information to aid comparisons among similar programs. While cost comparisons do not tell the complete story, wide differences in unit costs among similar programs (such as elementary schools) can be identified and investigated. It is very important to make sure that the comparisons are truly comparable, that is, that the types of students, the program objectives, the results, and the types of costs are similar. Otherwise, the unit cost differences may represent program differences rather than cost efficiencies or inefficiencies.

For example, the two elementary schools which are compared in Table 5.5 show sizable differences in their unit costs: School A has a higher unit cost per student, but School B has a higher unit cost per teacher. The causes of these apparently contradictory differences are probably that School A has a much lower student/teacher ratio than School B, but that School B has higher salaried teachers than School A. The lower student/teacher ratio drives up the cost per student in School A, while the seniority of the teaching staff in School B increases the cost per teacher.

Variable and Fixed Costs

It is frequently useful to distinguish between costs which are altered by a change in the level of activity of a program and those which are not. These costs have different characteristics and quite different implications for budget planning.

TABLE 5.5   Total and Unit Cost Example

	SCHOOL A	SCHOOL B
TOTAL COSTS	$396,000	$572,000
Number of Students	240	400
Unit Cost per Student	$1,650	$1,430
Number of Teachers	18	22
Unit Cost per Teacher	$22,000	$26,000
(Student/Teacher Ratio)	13.3	18.2

Variable costs. *Variable costs are those which change with the level of activity.* They are directly proportional to the level of activity. The more activity, the greater the variable costs are. Conversely, if the level of activity decreases, the variable costs will also decrease. For example:

> Textbook costs for students. If textbook expenditures are based on $16.00 per student, then ten more students will increase the textbook costs by $160.
>
> Mileage costs for itinerant teachers. At a reimbursement rate of $0.25 per mile, the more miles traveled by teachers, the greater travel costs will be.
>
> Tuition charges paid to a neighboring district. If fewer district students are placed in the educational programs of neighboring districts, the district's tuition payments will be reduced.
>
> Total district salary expenditures for instructional personnel. The greater the number of teachers employed by the district, the higher the total salary expenditures will be.
>
> Total district expenditures for school principal salaries. If two schools (each with one principal with a salary of $36,000) are closed, the expenditures for principals' salaries will be decreased by $72,000.

With variable costs it is necessary to specify the activity measure and to relate the unit variable cost to this measure. In the textbook and tuition examples above, the measure of activity is the number of students and the unit variable costs are the textbook cost and the tuition amount per student respectively. For the travel reimbursements for the itinerant teachers, the measure of activity is the number of miles traveled and the unit variable cost is the reimbursement amount per mile. For teacher salaries, the activity measure is the number of teachers and the unit variable cost is the average teacher salary; and for the principals' salary expenditures, the activity measure is the number of principals employed (or number of schools if each school has one principal assigned to it) and the unit variable cost is the average principal salary.

Fixed costs. *Fixed costs do not vary with a change in the level of activity of a program or operation.* They remain constant over the range of activity under consideration and are not influenced by the level of activity. For example:

> A teacher's salary in one classroom does not vary with the number of students in the classroom. The teacher does not get paid more if there are twenty-five students in the class rather than twenty-one students.
>
> The principal's salary in a given school does not change in relationship to the number of students or teachers in the school. The principal's salary is not reduced if the enrollment declines by twenty-five students during the year or if one teaching position is transferred to another school in the district.
>
> The district superintendent's compensation is fixed for the year and will not change if more or fewer students are enrolled, if the number of teachers change, or if schools are opened or closed during the year.

Fixed and variable costs.   How can you decide whether a particular cost is fixed or variable? The procedure follows from the definition of the cost types.

1. Identify the unit or level of analysis—generally student, teacher/classroom, school, support unit, or district.
2. Specify the measure of activity for the unit—the most representative indicator of the size, scope, or volume of the unit's operation.
3. Determine whether the cost item increases with increased activity and/or decreases with decreased activity. Do the total costs go up (or down) as the measure of activity for the operation goes up (or down)?

If it does, it is a Variable cost.

If it does not, it is a Fixed cost.

The fixed and variable cost relationship can be shown graphically. Figure 5.2 illustrates the relationship. Total costs are shown on the vertical axis and the level of activity is shown on the horizontal axis. Fixed costs, which do not change with the level of activity, are graphed as a horizontal line. They stay the same amount for the level of activity under consideration.

Variable costs, on the other hand, increase in proportion to the level of activity. The simplest type of variable cost relationship is a linear one in which the cost per unit remains constant. This is graphed as a rising line with the slope of the line equal to the variable cost per unit. More complex variable cost relationships are nonlinear and are graphed as curved lines.

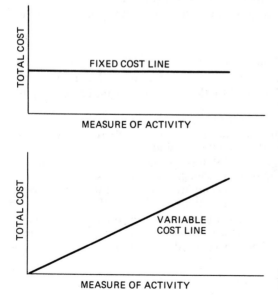

FIGURE 5.2
Fixed and Variable Cost Graphs

To demonstrate the application of fixed and variable costs, the hypothetical costs of an elementary school lunchroom are examined. Assume that the lunchroom has a capacity to serve 300 meals per day and that the fixed costs have been calculated at $300 per day; these include the lunchroom staff, utilities, and other costs incurred by simply having the lunchroom open. The variable costs, primarily food and serving supplies, have been estimated at $1.00 per student. Figure 5.3 shows the fixed, variable, and total costs for the relevant range of students in the lunchroom. Notice that even if no students are served there will still be a cost of $300 (the fixed costs). As the number of students served increases, the variable costs also increase and the total costs rise.

On the graph the fixed costs are shown first as a base cost amount (the horizontal line at $300). The variable cost line rises (at a slope equal to $1.00 per student) from the top of the fixed cost line beginning at the vertical axis. To plot the variable cost line it is only necessary to begin at this point, to calculate one more point on the line (that is, another point representing the total cost amount for a given number of students), and to con-

FIGURE 5.3 Fixed and Variable Cost Example for an Elementary School Lunchroom

CAPACITY:	300 STUDENTS PER DAY
FIXED COST:	$300 PER DAY
VARIABLE COST:	$1.00 PER MEAL

STUDENT MEALS	FIXED COSTS	VARIABLE COSTS	TOTAL COSTS
0	$300	$0	$300
100	$300	$100	$400
200	$300	$200	$500
300	$300	$300	$600

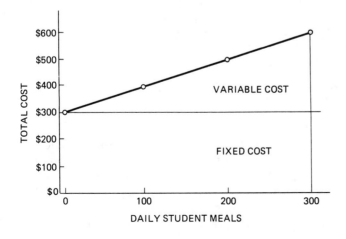

CAPACITY:	FIXED COSTS ($/DAY)	VARIABLE COSTS ($/MEAL)
300 Students per day	0 to 300 Students $300	$1.00
500 Students per day with Additional Fixed Costs	300 to 500 Students $100 Additional	$1.00

STUDENT MEALS	FIXED COSTS	VARIABLE COSTS	TOTAL COSTS
0	$300	$0	$300
100	$300	$100	$400
200	$300	$200	$500
300	$300	$300	$600
400	$400	$400	$800
500	$400	$500	$900

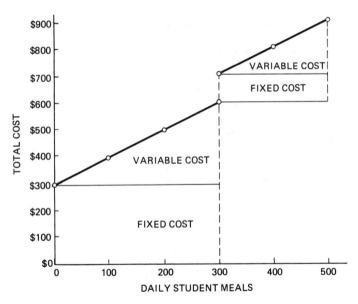

FIGURE 5.4 Fixed and Variable Cost Example with an Increase in Fixed
Costs for an Elementary School Lunchroom

nect the two points. In the figure, three more points on the variable cost
line are shown corresponding to the total costs for 100, 200, and 300 students. This procedure allows the sum of fixed and variable cost lines to
equal the total costs of operation for any given number of students. The
total cost amount for a specific number of students within the relevant
range can be read directly from the graph by taking the number of stu-

dents, moving vertically to the top of the graph (the variable cost line), and reading the corresponding total cost from the vertical axis scale.

This analysis assumes that fixed costs remain constant within the range of activity examined. If the analysis includes levels of activity outside of the range of constant fixed costs, then it is necessary to adjust the fixed cost amount to the new level. A common example in education is an increase beyond the original capacity of the number of students served in a program. At this point it may be necessary to increase the amount of fixed costs to accommodate the additional students. The additional fixed costs and the variable costs for the new students are added to the original fixed and variable costs at the unit's capacity level to arrive at the new total cost amount. Figure 5.4 illustrates these changes.

Break-even analysis. Another type of analysis using fixed and variable costs is the determination of the break-even point of an operation. This analysis is used in situations where revenues, as well as expenditures, are associated with a program. The break-even point is the level of activity where the revenues generated by an operation are equal to the expenditures caused by the operation. It is a point of "no profit or no loss," and the point at which the operation is self-sufficient. At a level of activity below the break-even point, expenditures are greater than revenues and the operation creates a deficit. At a level of activity above the break-even point, revenues are greater than expenditures and the operation creates a surplus.

The break-even analysis is illustrated through the continuation of the lunchroom example. The type of question which this analysis can answer is: How many meals must be served daily in order to cover all lunchroom costs? To answer the question, we first must know what the price charged per meal is. In the example, assume that the price is $2.00 per meal. Now with this price and the previous cost data, the break-even point of the lunchroom operation can be determined.

First, the definition of the break-even point is the level of activity where revenues equal expenditures.

Total Revenues = Total Costs

Total revenues are equal to the price charged per meal times the number of meals sold. Total costs are equal to the fixed costs plus the variable costs per meal times the number of meals sold.

$$\text{Revenue/unit} \times \text{Quantity}_{BE} = \text{Fixed Costs} + \text{Variable Cost/unit} \times \text{Quantity}_{BE}$$

Rearranging the equation and solving for the break-even quantity, the equation becomes

$$\text{Quantity}_{BE} = \frac{\text{Fixed Costs}}{\text{Revenue/unit} - \text{Variable Cost/unit}}$$

The revenue/unit minus the variable cost/unit calculation gives the amount of money from each unit sold that can be used for meeting fixed costs. It is also called the contribution/unit or the amount that each unit contributes toward covering the fixed costs of operation.

In the lunchroom example, all of the revenue and cost amounts are known. Substituting them into the equation and solving for the number of meals which need to be sold in order to have the lunchroom break-even is a simple matter.

$$\text{Quantity}_{\text{BE}} = \frac{\$300.00}{\$2.00 - \$1.00} = 300 \text{ meals/day}$$

Now, suppose that an average of 265 student meals/day are being purchased in your school's lunchroom and that the lunchroom is, therefore, operating below the break-even point and at a deficit. Assume that you have received a proposal to raise the price of lunch in the school to $2.50 per meal to cover the cost of operating the lunchroom. What would this do to the break-even point? How many lunches would need to be sold to cover the costs of operation?

$$\text{Quantity}_{\text{BE}} = \frac{\$300.00}{\$2.50 - \$1.00} = 200 \text{ meals/day}$$

The increased price per meal lowered the break-even point to 200 meals per day from the previous level of 300 meals per day. While this provides useful information for your decision, it does not make the decision for you. There is still the unanswered question of what the student response will be to the higher meal price: Will the higher price reduce the number of students who buy lunch and will the number drop below the break-even point of 200 students? Or will the reduction in student meals purchased be relatively slight and allow the lunchroom to operate above the break-even point and produce a surplus. The additional concern of the impact of the price increase on lower-income students' ability to afford the lunch must also be considered. If the $2.50 price is felt to be too high, then the analysis can be repeated for different prices and the break-even points determined for each. The break-even analysis can be a useful tool which allows you to understand the financial implications of the possible price changes.

The break-even analysis can also be shown graphically by adding a revenue line to the basic fixed and variable cost graph. The revenue line starts at the origin of the graph (where both the revenue and number of meals are zero) and rises with a slope equal to the revenue/unit (or price) of a meal. To plot the revenue line, select another level of activity toward the high end of the possible range of meals served and calculate the revenue generated at this level. Then plot this point (number of meals and total revenue amount) on the graph and connect it with the origin of the graph. *The*

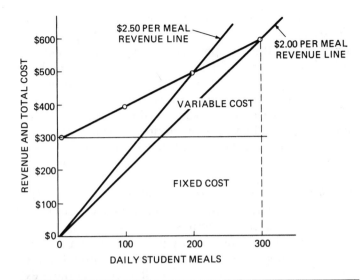

HOW MANY MEALS MUST BE SOLD TO BREAK EVEN AT A PRICE OF $2.00?
HOW MANY MEALS MUST BE SOLD TO BREAK EVEN AT A PRICE OF $2.50?

STUDENT MEALS	FIXED COSTS	VARIABLE COSTS	TOTAL COSTS	REVENUES $2.00	REVENUES $2.50
0	$300	$0	$300	0	0
100	$300	$100	$400	200	250
200	$300	$200	$500	400	500[a]
300	$300	$300	$600	600[a]	750

[a]BREAK-EVEN POINT

FIGURE 5.5 Break-Even Analysis of an Elementary School Lunchroom

break-even point on the graph is where the revenue line crosses the variable cost line. In the example in Figure 5.5, the break-even point is 200 meals for a price of $2.50 per meal and 300 meals for a price of $2.00 per meal.

Direct and Indirect Costs

Another type of cost distinction is that between direct and indirect costs.[1] This is a useful distinction when separating those costs which are central to an operation from those which support it.

Direct costs. *These are expenditures which are identifiable with a single program or activity.* There is a clear linkage or association between the expenditures and the program in question. Another way of viewing direct costs is that without the particular program the direct cost items would not be necessary or would not exist.

As an example, consider the transportation program of a school district. Direct costs of this program would include: drivers' wages and benefits; expenditures for gas and oil, tires, and replacement parts; insurance premiums; salaries for the transportation supervisor, dispatcher, and mechanics. These are costs which are directly connected to or caused by having the transportation program. If the district decided to eliminate its bus transportation service for students, then the district would not have these direct costs.

Indirect costs.   *These are costs which apply to several programs, one of which is the program being considered.* The activities for which these expenditures are made support or benefit several programs. There is an indirect relationship between the expenditures and the program in question and the expenditures cannot be identified solely with that single program. Indirect costs are sometimes referred to as overhead costs. To associate these expenditures with a particular program requires an allocation of a portion of the expenditures to the program.

Examples of indirect costs for the transportation program would include the costs of the personnel department (which hires the bus drivers and mechanics), the costs of the payroll department (which prepares the checks for transportation personnel), the costs of the purchasing department (which buys the gasoline, oil, and parts), and the costs of the insurance department or manager (which solicits and maintains the necessary insurance coverage). In each case, some of the work of these other departments does support the transportation department, but it is not the only activity in which they are engaged.

Once again the unit of analysis is an important consideration when determining whether a cost is direct or indirect. Costs that are indirect at a lower level of the district organization can become direct at higher levels which encompass all of the individual programs served by the costs. Table 5.6 illustrates direct and indirect costs at three different levels of a district's organization. The classroom teacher's salary is a direct cost at all three levels since it can be directly associated with a particular classroom, school, and district. The school nurse (assigned half-time to a given school) is an indirect cost at the classroom level since the nurse's salary cannot be specifically associated with one particular classroom, but it is a direct cost at the school level since it is assigned exclusively to the school. The school custodian's salary is similar to that of the school nurse. The business manager's salary and the costs of districtwide psychological testing are both indirect costs at both the classroom and school level, but direct costs at the district level. In fact, all expenditures within a district are direct costs at the district level.

TABLE 5.6 Direct and Indirect Cost Examples

COST	CLASSROOM	SCHOOL	DISTRICT
Classroom teacher	Direct	Direct	Direct
School Nurse (0.5 FTE)	Indirect	Direct	Direct
School Custodian	Indirect	Direct	Direct
Psychological Testing	Indirect	Indirect	Direct
Business Manager	Indirect	Indirect	Direct
School Board	Indirect	Indirect	Direct

Allocation of indirect costs.   The allocation of indirect costs from supporting programs to operating programs is generally not done in educational budgeting. The expenditures of the supporting programs are maintained separately in the district accounting system. This allows managers to plan and budget for their programs and to be held accountable for controlling expenditures. The calculation of the amount of the central office or other support program expenditures which should be allocated to each school or each child is an interesting and sometimes enlightening analytical exercise. However, the administrator in charge of the operating program generally has little or no control over the indirect costs incurred by other program units. For example, a high school principal has no authority over of even knowledge of the expenditures of the district's personnel office. Therefore, the overhead amount, if it is charged to operating programs, is largely a paper calculation.

The exception to this situation is when the school district provides services to outside funding agencies. If the activities or programs provided by the district require support services, then the district may be allowed to charge a portion of its indirect costs to the funding agency along with the direct costs of the program. For example, if a large district is providing educational services for certain types of handicapped students from surrounding smaller districts, then the tuition charges for students could include not only the direct instruction costs, but also an amount for the larger district's support and administrative costs. In certain programs involving federal funding the district may have to establish and document an indirect cost recovery rate which is used to determine the allowable overhead amount.

The goal in allocation of overhead costs to operating programs is to have each operating program bear an equitable share of the indirect costs. This is done by establishing a reasonable basis for the allocations. The preferred standard for "reasonable" is in the proportion that each operating program causes the indirect costs to be incurred. If it is not feasible to determine this directly, then the allocations are usually made on some basis that represents most closely the magnitude of the program's operation. Examples of suggested allocation bases for various types of educational services within a school district are shown in Table 5.7.

The sum of the direct costs of a program and the indirect costs allocated to a program is termed the *full cost*. With the calculation of full cost amount, the total cost of each program consists of the direct costs associated with the program and a "fair share" of the indirect costs of the other programs which support it.[2] However, administrators should note that many of the indirect costs allocated to the program are in essence fixed costs from the operating program's perspective and could remain even if the program were canceled.

A classic mistake in this area is to treat indirect costs as variable costs of the programs to which they are allocated. Table 5.8 provides an illustra-

TABLE 5.7   Indirect Cost Allocation Bases

TYPE OF SUPPORT SERVICE	SUGGESTED BASES FOR ALLOCATION
Accounting	Total Dollar Volume or Number of Transactions Processed
Auditing	Direct Audit Hours
Data Processing	Direct Identifiable Hours of Employees of Central Budget
Disbursing Services	Number of Checks or Warrants Issued
Employee Benefits Administration	Number of Employees Contributing
Insurance Management Service	Dollar Value of Insurance Premiums
Legal Services	Direct Labor Hours
Mail and Messenger Service	Number of Documents or Employees Served
Motor Pool Costs	Miles Driven/Days Used
Equipment Repairs	Direct Hours
Space Use (Operation, Maintenance, Depreciation)	Square Feet of Space Used (For Instruction: Sq. Ft. per Pupil per Hour)
Utilities and Fuel	Time Consumption
Management Services	Direct Hours
Payroll Services	Number of Employees
Personnel Administration	Number of Employees
Printing and Reproduction	Direct Hours, Job Basis, Pages, Etc.
Procurement Services	Number of Transactions
Local Telephone Service	Number Telephone Instruments
Health Services	Number of Employees or Pupils
Fidelity Bonding Program	Employees Subject to Bond or Penalty Amounts
Transportation	Number of Pupils Enrolled
School Administration	Number of Employees Supervised
Moveable Equipment	Hours Used
Pupil Services	Average Daily Membership
Instructional Services	Learners Served (Average Daily Membership)

Source: Financial Accounting: Classifications and Standard Terminology for Local and State School Systems, Handbook II, revised.

TABLE 5.8   Indirect Cost Allocation Example
(Dollars in Thousands)

	PROGRAM A	PROGRAM B	TOTAL	PROGRAM A ONLY
Revenue from State	$200	$200	$400	$200
Direct Costs	100	150	250	100
Indirect Costs (Percent of Direct Costs)	48	72	120	120
Full Costs	148	222	370	220
Surplus (or Deficit)	$52	($22)	$30	($20)

tion of the difficulties that this misunderstanding can cause. Consider a district with two programs, each receiving $200,000 in state aid. Program A has direct costs of $100,000 and Program B has direct costs of $150,000. District indirect costs totaling $120,000 are allocated to these two programs on the basis of their total direct costs; Program A has 40 percent of the total direct costs of the two programs ($100,000/$250,000), and it has $48,000 allocated to it, while Program B has $72,000 as its indirect cost allocation. The full costs of each program are the sum of the direct and indirect costs. Without an understanding of direct and indirect costs an administrator might be tempted to conclude that Program A shows a surplus for the district, while Program B costs the district money and should be eliminated. This erroneous conclusion is based on the mistaken assumption that if Program B is dropped that the full costs will be saved. Rather, all that would be saved would be the direct costs of the program; the indirect costs that were allocated to the program will still exist and now will simply be reallocated to the remaining program. With the elimination of Program B, Program A now must bear all of the indirect costs alone and now the district really does lose money.

Average and Marginal Costs

The final type of cost categorization is the difference between average and marginal costs. This distinction is particularly useful when trying to determine the actual cost change which would result from changing the size of a program. An understanding of average and marginal costs can make cost projections much more accurate.

Average costs.   The average cost, as the name implies, is simply the average cost of some unit of operation. It is calculated by dividing the total cost by the number of units. It is the same as the unit cost discussed earlier. The costs involved can be either the direct costs alone or the full costs of a program. An average cost establishes what it costs to provide educational services to a group. For example in the particular school district illustrated in Table 5.9, it costs an average of $3,550 per student (full costs) to educate elementary students, an average of $39,000 per teacher for salary and benefits (direct costs), an average of $850,000 per middle school (direct costs). Such average costs can be helpful in comparing similar educational operations; however, care must be taken that the comparisons are valid and that the same operations and costs are included in all comparators.

Marginal costs.   *The marginal cost is the additional cost actually incurred (or saved) to serve one more (or less) unit or to provide one more (or less) unit of service.* It is the incremental cost (or savings) of small changes in the magnitude of the operation.

In the average cost example above, it certainly does not cost $3,550 to add one more student in a second grade classroom. Assuming that there is space in the classroom, the actual additional costs of one more student will be quite small because most of the classroom costs are fixed—no additional teacher salary or benefits, school administration expenditures, or classroom operating and maintenance costs. Probably a slight increase in the expenditures for supplies and equipment for the additional student is the most that will be needed.

In general, as long as the change in magnitude in operation does not change the relevant range of fixed costs, the incremental costs will equal the variable costs. These are the costs that change in direct relation to the volume or level of activity of the operation. While average costs include

TABLE 5.9   Average Cost Examples

Total Direct Elementary School Costs	$2,002,200
Allocated Indirect Costs	$1,334,800
Total Full Elementary School Costs	$3,337,000
Number of Elementary School Students	940
Average Cost per Elementary School Student	$3,550
Total District Teacher Salary Costs	$29,250,000
Total District Teacher Benefits Costs	$9,750,000
Total District Teacher Costs	$39,000,000
Number of Teachers	1,000
Average Cost per Teacher	$39,000
Total Direct Middle School Costs	$3,400,000
Number of Middle Schools	4
Average Cost per Middle School	$850,000

both fixed and variable costs in their calculation, marginal costs usually include only the variable costs. Consequently, marginal costs are typically lower than average costs, particularly for small changes in the level of operation. This is an important consideration to remember when planning for future operations based on changes from existing programs.

However, there is one significant exception to this situation and that is when the change in level of activity pushes the operation out of the relevant range of fixed costs and into another range of fixed costs. In addition to changes in the variable cost amounts, a change in operation of this sort requires a shift in the amount of fixed costs. This has a profound effect on the marginal costs of this change. Since the definition of marginal cost is

FIGURE 5.6 Marginal Cost Example

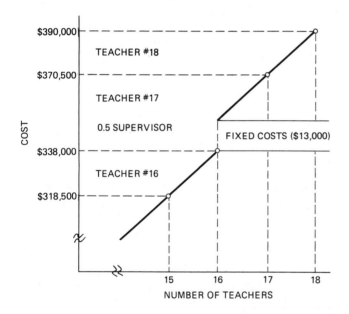

WHAT IS THE MARGINAL OF ADDING A TEACHER TO THE INSTRUCTIONAL STAFF?

COST OF TEACHER	$19,500	SUPERVISION STANDARD:
COST OF SUPERVISOR	$26,000	0.5 SUPERVISOR FOR EVERY 8 TEACHERS OR FRACTION OF 8 TEACHERS

TEACHERS	SUPERVISORS	TOTAL COSTS	MARGINAL COSTS	AVERAGE COSTS
15	1.0	$318,500	$19,500	$21,233
16	1.0	$338,000	$19,500	$21,125
17	1.5	$370,500	$32,500	$21,794
18	1.5	$390,000	$19,500	$21,667

the increase (or decrease) in the actual costs needed to serve or produce one more (or one less) unit, the marginal cost of a change requiring a shift in fixed costs must include both the amount of fixed cost change and the variable cost of the unit. For this change in the level of operation, where a cost transition point is crossed, the marginal costs are quite high and will exceed the average cost.

Consider the example in Figure 5.6 involving the marginal cost of adding additional teachers where there is a supervisor required for every sixteen teachers. Assume that for every eight teachers or fraction of eight teachers contract provisions require that a half-time supervisor must be hired. Under these conditions, the marginal cost of the fifteenth teacher is just the cost of the teacher ($19,500). The same is true for the sixteenth teacher. However, when the seventeenth teacher is hired, additional supervision is required. As a result, the marginal cost of the seventeenth teacher is the cost of the teacher (variable cost) plus the increase in supervision costs ($19,500 + $13,000 = $32,500). Once this new fixed cost level is reached, the marginal costs of additional teachers will again equal the variable cost of a teacher until another half-time supervisor is required (at teacher number twenty-five). Graphically, this is shown by beginning another fixed and variable cost diagram at the cost transition point at the uppermost point of the previous cost diagram.

Summary Illustration of Cost Categories

As a means of summarizing this cost analysis section, an example illustrating the various types of costs is presented and discussed below. The example used is an educational program consisting of one classroom unit as shown in Table 5.10. In this classroom, which is the level of analysis, the relevant costs are for the teacher, employee benefits for the teacher, supplies, and equipment. The classroom has a capacity of thirty students, but there are only twenty-five in it. The unit prices are given for each of the resources and the total cost for the classroom with twenty-five students is calculated at $32,350.

The fixed costs are those which do not change with a change in level of activity within the capacity of the unit. In this case the level of activity is measured by the number of students enrolled in the classroom. For up to thirty students, the fixed costs are those for the teacher and employee benefits since their amounts will not vary whether there are one or thirty students in the classroom. They total $28,600. The variable costs are those which are directly related to the number of students in the classroom—the more students, the higher the costs. The variable costs in this example are those for supplies and equipment; they are expressed in dollar per student terms rather than a total dollar amount since that amount of variable costs will depend on the number of students in the classroom. The variable costs for the unit are $150 per student. The total unit cost for the classroom at its capacity of thirty students is $33,100, which is the sum of the fixed costs and the variable costs for thirty students.

The marginal cost is the additional cost caused by adding (or subtracting) one student. The marginal cost amount will usually equal the variable cost per student as long as the increase (or decrease) does not change the range in which the fixed costs remain constant. In this example, the classroom has a capacity of thirty students. Additional students beyond the capacity will require another classroom to be added. Consequently, the marginal cost of the twenty-ninth and thirtieth students will be $150 each (the variable cost per student) as they can be accommodated in the original classroom. However, with the addition of the thirty-first student the total number of students cannot all be served in one classroom and another classroom must be added. Therefore, the marginal costs for the thirty-first student are the additional fixed costs of the second classroom ($28,600) plus the variable costs for that student ($150) or a total of $28,750. The second classroom provides capacity for an additional thirty students, so the thirty-second student can be accommodated in this classroom with only an additional cost of $150 (the variable cost per student).

To calculate the total costs for program levels requiring the second classroom it is necessary to account for the required number of fixed and variable cost amounts. This can be done in several ways as shown in the example for thirty-one students. One possibility is to add the marginal cost of the thirty-first student to the unit cost (for thirty students). Another is to take the unit cost for the first thirty students and add to it the fixed cost amount for the new classroom and the variable costs for the additional student. A third procedure is to add the required number of fixed cost amounts (two) and the required number of variable cost amounts (thirty-one). In all three cases the result is identical. The total cost calculation for forty-five students uses the second procedure to determine the costs.

The average costs are the total costs divided by the number of students. For twenty-five students the average cost is $1,294 per student and for thirty students the average cost is $1,103 per student. The average cost is higher for twenty-five students than for thirty students because the fixed costs are spread over a fewer number of students.

In this example, all of the costs have been been direct costs at the classroom level. That is, they can be identified specifically with the classroom and serve no other program. Examples of indirect costs at the classroom level would be school level expenditures for school administration, operation and maintenance, and for instructional and support activities

TABLE 5.10 Illustration of Cost Categories

FOR AN EDUCATIONAL PROGRAM OF ONE CLASSROOM

LEVEL OF ANALYSIS:	Classroom
CAPACITY:	30 Students
ACTUAL ENROLLMENT:	25 Students

RESOURCES IN CLASSROOM	UNIT PRICE OF RESOURCE		COST
Teacher	$22,000	per Teacher	$22,000
Employee Benefits	30%	of Salary	$6,600
Supplies	$90	per Student	$2,250
Equipment	$60	per Student	$1,500
Total Cost For	25 Students		$32,350

FIXED AND VARIABLE COSTS

Fixed Costs:	Teacher	$22,000	
	Employee Benefits	$6,600	
	Total Fixed Costs	$28,600	
Variable Costs:	Supplies	$90	Per Student
	Equipment	$60	Per Student
	Total Variable Costs	$150	Per Student

UNIT COST

Classroom at Capacity: 30 Students

$$\text{Fixed Cost} + 30 \times \text{Variable Cost}$$
$$(30 \quad \$150)$$
$$\$28,600 + \$4,500 = \$33,100$$

MARGINAL COSTS

What are the marginal costs of the 29th, 30th, 31st, and 32nd students?
 Students 29 and 30 can be added to the existing classroom.
 With the addition of student 31 the capacity of the first classroom is exceeded and another classroom is required.
 Student 32 can be added to the second classroom.

NUMBER OF STUDENTS	ADDITIONAL COSTS VARIABLE	FIXED	MARGINAL COST
29	$150	$0	$150
30	$150	$0	$150
31	$150	$28,600	$28,750
32	$150	$0	$150

TOTAL COSTS

FOR 31 STUDENTS

Unit Cost	30	Students	$33,100
Marginal Cost of	31st	Student	$28,750
or			$61,850

TABLE 5.10 (*Continued*)

Unit Cost	30	Students	$33,100
Fixed Costs	1		$28,600
Variable Costs	1		$150

or			$61,850

Fixed Costs	2		$57,200
Variable Costs	31		$4,650

			$61,850

FOR 45 STUDENTS

Unit Cost	30	Students	$33,100
Fixed Costs	1		$28,600
Variable Costs	15		$2,250

			$63,950

AVERAGE COSTS

NUMBER OF STUDENTS	TOTAL COSTS	AVERAGE COST
25	$32,350	$1,294 per Student
29	$32,950	$1,136 per Student
30	$33,100	$1,103 per Student
31	$61,850	$1,995 per Student
32	$62,000	$1,938 per Student

DIRECT AND INDIRECT COSTS

All costs in this example are direct costs at the classroom level.

Indirect Costs:

School Support Costs	$19,000	
School Administrative Costs	$61,000	
Total School Level Indirect Costs	$80,000	
Number of Classrooms in School	16	
Indirect School Level Costs	$5,000	per Class
District Support Costs	$2,400,000	
District Administrative Costs	$1,200,000	
Total District Level Indirect Costs	$3,600,000	
Number of Classrooms in District	400	
Indirect District Level Costs	$9,000	per Class

FULL COST (FOR 25 STUDENTS)

Direct Classroom Costs	$32,350	per Class
Indirect School Level Costs	$5,000	per Class
Indirect District Level Costs	$9,000	per Class
Full Cost of Classroom	$46,350	per Class

which are not classroom specific, such as a music teacher, gym teacher, or library expenditures. District level expenditures for activities which support all district pupils, personnel, or schools are also indirect at the classroom level. If it is desired to associate these costs with the classroom or even student level then they must be allocated to these levels using some reasonable basis. With additional information on the magnitude of support and administrative costs at the school and district levels, along with the number of classrooms in the school and in the district, the indirect costs can be calculated at the classroom level. When the indirect costs are added to the direct costs, the full costs at the classroom level are determined.

The fixed, variable, total, unit, and marginal costs are shown graphically in Figure 5.7. Note that all of these costs are direct costs and do not include any allocated amounts. For the first thirty students, one classroom with its fixed and variable cost components will be sufficient. The total unit cost is the amount at the full capacity of thirty students (33,100). When more than thirty students are to be served, a second classroom unit must be

FIGURE 5.7   Illustration of Cost Categories

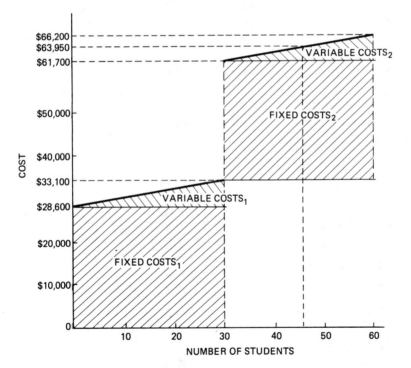

added with its additional fixed cost amount and the variable costs for each student. The total costs for students in the thirty-one to sixty range are calculated in the same manner as those for the first classroom. The total cost for any number of students can be determined from the graph by reading up from the number of students to the total cost line (fixed plus variable costs) and over to the cost axis. For example, the total cost for forty-five students is $63,950.

Managerial Uses of Cost Analysis

Cost analysis techniques can be used by administrators for a variety of purposes. On a conceptual level, an understanding of the differences between fixed and variable, direct and indirect, and average and marginal costs can clarify the relationships between programs and their costs. This is particularly true for recognizing the cost effects of changes in educational programs. With understanding comes a greater ability to plan future activities with increasing accuracy and to explain the cost implications of program changes to other school personnel, school board members, and district patrons with more clarity and persuasiveness.

On an operational level, cost analyses can provide information to help administrators make better decisions. Cost estimates for future operations which involve changes in existing programs can be made with greater accuracy by considering marginal costs as well as identifying the fixed and variable costs which are involved. The same is true for projecting the costs for new programs which the district may wish to undertake.

Development of annual budgets can utilize, explicitly or implicitly, all of the cost concepts discussed in this chapter. If there is uncertainty over the future level of a program's operations, then a series of cost estimates can be calculated over the expected range of activity. Again, the recognition of fixed and variable costs, marginal costs, and direct and indirect costs will prove very useful. If revenues are involved in the program's operation, a break-even analysis can provide vital information on the feasibility of the program and the anticipated surplus it will yield or subsidy it will require.

Unit costs enable administrators to compare similar programs along the cost dimension. Here, however, any differences among the population served, program objectives, types of costs included, size of operation, organizational structure, or other relevant aspect of the programs must be clearly identified.

In summary, knowledge of costs—both the concepts of the different types of costs and the ability to perform useful analyses—can be a highly useful and important tool for successful administrators.

PROBLEMS

5.1   WEBSTER SCHOOL DISTRICT
    The annual presentation of the proposed budget in Webster School District
went quite smoothly. With the exception of two accounts for the middle schools,
the school board appeared satisfied with both the amounts and the explanations for the budgeted expenditure items. They could not understand the substantial increase in the amount for Overtime Salaries. This account reflects the
costs of overtime pay for middle school teachers for parent conferences which
are held after school hours. Also, the decrease in the amount for data processing services, while not large, was puzzling in a time of increasing computer
useage. The data processing expenditures are for the costs of individual student reports which are prepared by an outside computer services company.
    Prepare a brief report analyzing the causes of the changes in the budget
amounts for these two items. Calculate the amount of change due to changes in
workload, price, and program standard and write a brief description explaining
the nature of these changes.

Webster School District Budget Data

		CURRENT YEAR	BUDGET YEAR	CHANGE
1120	Middle School Instruction:			
131	Overtime Salaries	$108,000	$288,000	$180,000
316	Data Processing Services	$4,860	$2,880	($1,980)
Other Budget Information:				
Number of Students		10,800	12,000	1,200
Overtime Pay Rate ($/hr)		$20.00	$24.00	$4.00
Parent Conferences per Year		1	2	1
Conference Length (hours)		0.5	0.5	0
Cost per Student Report		$0.05	$0.06	$0.01
Student Reports per Year		9	4	−5

5.2   SHOTGUN UNION SCHOOL DISTRICT
    The administration of Shotgun Union School District presented its proposed
budget to the Budget Committee last week. The budget message, the overall
level of proposed expenditures, and the amount required for the tax levy were
all well received by the committee members. However, a new budget committee member, I. M. Hardnose (who had been a frequent past critic of district
spending policies), questioned several items. The two items, custodial salaries
and postage for the schools, are shown below. He pointed out that even though
the district closed one school for the upcoming year and fewer students were
expected, both of these cost items increased. These he claimed were typical of
the unnecessary expenditures which the district continued to make.
    The superintendent wishes to make no changes in these items as she be-
lieves that the expenditures are needed and proper. She wants to take this opportunity to educate the budget committee members, and Mr. Hardnose in par-

ticular, as to the reason for these expenditures. She has asked you to provide her with an analysis which she can present to the next budget committee meeting which explains the reasons for the changes in the budget amounts for the two items questioned by Mr. Hardnose. The presentation should be brief: a numerical analysis of the causes of the budget changes and a narrative of less than one page succinctly explaining them.

Shotgun Union School District Budget Data

		CURRENT YEAR	BUDGET YEAR	CHANGE
1110	Elementary Instruction			
353	Postage	$3,150	$5,400	$2,250
2542	Custodial Services			
112	Noncertified Salaries	$336,000	$412,500	$76,500
Other Budget Information:				
Number of students		6,300	6,000	(300)
Mailings per year		2	3	1
Cost per piece mailed		$0.25	$0.30	$0.05
Square feet to be cleaned		360,000	330,000	(30,000)
Average custodian salary		$14,000	$15,000	$1,000
Cleanings per week		1	5 times in 4 weeks	

A single custodian can maintain 15,000 square feet per week.
This capacity will not change from the current year to the budget year.

5.3 KINDERGARTEN PROGRAM IN EDISON SCHOOL DISTRICT

At a recent meeting of the School Board of Edison School District, the budget for the upcoming school year was presented by the superintendent and other staff members. As the Director of Elementary Instruction, part of your presentation covered the budget for the kindergarten program. Several members of the Board had questions about some of the proposed expenditures. In particular, they questioned the changes in the Certificated Salaries, Noncertificated Salaries, and Instructional Supplies accounts. They could not understand what caused the changes in these accounts from the current year to next year.

Kindergarten Program in Edison School District: Budget Data

		CURRENT YEAR	BUDGET YEAR	CHANGE
1110	Elementary Instruction:			
111	Cert. Salaries	$1,320,000	$1,108,800	($211,200)
112	Noncert. Salaries	$360,000	$616,320	$256,320
430	Supplies (Paper)	$1,890	$1,728	($162)
Other Budget Information:				
Students		1,260	1,200	(60)
Teachers		60	48	(12)
Instructional Aides		30	48	18
Reams of Paper Purchased		1,260	1,440	180

The superintendent has asked you to prepare a brief report which explains the causes of the expenditure changes in these three accounts. A copy of the budget accounts and some related programmatic information are given below. Calculate the amount of the change in each account which is due to changes in workload, prices, and district program standards. Present your results in a short report and include your calculations.

5.4 ACE PROGRAM IN CANASTA SCHOOL DISTRICT

Canasta School District operates the ACE program for gifted students. ACE teachers give special, higher level instruction to those children who qualify. ACE teachers in the program are assigned to individual schools and the students leave their regular classrooms and report to the ACE teacher in a special room set aside for this purpose. They receive additional assistance in their regular classroom from an ACE aide.

Full-time teachers and part-time aides are hired to teach in this program. Each teacher has a maximum of twenty students at any given time. Each student is seen twice a week for one-half hour on a one-to-one basis by the teacher. The daily teaching schedule is ten students per day—four days per week. One day a week is used for teacher preparation. The aides work one hour per week in the regular classroom with each student seen by the ACE teacher. The school year is thirty-six weeks long.

The cost items for this program are:

Teacher salaries	$19,000/teacher per year
Aide wages	$10/hour (paid for time working with students only)
Employee benefits	30% of salary for teachers
	22% of salary for aides
Instructional supplies	$60/student per year
Books	$40/student per year
ACE room	$3,200/year

Consider the unit of analysis to be the individual ACE teacher and the level of activity measure to be the number of students served by the teachers.

1. What are the fixed costs of one unit of this program (name and amount)?
2. What are the variable costs of this program (name and amount/level of activity)?
3. Specify the total unit cost for one unit and diagram the fixed and variable costs for two units on a graph.
4. What is the average cost of one student in a full unit?
5. What would the cost be to serve thirty students in the program?
6. If 470 students were being served by the district this year, what would be the marginal costs of serving fifteen more students next year?

5.5 NIGHTINGALE EDUCATIONAL SERVICE DISTRICT

The Nightingale Educational Service District is a countywide agency which was established to coordinate and provide regional services for low incidence handicapped students. The district operates a Home and Hospital Instruction program in which teachers instruct students who, through temporary or long-term disability, are unable to attend regular school programs in their home district. The teachers in the program visit students at home or in medical institutions. Each student has a medical examination to determine eligibility for the program.

Full-time teachers are hired on annual contracts to teach in the program and each teacher has a maximum caseload of twelve students at any given time. Each student in this caseload is seen once per week for two hours on a one-to-one basis. The daily teaching schedule is three students per day; one day per week is provided for teacher preparation. The length of the school year is thirty-six weeks. Teachers use their own cars to travel from the district office to their student's locations and are reimbursed by the district at the rate of $0.25 per mile. Over the year, home and hospital teachers average thirty miles of reimbursable travel per day when they visit three students.

The cost items for this program are:

Teacher salaries	$22,000 per teacher
Employee benefits	22 percent of salary
Instructional supplies	$50 per student
Medical evaluation	$100 per student
Travel reimbursements	as described above

In answering the questions below, consider the unit of analysis to be the individual teacher unit, the level of activity measure to be the number of students served by the teacher, and the time period to be one year (that is, use annual costs).

1. What are the fixed costs of one unit of this program (names and amounts)?
2. What are the variable costs of this program (name and amount per level of activity)?
3. What are the total costs for one unit of the program? Diagram the fixed and variable costs for two units of the program.
4. What would be the costs to serve thirty-four students in the Home and Hospital program?
5. If thirty-nine students were the total number that were being served by the district in the Home and Hospital program this year, what would be the marginal cost savings of serving five fewer students next year?

5.6 COST ANALYSIS IN WESTERN SCHOOL DISTRICT

Use the following data to analyze the costs in Western School District:

District level data:

4,936 students enrolled in the district

9 schools of 20 classrooms each

2 schools of 36 classrooms each

247 teachers employed

Maximum class size permitted is 20 students/classroom

Average teacher salary is $22,500

Employee benefits average 35 percent of salary

District level support service expenditures $466,200

District administrative expenditures $248,500

Emerald School data:

396 students enrolled

20 teachers in 20 classrooms

*Instructional supplies expenditures $45,540

*Textbook expenditures $19,800

Building operating and maintenance expenditures $46,000

School administration expenditures $96,000

*These items are ordered by individual teachers based on their class size and instructional needs.

1. Identify the specific cost items which are direct costs for a classroom in Emerald School. Calculate the direct unit costs for a classroom of twenty students. Use the format shown below.

Cost Type (Direct or Indirect)	Cost Item	$/Classroom	Calculation Basis

2. Allocate all indirect costs from the school and district level which are listed in the data section to the classroom level. Use the same format as for Question 1. Calculate the full unit cost of a classroom in Emerald School.

3. Now, using the school as the level of analysis, specify the direct costs for Emerald School. Use the same format as the previous questions. Allocate all district support and administrative costs to the school level and indicate the basis for each allocation. Calculate the full cost for Emerald School.

4. At the classroom level in Emerald School which of the direct costs are fixed and which are variable? Specify the cost items and amounts.

5. Graph the fixed/variable cost relationship as the number of students goes one to forty-five. Use the number of students as the horizontal axis and the cost as the vertical axis.

6. What would be the direct classroom costs of serving thirty-five students?

7. What is the average cost per student (full cost) in Western School District? Assume that Emerald School costs are representative of other schools of its size in the district and that district support and administrative costs include all costs above the school level.

8. What is the marginal cost to the district of adding seven new students?

NOTES

1. Robert N. Anthony and Regina Herzlinger, *Management Control in Nonprofit Organizations* (Homewood, IL: Richard Irwin, Inc., 1975), p. 122.

2. Ibid.

6

BUDGET ADJUSTMENTS

The basic requirement in budgeting is balance; that is, that projected revenues be equal to or greater than planned expenditures. This is not a matter of choice, but a requirement imposed by state statutes. School districts are not allowed to engage in deficit financing.

In achieving a balanced budget, administrators must deal with three types of budget adjustments: budget reductions; budget increases; and budget shifts. Budget reduction is the focus of this chapter. It is the situation that administrators will face most often; it is also the most difficult task for administrators and one that is highly volatile. Other types of budget adjustments may be necessary if revenues are sufficient to allow an increase in the budget or if resource shifts among district programs are desired.

The adjustments can take place at any time during the budget cycle—from during the development process to the end of the operating year. Adjustments in the development period are the simplest to make because changes can be implemented at the planning stage before actual operations begin. Nevertheless, it may be difficult if significant changes in planned expenditures are required as a result of the adjustments.

The requirement for a balanced budget does not disappear once the budget is adopted and the operating year begins. The school district cannot spend more money during the year than it actually collects.[1] This means that if actual revenues are much less than those which were projected or if actual expenditures were much greater than estimated, budget reductions must be made during the operating year to bring revenues and expenditures back into balance. These adjustments can interrupt or cancel programs or services already in operation. If required during an operating year, budget reductions may necessitate cutting back or eliminating programs and services which are currently provided, laying off of currently employed personnel, and canceling vendor contracts.

What can cause an imbalanced budget for a school district? After all, the budget was in balance last year; won't the normal inflationary increases in both expenditures and revenues keep it in balance next year? There are a number of conditions which could put the budget out of balance. State revenues may be restricted or even reduced due to declining district enrollments or state economic problems. Federal revenues may be cut back. Local property tax collections may not be as great as anticipated. On the expenditure side, a salary increase negotiated several years before may be larger than the gain in revenues anticipated next year. Some essential items, such as energy costs or insurance rates, may have experienced severe price increases. The district may require new equipment, such as computers, or have nonpostponable maintenance needs, such as leaky roofs which are damaging classrooms, gymnasiums, or offices.

Whatever the causes of an imbalanced budget, if expenditures are greater than revenues, one of two things has to happen: expenditures must be reduced; or revenues must be increased. Frequently, a combination of these approaches is employed by school districts to balance their budget.

TYPES OF BUDGET ADJUSTMENTS

Although the most common form of budget adjustment is to reduce the size of the budget, two other forms of adjustment may arise—budget increases and budget shifts among programs.

Budget Increases

When revenues are anticipated to be significantly greater than expenditures, it may be appropriate to consider increasing the budget. Having to adjust a school district budget by increasing it is generally a more pleasant situation than having to reduce it.

Where would these additional revenues come from and when would the school district know about them? If higher than usual revenues are estimated during the budget development process, then the normal matching of revenues with expenditures will balance the budget before the operating year begins. However, if additional, unanticipated revenues come in during the year—higher level of state aid, greater percentage of tax collections, or a substantial gift—then adjustments, if they are made, must be implemented during the operating year. These adjustments usually require school board action to authorize the expenditure of the additional monies in approved ways. Such authorization requires scrutiny of the proposed increases to determine that the monies will be spent wisely and in accord with district objectives.

There are, however, two alternatives to automatically committing the surplus revenues to increasing expenditures. One possibility is to return the surplus to the local taxpayers in the form of lower property taxes. This reduces the revenues available to the school district and can align revenues and expenditures more closely. It is also popular with the taxpayers and may build trust and goodwill for future tax increase requests. It has the obvious disadvantage of removing revenues from the school district which could be used to improve or expand programs in the current year or may be needed in future years.

The second alternative is to keep the excess revenues in an uncommitted reserve account—a rainy day fund—for use in future years when additional revenues may be needed to balance increased expenditures. In this case the district keeps the monies under its control, but does not spend them in the current year. This has the effect of reducing future year taxes.

Budget Shifts Among Programs

Another type of budget adjustment is shifting of monies among district programs. This procedure does not require a change in the size of the overall budget, but rather is a redistribution of the existing resources. In the budget development process it can be used to realign spending patterns with district priorities without increasing total expenditures. For example, districts can use this approach to shift the curriculum emphasis in the district. Allocations for teaching positions and monies for supplies and equipment can be transferred from curriculum areas of reduced emphasis, such as vocational education in some districts, to areas of increased emphasis, such as math and science. This approach can also be used to finance new programs, such as computer science, without a budget increase.

Since there are no new dollars added to the budget, there are both winners and losers as a result of the shifting of monies. Those programs which gain resources should be those which are believed to be of greater importance, are more central to the mission of the school district or are mandated by state or federal statutes and regulations. Conversely, those programs which lose resources are presumed to have lower priority for district attention. Obviously, if sizable or influential groups object to the losses for programs that they believe important, these shifts can cause political difficulties. A board member or members with a strong belief in vocational education, for example, may be an effective advocate for maintaining funding levels for those programs. Similarly, internal groups of teachers or administrators may lobby strenuously to prevent losses to their programs.

These actions are part of a normal democratic budget development process, but they can inhibit budget adjustments which modify current district practices.

Another type of budget adjustment occurs during the operating year, most frequently close to year end: shifting of remaining monies from one account to another in order to spend the available budget. This is an ongoing and regularly practiced form of budget adjustment. These transfers typically involve smaller dollar amounts. As a result, they are usually less visible to the board or public and are less controversial. Since the budget was developed up to eighteen months in advance of actual expenditures, circumstances change and the need for expenditures in various district programs may decline or increase. Within district policies, administrators are often permitted to shift budgeted expenditures from one area to another to meet current district or school needs. For example, the transfer of monies allocated for supplies from one high school instructional department to another is frequently done at the principal's discretion. On the other hand, transfers of monies into or out of salary accounts (for example, purchasing a computer with funds originally budgeted for a secretary) may require central office or even school board approval.

The process may accelerate as the end of the operating year approaches. In some budgeted accounts not all of the monies originally allocated to them will have been spent, while other accounts will have been overspent. Usually, this is not a problem if the unspent amounts can cover the overspent accounts. In fact, administrators should monitor budget accounts under their supervision to determine the status of all important accounts; they may even initiate such account transfers in order to enhance the operations of their programs. For example, if the math department in a high school has not spent its budgeted equipment amount as the end of the year nears and has no plans to do so, the principal could approve a request by the English department to transfer those funds to its account in order to purchase a microcomputer for students to use in a creative writing class. With an overall understanding of the status, plans, and needs for each department the principal is in an excellent position to initiate and direct the budget adjustment process at the school level.

Budget Reductions

Budget reductions are necessary when projected expenditures are greater than available revenues. This situation creates an unbalanced budget which must be corrected. The adjustments made to reduce expenditures (and to a lesser extent, to increase revenues) comprise the process of budget reduction.

Cutback management is a term applied to the administration of program reduction.[2] Ideally, it should be planned, rational, and carried out in the least disruptive manner. Actually, it is usually a more messy and complex process. A condition requiring significant reductions is the most difficult situation for school boards, administrators, district personnel, students, parents, and the public to deal with. Unlike budget increases and even budget adjustments, there are no real winners in the educational system in this process. Winning may mean that your program does not get cut as much as some others, or at best, that your program was spared the axe.

TYPES OF BUDGET REDUCTIONS

There are two principal types of budget reductions:

1. Cost reductions through improved efficiencies.
2. Program reductions.

The first type of reduction occurs because of an improved efficiency in district operations which does not affect the delivery of instructional programs or services. The reductions are cost savings which result from changes in operating procedures that have little direct impact on instruction or student services, at least in the short run. From an educational and management point of view these are the most desirable types of reductions. The costs of operations are reduced, but the educational programs are largely unaffected.

In contrast to improved efficiencies, the second type of cost reduction is that of program reduction. These reductions result in a cutback in the quantity or quality of programs and services provided by the school district. After the program reduction, a lower level of service is provided than before. This is undesirable, but sometimes necessary. Or, in the words of a high-school principal facing a central office mandate to reduce expenditures for supplies and equipment by fifty percent, "Do we like it? No. Will we do it? Yes."

Continuum for Budget Reduction Alternatives

Between the the poles of improved efficiencies and program reductions there is a range of types of reductions which are possible. Administrators who have to recommend or decide which budget reductions to implement should consider the continuum shown in Table 6.1. One or more types of reductions may be necessary to reach a balanced budget.

The continuum is arranged in more or less ascending order of severity. The conventional wisdom of making the cuts as far from the classroom as possible is generally followed by school administrators. Instructional programs usually receive priority over support services or administration, and personnel expenditures are maintained in preference to capital outlay.[3] In accordance with this order, the first efforts in budget reduction

TABLE 6.1   Continuum for Budget Reduction Activities[a]

1. OBTAIN REDUCED PRICES FOR SAME SERVICES
     Competitive bidding
     Salary adjustments
2. INCREASE PRODUCTIVITY
     Economize
     Combine similar functions
     Modify instructional and/or support approaches
     Reduce support and administrative personnel and increase responsibilities for
       those remaining
3. DEFER SPENDING
4. MAKE ACROSS-THE-BOARD CUTS
     All programs and services reduced approximately equally
     Differential reductions favoring instruction
5. ELIMINATE "NONESSENTIAL" SERVICES
     Make selective reductions
     Reduce or drop optional or nonmandated programs and services offered by the
       district
6. REDUCE INSTRUCTIONAL POSITIONS AND PROGRAMS
     Make selective reductions
     Increase class size and/or instructional caseloads

[a]This list is based on *Managing Costs Creatively* (Salem, OR: Oregon Department of Education, 1982).

should be locating and making changes which increase operating efficiency or productivity. These activities should yield cost reductions which have the least impact on instructional programs and services.

Reduce prices for services.   Administrative efforts devoted to reducing the costs of various purchased services through competitive bidding can have significant financial payoffs. Shopping around for the best price for services (such as insurance, data processing, and transportation) that the district may purchase from outside firms can result in lowered costs for the same service. Cooperative purchasing arrangements with other districts can achieve high volume orders which qualify for quantity discounts from suppliers.

Another form of price reduction which can have a substantial impact on the budget is an adjustment in personnel salaries. This may be very difficult or even legally impossible for some districts, but if salary costs are reduced without reducing the number of personnel the district can provide the same level of programs and services at a lower cost. Several possibilities exist for salary adjustments: a reduction in the increase planned for next year (for example, 3 percent increase in the salary schedule rather than a 6 percent); a salary freeze or no increase; and an actual reduction in salary level for employees. This approach also has the advantage of spreading a relatively small individual financial impact over most or all district employees rather than placing a much larger financial burden on a smaller number of employees who might lose their jobs in order to provide or maintain salary increases for their colleagues.

Increase productivity of district operations. Productivity increases can occur if existing tasks can be accomplished more efficiently. This can be achieved through efforts to economize in the consumption of resources. Examples could include a reduction in the quantity of various supplies and materials used in both instructional and support operations. Energy conservation is also an important source of cost reduction; however, some savings in this area are long term and require an investment in weatherization, insulation, or energy efficient equipment.

It may also be possible to provide equivalent services in a different format or using a different approach. Positions with similar responsibilities can be consolidated resulting in personnel savings; cooperative arrangements with nearby districts can combine identical functions, such as purchasing; modifications to instructional or support service programs may yield the same results, but at a lower cost; and personnel may be asked to take broader responsibilities as part of their employment.

Defer spending. Another means of reducing budgeted or actual expenditures is to defer spending from this year to a later year. This approach calls for staff and students to make do with existing facilities and equipment for another year. Sometimes this is possible, sometimes it is not. For example, replacement equipment requests for a high school can be categorized according to the condition of the existing equipment as: Top Priority—Replace (current equipment dangerous for students, broken or irreparable equipment); 2nd Priority—Replace if funds available (current equipment worn, but possible to last another year); 3rd Priority—Defer if necessary (current equipment out-of-date, newer and improved equipment available).

Make across-the-board reduction. This approach involves cuts, usually small, applied to all programs. By definition, a straight across-the-board reduction will affect all areas, including instruction. If the board instructs the superintendent to make a 4 percent across-the-board cut in the budget, they can avoid specifying exactly which cuts are to be made. It is frequently more politically palatable for district policy makers to use this approach. In this manner every program and everyone bears part of the budget reduction burden. It is less divisive than singling out particular programs for reductions while sparing others. The assumption, explicit or implicit, is that all programs will be able to continue in operation with a small, but manageable reduction in available resources and that the programs and services will not be seriously affected. While this may be true for a year or two in some districts, continued application of this approach will slowly starve the district's programs and negatively impact the quality of education provided.

Another difficulty with this approach is that programs have differential abilities to absorb across-the-board cuts. Large programs may be able to share the percentage reduction among more staff members and larger supply and equipment allocations. Small programs, where the staff members and other resources are fewer and less divisible, may find the same percentage reduction cut would require expenditure reductions which would eliminate an essential component of their program. For example, a high school foreign language department required to reduce its allocated teaching positions by 0.5 FTE as part of an across-the-board reduction order may have to cut its only French teacher (a half-time position); this reduction would eliminate French instruction in the high school entirely.

A modification of the strict across-the-board approach is to have differential reduction percentages applied to instruction and to other areas. While a lower reduction rate for instruction favors instruction, including this large and significant portion of the budget in the areas for reduction avoids larger and more severe budget cuts in the support and administrative areas.

Eliminate "nonessential" programs.   Some of the programs and services provided by school districts are not required by statute or regulation. Since they are not mandatory, the district has the option of reducing or eliminating these "nonessential" services, even though they may be helpful and have come to be expected by the public. While the list will vary from state to state, examples of nonmandated programs may include home-to-school transportation, food services, intramurals, athletics, and student body activities. On the instructional side, the list could be broadened to include elective courses not required for graduation. As is obvious from the services listed above, the elimination of many of them would cause significant controversy and potential political problems for the district.

In contrast to the across-the-board cut approach, these reductions are selective; they target some programs for deep cuts or elimination, while others are untouched or reduced only a little. This technique permits policy makers to identify specific reductions from the budget which are the farthest from the central goals of the district.

Reduce instructional programs.   The final type of budget reduction is to reduce programs and positions in the instructional area. These reductions are typically saved for last, but if the amounts to cut are significant, they often cannot be avoided. Education is a labor intensive business. Eighty percent or more of the costs of education in a district are for personnel related expenditures and the bulk of these are in the instructional area.

Consequently, for large budget reductions, it is almost inevitable that instructional personnel will be reduced. This reduction-in-force will result in increased class sizes and greater instructional caseloads for the remaining staff, both educationally undesirable conditions.

Immediate versus Long Term Reductions

In order to balance the budget *during the development process*, reductions need to be made to the budget for the upcoming year. To bring a budget into balance *during the operating year* reductions have to be made in the current year's budget. In both cases there is a need for immediate impact. Cuts have to be implemented that will decrease expenditures in the next or current year.

By contrast there are some budget reduction activities which will have an impact in future years. These are adjustments which decrease expenditures in the long term. Rather than showing immediate reductions, some of these activities may require additional current expenditures to invest in cost saving equipment, training or retraining, or start-up requirements. These reduction activities generally will not help in cutting the current budget although they are expected to yield savings in the future. If the district is in a budget cutting mode by necessity, then such projects are difficult to justify in the current year, even though significant cost savings may be anticipated in future years. In any event, the district should carefully analyze any such request to ensure that the long term savings justify the current costs. An analysis of the anticipated investment and subsequent future year savings should include net present value calculations to account for the time value of money to the district.[4]

BUDGET REDUCTIONS THROUGH IMPROVED EFFICIENCIES

These are reductions in district expenditures which are a result of changes in operating procedures. They encompass reductions from reduced prices, increased productivity, and deferred spending from the continuum above. Their common characteristic is that they have relatively little direct impact on the instructional program or student services in the immediate future. Some of the most prominent examples are described below.[5]

Energy conservation.   Energy costs are among those rising most rapidly. A energy conservation program can yield large dollar saving. Not heating or lighting unused spaces and lowering thermostat settings are two of the most common and simplest activities in this area. Another source of information and energy savings suggestions is the local power company; frequently, they will conduct an energy audit for large users.

This area also has the possibility for investments in energy saving devices which will increase costs in the short term, but reduce costs in later years. Examples include switching to fluorescent lighting, weatherizing buildings, weatherstripping doors, double glazed windows, additional insulation, landscaping, and solar energy generation.

Risk management. Insurance costs are also among the most rapidly increasing of district expenditures. Typically, school districts require a variety of policies to cover different types of risks: property and casualty, group health, student accident, automobile, other vehicle, errors and omissions, boiler, computer, workmen's compensation, unemployment compensation, vandalism, and liability.[6] The district's existing insurance coverage in each of these areas should be examined for appropriateness and adjusted if necessary. Competitive bidding for providing the desired coverage should be utilized in order to obtain the lowest cost consistent with the coverage specifications.

A self-insurance component of the insurance program may reduce premiums significantly. This can be done through high deductible amounts for certain policies and through a self-insurance consortium in which several district pay amounts into a funding pool which is used to cover losses of the members.

Purchasing. Competitive bidding for necessary items can result in cost savings in a market where there are several suppliers. Volume purchasing, made possible by several smaller districts pooling their purchase requests, can give the consortium additional power to negotiate lower prices with suppliers. The tradeoff in a consortium is the necessity for member districts to agree upon a particular brand or product for common items in their purchase requests. The individual items may be minor—ball point pens, grade of paper—but a single selection for the consortium may require some members to make changes from particular products with which they are familiar and comfortable.

Make or buy decisions. Make or buy decisions refer to the district choice of whether to provide the service in-house (with its own personnel) or to contract with an outside company to provide the service for the school district. Examples of services which could be done either by the district or purchased from an outside company are transportation, building maintenance, grounds maintenance, equipment maintenance, vehicle maintenance, food service, printing, and data processing. However, there many more considerations than cost when deciding whether to provide or contract the service. The quality of the service, control over the timing, ability to make rapid adjustments in schedules, and selection and qualifications of personnel are also part of the decision.

Training for nonteaching staff.   Inservice training for classified personnel can increase both their productivity and efficiency. For example, cost savings are possible through less waste and spoilage in the food service operations, through reduced fuel consumption by district vehicles, more efficient procedures in district warehouse operations, and faster turnaround time for repairs in the district maintenance shop.

Deferral of expenditures.   Delaying some expenditures is a widely used tactic for reducing a budget. Typically, maintenance and capital outlay are areas which experience deferrals. While it may be expedient or even necessary to defer maintenance or new capital outlay requests, this is a short-term strategy. In the long run it can be very expensive to correct the results of many years of deferred maintenance. Repeated yearly deferrals open the possibility of serious damage to facilities through inattention. Delays in purchasing new capital equipment mean that the district students and employees work with possibly outdated and inefficient existing equipment.

Use of more efficient procedures or equipment.   In some cases it is possible to increase the utilization of existing equipment or facilities through a modification in operating procedures; this can allow a decrease in cost, prevent an increase in costs, or even provide an increase in service for the same expenditure. Several examples of this type of opportunity are found in the transportation area. Staggering school starting and dismissal times within the district can allow school buses to make multiple runs in both the morning and afternoon. With this procedure fewer buses and drivers are required and the process operates more cost efficiently. Other possibilities in transportation include using newly developed computer programs to determine the most efficient route schedules for buses and the use of diesel rather than gasoline buses to lower operation and maintenance costs.

Similar opportunities for improving the efficiency of other district operations may exist in instruction (for example, coordination of specialized courses, such as in the science curriculum), school administration (student scheduling for maximum utilization of scarce or expensive equipment and facilities), and district administration (reorganization of administrative and classified staff to reduce the total number of personnel while performing the same functions).

Early retirement for long-term staff.   If long-term staff members retire and are replaced by less senior personnel the district may recognize some significant cost savings. This is particularly true in the instructional area where teachers at the top of the salary schedule are paid approximately twice the amount of beginning teachers. The difference between the top level salaries and the beginning ones leaves significant money available to provide incentives for early retirement, yet still obtain overall cost savings in personnel.

Caution should be exercised in using this strategy, however. A wholesale turnover of senior staff would deplete the district of many of its most experienced and valuable teachers and other staff. Rebuilding both the credibility and competence of the district personnel could be a difficult and long-term process.

Lower salary increases. A potentially cost-effective expenditure reduction, but one that may be politically difficult to achieve, is that of lower salary increases. For example, a 2 percent overall increase in the district's teacher salary schedule instead of a 5 percent increase will save the district a significant amount. With no other changes, there will be the same number of instructional personnel next year and for the most part the same people in the classrooms. Except for some possible loss in morale, instructional services should not be greatly affected. All instructional personnel who have increased their educational level or are not at the maximum number of years on the salary schedule will receive additional step increases as they move through the schedule so their actual increases will be greater than the 2 percent schedule increase. The same tactic can be applied to other employees as well. In fact, if the major employee group (teachers) is to accept a lower increase, it may be necessary that other groups, such as administrators and classified employees, receive similar treatment.

Reduction of cash carryover amount. The cash carryover or unencumbered fund balance is the amount of money that the district has budgeted with which to end the fiscal year. This is money that the district will use to meet its obligations until revenues are received in the coming year. The cash carryover is a regular and ongoing item in the budget and provides a transition from one budget year to the next. The current year's cash carryover reduces the need for other revenues in the next or budget year, and next year's cash carryover amount reduces the need for other revenues the following year. If the cash carryover amounts are similar from year to year, there is little net impact on the budget. This year's cash carryover is treated as a revenue in the budget for the upcoming year and is largely offset by the projected ending cash carryover amount which is treated as an expenditure in the same budget.

However, a lesser amount budgeted for the ending cash carryover for next year is the equivalent to a one year expenditure reduction for the coming year. If the district can operate adequately with a lower cash carryover amount the net effect is a reduced total budget. Unless the district intends to maintain this lower amount permanently, this is a short-term strategy. The following year's expenditures will have to be increased beyond their normal level if the cash carryover amount is to be built up again.

BUDGET REDUCTIONS THROUGH PROGRAM REDUCTIONS

Another approach to decreasing the budget is to reduce the quantity or quality of programs and services offered by the school district. Budget reductions of this type result in a lower level of service. The lower cost corresponds to a reduction in district operations. These are the most painful budget cuts to make for they directly affect the operations of the district. However, they are sometimes necessary in order to keep the planned expenditures in line with the estimated revenues.

If it becomes necessary to employ program reductions, it is frequently helpful to illustrate their impact in programmatic terms. This makes the school board members (who are ordering the reductions) or the district patrons (who may be unwilling to vote for a higher budget levy) aware of the changes in program operations which will result from the lower budget. For example, descriptions such as an increase in average student/teacher ratio from 21:1 to 23.5:1; or 92 teachers laid off; or 450 high school students unable to take advanced science, mathematics, and foreign language courses put the results of a programmatic reduction into immediate educational and human terms. Programmatic measures convey the real meaning of the budget reductions much more thoroughly than do dollar amounts.

Reduction of instructional staff. The largest single expenditure in school districts is for instructional personnel. As a result, if significant budget reductions are required a reduction in instructional staff will have to be considered. Eliminating teaching positions will increase the student/teacher ratios in classrooms. Reducing the number of other direct instructional staff, such as remedial reading teachers, will restrict the services provided by these personnel and place additional burdens on the classroom teachers.

The least disruptive means of reducing staff is by attrition; that is, by not replacing staff members who leave their positions for retirement or other reasons. If additional reductions are needed, the district may need to lay off some teachers. Usually the district has established reduction-in-force policies for determining the order of layoff, primarily based on seniority. The remaining, more senior teachers may be required to change their existing teaching assignments to match those available in the district. The result can be a "bumping" process in which highly qualified teachers in some areas are replaced by marginally qualified, but more senior teachers. Personnel layoffs are a difficult and painful process.

Reduction of course offerings. One of the common impacts of staff reduction is a corresponding reduction in the number and variety of courses offered, particularly at the high school level. With fewer classroom teachers, decisions have to be made how to utilize those available positions.

Frequently, low enrollment courses are the first eliminated. These typically are the advanced and elective courses which attract relatively few students. While fewer students may be affected with this approach, those whose classes are eliminated lose needed instructional opportunities.

Another means of reducing the number of classes to match the available teaching staff is to reduce the number of sections offered of the required or core classes, such as math, English, social studies. The net effect is to increase the class size of the remaining sections. For example, a high school with 500 ninth graders, each of whom is required to take an English class, would require twenty sections of English, with an average class size of twenty-five students. If only seventeen sections were offered, the average class size would be over twenty-nine students and three teaching periods (or approximately a half-time position) would be eliminated.

Some of the teaching time freed up by larger class sizes in required courses can be used to offer other courses, such as electives, which otherwise would not be available. This tactic does not maximize the reduction in the number of teaching positions nor, consequently, the reduction in the budget. It represents a partial shift of budget resources and transfers the burden of reduced service quality (higher class sizes) to a larger number of students to provide additional instruction to a smaller group. This approach also gives administrators a potentially attractive proposal to some teachers. In return for slightly higher class sizes in required courses, they will also be assigned to teach a smaller, specialized class more to their interest.

Reduction of support staff. A common place for districts to look for reductions is among the support activities provided to students and instructional staff. A rationale for reductions in these areas is that they are not directly involved in instruction and that the student's educational programs will be less affected by cuts here. This may be true in the short run, but the long term effects of fewer guidance counselors, librarians, school psychologists, school social workers, school nurses, speech pathologists, audio-visual specialists, and computer-based instruction specialists will certainly affect the educational programs provided in the district. Fewer services will be available to students and those services that are provided may be oversubscribed by students. Further, if teachers are called on to do some of the activities previously carried out by support staff, teachers will have less time for instruction and students will be receiving services from persons not necessarily trained in those areas.

Reduction of administrative staff. Even more popular than the reasoning for decreasing support staff is the call to reduce administrators in the district. "Get rid of the administrative fat in the district budget" is a common demand. This stems from a widespread assumptions that administrators add very little to the educational process, that they probably hinder teachers in trying to work with their students, and as a result, that the district would generally be better off with fewer administrators. In most school districts these assumptions are not true. Administrators are necessary to direct the district's operations, to establish and monitor policies, and to obtain and distribute resources to carry out the educational programs of the district.

However, administration is not immune from budget cuts. If instructional programs are being cut, it may be appropriate from several perspectives to cut administrative expenditures as well. District priorities properly favor instructional activities and administrative expenditures are considered less crucial to the students' welfare. Politically, administrative budgets often need to show reductions at least as great as those in instruction to counter charges of administrators firing teachers in order to protect their own positions.

Like other areas, if administrative positions are reduced there will also be a reduction in the services provided. A district office with fewer people has less capacity. Some efficiencies may be recognized if there is an excess of staff, but some activities may have to be eliminated or reduced. At the school level, there are also possibilities for reducing of administrative staff, but with corresponding reductions in services. For example, vice principal positions can be reduced from three to two in high schools, secretarial positions can be cut back, one principal can be responsible for two smaller elementary schools. The schools will still function under these conditions, but the remaining personnel will need to extend their activities to include the essential elements of the eliminated positions; this may affect their ability to carry out all of their expanded responsibilities adequately.

Reduction of nonessential services. State requirements mandate that school districts provide certain educational and educationally related services in their operation. However, districts typically go beyond the basics to provide other services, which, although not legally mandated, are believed to be beneficial to the educational process. Examples of common, but not strictly required services could include home-to-school transportation, interscholastic athletics, and most extracurricular activities. A reduction or elimination of some of these activities will also reduce the expenditures for them and, in turn, reduce the district's budget.

An increase in the walking distance to school from one-half mile to one mile will decrease the number of students transported daily, require fewer school buses in operation, and reduce the district's transportation expenditures. Athletics and club activities are an important aspect of many districts' overall program, providing significant educational, social, and public relations value. They are, however, generally optional activities, not required by state statutes or regulations.

If the district is facing a severe fiscal crisis, first in line for funding are the mandated items. Nonmandated activities, no matter how important to the district, cannot take precedence over those legally required. Unfortunately, district patrons do not always understand the distinction, and district warnings about the possibility of cutting football and basketball programs are sometimes viewed as threats to force voters to approve district tax levies or budgets.

INCREASING REVENUES TO AVOID EXPENDITURE REDUCTIONS

Increasing revenues is an alternative which has the same impact on balancing the district budget as reducing expenditures. The additional revenues will support activities which otherwise would be eliminated in order to balance the budget. Assuming that the district is levying the maximum property tax available to it and that the amount of state aid the district is to receive is fixed, additional revenue amounts feasible for the district to raise are somewhat limited and mostly focused on local revenue sources. However, some additional revenue raising activities are not insignificant and can make it possible for desired district programs to be continued and improved.

Improved cash management.   The receipt of revenues by the district and the need for cash to pay its obligations are not usually simultaneous. State aid comes in regular intervals during the school year and property tax payments are generally received only during several periods. On the other hand, most district expenditures occur in a more steady monthly pattern. This nonmatching of revenues and expenditures creates times during the school year when the district has excess cash in its accounts and other times when it is short of money.

A cash management system is designed to smooth out these differences and to earn the district additional revenues at the same time. This is done by investing the excess cash in interest earning short-term investments and withdrawing it as needed to pay obligations when they are due.[7] An effective cash management system will always have cash available as needed, but it will also maximize the yield on the investments made by the district and lower the district's borrowing costs (if any). The interest amounts earned through improved cash management provide additional revenue to the district and can be used to maintain programs or activities which otherwise would be reduced.

Charges for services provided.   A school district may provide certain services to other districts or to other public or private agencies. Examples of such services could include regular education programs, special education programs, specialized classes, purchasing, computerized information management and data processing, printing, vehicle maintenance, and transportation. Typically, the providing district is already engaged in the activity for its own students and is able to include students or work activities from other districts or agencies in its own operation in an efficient manner through economies of scale. The charges for these services should be reviewed to see if they are appropriate or if some modification needs to be made. Charges that are too low mean that the providing district is subsidizing other agencies' operations, while charges that are too high may be inhibiting additional agencies from purchasing services from the district. At a minimum the charges should cover the direct costs of the providing district and more appropriately could include the indirect or overhead costs associated with the activity.

Charges for nonacademic activities.   Certain activities are not required in the academic program, but are optional for students. Even so, the activities require expenditures and students receive benefits from them. Primary among these are athletics, although there are a number of extracurricular activities which also fall into this category. One approach to raise money to meet some of the expenditures is to charge a participation fee for students, such as an athletic fee for playing a sport. While revenues from such fees will probably not cover the full cost of providing the activity, they do reduce the cost to the district. However, care must be taken that low income students are not prohibited from participating in fee activities; this can be done by utilizing a sliding scale fee structure or having a fee waiver policy based on family income.

Another revenue raising tactic, particularly in high schools where extracurricular activities are numerous, is to charge a fee to all students for a student body card. The revenues are used to finance extracurricular activities and the possession of a card admits students into school events. Again, provisions should be made for low income students to obtain reduced cost or free cards.

Donations from local businesses and organizations.   A frequently untapped resource for school districts is the local business community. Approached properly, individual businesses and organizations may be willing to contribute to the school district. Such contributions can be in a variety of forms: unrestricted money; funds for specific purposes or items; new or used equipment; supplies; and personnel. These donations can replace expenditures which otherwise might have been necessary and they can maintain and expand existing activities or initiate new ones. The donations are generally tax-deductible for the businesses and the publicity value can be used as a further argument in soliciting contributions.

Volunteers.   Patrons of the school district have many different talents and skills which they may be persuaded to provide the school district for use in its operations. Classroom and library aides are common examples of areas in which volunteers can provide useful assistance in the instructional area. Other examples include a piano accompanist for music teachers, craft demonstrations and instruction, story and poetry readings, special tutoring, and nurse's aide. Extracurricular activities can also benefit from volunteers to provide specific skill training, supervision, and additional labor as needed. Payoffs to the volunteers range from obtaining experience which can be used for later employment to a feeling of being useful. An active program which encourages, recognizes, and rewards volunteers can pay significant benefits in the form of additional resources and lower costs to the school district.

BUDGET REDUCTION PROCESS

Budget reductions do not happen automatically; decisions, often difficult ones, must be made among alternative types of reductions and the programs affected. The process of managing budget reductions is an important one—both for the ultimate impact on the educational program in the district and for obtaining staff and community support for the necessary cuts. The questions of what type of process to utilize to obtain budget reductions and how to implement the process are crucial ones for school administrators facing this task.

The overall process for deciding on budget reductions can range from a directive issued by the school board or district superintendent to district staff involvement to community participation. The procedures used will depend on several factors. The magnitude of the cuts required is a key issue. Minor reductions which will not impact programs significantly do not call for elaborate, high involvement processes. With nothing else to the contrary, small reductions may be handled most efficiently by the district administration with input from school building and central office administrators. On the other hand, if the reductions are significant and will require elimination or large scale reductions in district programs, then it is logical to consider involving the community in reaching the decisions.

The budget development process will also influence the budget reduction process. If budget requests have been prioritized, then reductions can be based on eliminating the lowest priority items in the original budget. Further, if the community, through budget committees and hearings, has an expectation for participating in budgetary decisions, it is both useful and politically wise to include community representation in the budget reduction process as well.

The history and tradition of the district are also important in establishing a budget reduction process. If the need to make reductions is a regular occurrence, district staff and the community will have experience in the process and expectations about how to proceed. A district facing nontrivial reductions for the first time may find it necessary to communicate the magnitude and seriousness of the reductions to both staff and community as a first step in initiating the budget reduction process.

Reductions tend to bring out fears in those potentially affected. This can lead to protective behavior for individual programs and conflicts among various factions in the district and community. Old animosities can surface and contaminate an already difficult process. While the past cannot be changed, a focus during budget reduction on a rational and equitable basis and process for deciding budget cuts can help to minimize frictions.

The stage in the overall budget process when the reductions have to be made will also affect the design of the budget reduction process. If the need for cuts becomes known before the budget has been completed, then the budget development procedures will be used to reduce the proposed expenditures to achieve a balanced budget. This, in effect, becomes another iteration in the budget development process. However, if it becomes necessary to reduce the budget during the operating year (for example, if projected revenues do not materialize or certain expenditures are higher than expected and the budget becomes out of balance), then there may not be time to implement a full fledged participatory process. In this case, reduction decisions tend to be made administratively with input from district staff and approved by the school board.

Criteria for Budget Reduction Process

In order to avoid many of the difficulties common to budget reduction efforts, it is helpful to establish principles or criteria which will guide the process when conflict arises over either the procedures for deciding on reductions or the specific reductions themselves. This gives administrators a basis for resolving disagreements and for keeping the process on track. One such set of criteria, which was developed by a large school district facing significant budget cuts, is shown below. As is clear from the criteria, this district chose a process which involved administrators, district staff, and widespread citizen participation.

1. Budget reductions should be based on principles that make clear the basis for all final decisions by the board of education.
2. Multiple opportunities should be provided for citizens to express themselves regarding budget priorities at the local school level as well as at the district level.
3. Budget reductions that have districtwide effects should be recommended at the superintendent's level.

4. Principals and department heads should recommend specific budget reductions in programs and services within their respective operations, tempered by districtwide considerations.

5. Ultimately, a full range of options for budget reductions should be administratively determined using citizen input tempered by professional judgments.

6. The board of education should have available multiple options and related impact statements in making final decisions regarding specific budget reductions.[8]

Limitations on the Budget Reduction Process

Even with a well-developed rationale for the process and a firm administrative resolve to conduct the reduction process in an equitable and participatory manner, there are significant limitations on the type of process and extent of participation. District contracts with employee groups may direct the procedures for any personnel reduction-in-force or layoffs which are selected. Further, individual personnel decisions are almost always made administratively; most administrators feel that it is inappropriate (and in some cases, may not be legally permissible under collective bargaining contracts) to share personnel decisions with colleagues of those affected.[9]

The timing for making the the reduction decisions may also restrict outside participation. Decisions which have to be made quickly limit district administrators' ability to involve others, while decisions with long lead times allow more opportunity for others to participate. For example, the district may receive new information in early August from the state department of education announcing the reduction in the estimate of state aid provided to the district. The new and reduced revenue estimate unbalances the budget. Further, in this case, it arrives when most teachers are not on duty and many patrons are out of town. In order to rebalance the budget before school begins, district administrators together with school principals may unilaterally decide (with school board approval) to reduce supply and material allocations below those previously approved. Situations with longer timelines may involve a different process and include district staff, parents, students, and community members in the decision.

A final limitation is that of the logistics of information. The more people involved, the more difficult it is to see that all have and understand the necessary financial and programmatic data to make the cuts in a knowledgeable fashion. This limitation interacts with the timing constraints, if any, so that a process involving large numbers of people analyzing significant budget reductions will require a lengthy and well-planned time period to complete successfully. On the other hand, the budget reduction process can be carried out relatively quickly if only a few people are involved.

SUMMARY

Whenever expenditures exceed revenues, a school district is required to take some corrective action. This can be in the form of raising additional revenues, but the most common action is to reduce expenditures. There are two primary types of budget reductions: those which result from greater efficiencies in district operation; and those which require program reductions. Efficiency oriented reductions are generally the first choice of administrators for they leave the district's programs and services intact. However, if the required reductions are large, it may become necessary to implement program reductions to bring expenditures back into line with revenues.

Reduction can be required during the development process when the next year's budget is assembled or during the school year when the actual operating results are significantly different from those projected. Whenever budget reduction is necessary, school administrators need to put into place an appropriate process to arrive at the needed decisions on the amounts of the cuts and where they will be made. The process may be a full-blown citizen participation effort if the required reductions are significant and there is time to implement the process. If time is short and the cuts are not too great or potentially disruptive, then the process may be less participatory involving mostly administrators and the board of education with district staff input.

However once the process is implemented, administrators must have a clear understanding of what they want to accomplish in terms of budget reductions and how they intend to create and manage the decision process. Good advice is provided by two administrators who directed a major budget reduction process in a large urban school district.

> Clear, concise information that distinguishes among *instruction, support,* and *management* functions, together with accompanying "impact statements" that give precise information about lost services, staff reductions, and other variables, become invaluable *administrative* and *board* tools in the decision-making process. The additional contributions of citizen budget committees provide a critical perspective by which the administration and board of education can test their perceptions of what is of ultimate importance to the welfare of children.[10]

PROBLEMS

1. Budget Reduction in Dunn School District

    Shortly after Dr. Kirk had completed her budget for the special education programs in Dunn School District, the tax levy for the district was defeated by a substantial margin. (Refer to Chapter four, Problem 4—Special Education in

Dunn School District—for budget data for this problem.) The following week in a memorandum to all principals and department heads, the superintendent announced that substantial reductions must be made in the district's budget before resubmitting the tax levy to the voters at the next election date in two months. The memorandum provided specific targets for each budget area. By prorating the total dollar reduction target for the general fund among the district's various programs, the maximum allowable budget for the three special education programs in Dunn School District was set at $1,080,000.

Prepare a revised budget for the special education programs in Dunn School District to stay within this reduced budget target. Use a standard budget format with account codes and titles as well as amounts. Include your calculations as a separate worksheet attachment. For presentation purposes, show the account number, account title, original budget amount, the revised amount, and a brief comment on the cause of each reduction. Use the format below as a guide.

Account Code	Account Title	Original Budget	Revised Budget	Comment
XXX	Name	$ XX,XXX	$ YY,YYY	Reason for reduction

Dr. Kirk was unsure where to begin reducing the special education budget. She knew that the district had contacted the teachers' association and they stated that they were unwilling to renegotiate the salary increase or benefit provisions of the new contract. Further, shortly after the superintendent's memorandum, she received a call from POPHS (Parents of Physically Handicapped Students) expressing concern that special education programs and students might be forced to bear the brunt of any cost reductions. The president of POPHS reminded her that both federal and state laws required the district to provide an appropriate education to handicapped students and that the programs established for the physically handicapped students, including physical therapy and transportation, had been written into each child's educational plan by the district as necessary.

NOTES

1. Short term borrowing may be permitted to ease a cash flow problem during the operating year, but later revenues from that year should be available to repay the borrowed amount.

2. Cutback management is defined as "managing organizational change toward lower levels of resource consumption and organizational activity," by Charles Levine, "More on Cutback Management: Hard Questions for Hard Times," in *Managing Fiscal Stress: The Crisis in the Public Sector*, Charles Levine, ed. (Chatham, NJ: Chatham House, 1980).

3. William Hartman and Jon Rivenburg, "Budget Allocation Patterns: School District Choices for Available Resources," *Journal of Education Finance*, 11 (Fall, 1985), 219-235.

4. For a discussion of net present value concepts and techniques see Edith Stokey and Richard Zeckhauser, *A Primer for Policy Analysis* (New York: Norton, 1978), Chapter 10.

5. Oregon Department of Education, *Managing Costs Creatively* (Salem, OR: Oregon Department of Education, 1982) provides an excellent compilation of cost-saving measures of all types. Many of the examples in this section and the two succeeding ones are derived from this source.

6. Thomas Glass, "Developing a Risk Management Program," *School Business Affairs*, 50 (June 1984).

7. Frederick Dembowski, *A Handbook for School District Financial Management* (Parkwood, IL: Research Corporation of the Association of School Business Officials, 1982) provides a description of the concepts, terminology, and practices of school district cash management.

8. Victor Doherty and James Fenwick, "Can Budget Reduction Be Rational?" *Educational Leadership* (January 1982), pp. 253-257.

9. William Hartman, "Resource Allocation in High Schools" (Eugene, OR: Center for Educational Policy and Management, University of Oregon, 1985).

10. Doherty and Fenwick, "Can Budget Reduction Be Rational?" p. 257.

7

BUDGET ELECTIONS

INTRODUCTION

The subject of this chapter is the budget election process and strategies for gaining support and approval of the electorate at a budget election. In a sense, a fiscal election to approve the budget or a tax levy is the ultimate political event for a school district. To be successful in the election requires a clear understanding of the district's economic and social situation, careful planning of the election, a well designed and executed campaign strategy, and a commitment to communicating the district's educational needs to the public. While educational administrators in states without the requirements or necessity for local fiscal elections need not concern themselves with this topic, for others it can be the crucial factor in being able to provide and operate adequate educational programs in the district.

Budgeting is inherently a political process. Almost anything having to do with raising, distributing, and spending public funds involves public review and approval, and education is no exception. This is especially true when the district is required to hold a fiscal election. At this point the budget process becomes overtly political and requires conducting a successful political campaign. Even though a fiscal election is time consuming, educators should not view it as improper or inappropriate; rather it is an opportunity to increase the public's awareness and appreciation of the importance of schools to the community. More importantly, administrators must

understand the activities they need to undertake in order to work successfully within the political environment.

The bulk of local funds for education comes from the local property
tax, a tax on real property located within school districts. To raise these
funds school districts levy a tax on the taxable property within their boundaries. There is substantial variation in the flexibility or authority available
to the local districts to set their individual levels of taxation. In some states
each local school board has the authority to establish the level of local taxation for its own district. Other states have established limits on the amount
of revenue which a district can raise or spend. Frequently, this has been in
reaction to court suits challenging the constitutionality of the school finance
system in the state. Property tax limitation measures,[1] such as Proposition
13 in California or Proposition 2½ in Massachusetts, also have established
ceilings on permissible tax rates. As a result, in states where laws limit local
taxes or tax rates and the district is planning to levy the maximum amount
allowable, the decisions involved in establishing the level of property taxes
may be largely circumscribed.

To levy and collect property taxes, school districts require some type
of formal public approval. Without this approval, school districts do not
have the legitimacy or authority to collect and spend these public monies.
State laws and regulations vary widely on the type of public approval which
is required and the procedures for obtaining it. In some states the only requirement is that the school board approve the budget and set the tax rate
or amount of local tax dollars to be raised. With school board approval, no
further authorization is needed for the district to levy the necessary taxes
and spend them as specified in their budget document. In these cases it is
assumed that the board represents the wishes of the majority of the district
voters and if not, new board members will be elected. This approach is
based on a representative democracy model and, at the local level, parallels
the state and national legislatures.

In other states, noneducational public bodies, such as city councils,
may have the authority to approve or disapprove the district's budget. In
these cases, educational issues may not be the primary concerns; instead
social, economic, or political issues could dominate. There is also the dan-
ger that the priorities and values of the other public agency board members
will differ from those of the school board which has primary responsibility
for overseeing education in the district.

In many states, however, the final approval of a school district's budget or property tax level is in the hands of the district patrons. These states
require a district fiscal election which allows all qualified voters in the
school district to vote on the budget. State statutes differ on the form of the
election: some require voter approval of the district budget itself; others
require approval of the amount to be raised from local property taxes to
support the budget; while others mandate approval of a tax rate to be ap-

plied to all taxable property in the district. Whichever form the elections take, the voters have the last word on the amount of local funding for their district. Because of the relatively small geographic size of most school districts and the manageable election logistics at the local level, it is possible for citizens to vote directly on fiscal issues (and often by implication educational program issues as well) rather indirectly than through elected representatives. It is one of the few times in which citizens have the opportunity to vote directly on measures which affect their pocketbook.[2] This fact alone can make school district fiscal elections difficult to win, particularly in uncertain economic times.

States which do have budget elections differ considerably on the permitted number of annual elections to pass a budget measure and on the consequences if the measure fails. In some instances, a district may have only one or two opportunities to pass a fiscal election. On the other end of the scale, Oregon districts have six possible election dates each year with the possibility for additional special elections if approved by the State Superintendent of Public Instruction. What happens if the district loses the election again varies from state to state. At one extreme, state statutes may permit the fiscal authority (for example, city council) of a financially dependent district to override a vote of the public and approve the district's budget even if the voters have turned it down. At the other extreme, in several states school districts have closed down their schools completely for weeks or longer because failed budget levies left them without sufficient funds to meet operating expenses (such as personnel salaries, supplier invoices) beyond that date.[3]

POLITICAL CONSIDERATIONS FOR BUDGETING

The budget represents many things to the school district. It helps establish district priorities, develops the educational plan for the upcoming year, projects the available funds to support the district's operations, allocates resources in accordance with priorities and educational objectives, controls expenditures during the year, and provides a target for evaluation of performance in the fiscal area.

The budget is also is a political document. As such, it is an attempt to reach an acceptable balance between educational goals and the fiscal reality facing the school district. However, there are usually many different views and priorities among the patrons of the school district, often in direct conflict with one another. For example, some patrons may be strongly in favor of increasing expenditures to improve the breadth and quality of the programs provided by the district, while others may be just as outspoken on the need to reduce expenditures in order to lower property taxes. Nevertheless, there is a strong underlying belief in society that education is an essential service. Public opinion polls consistently show that education ranks closely behind police and fire protection and ahead of health and hospitals, parks and recreation, sanitation, and social services as a government service which should be maintained or increased.[4]

Critics of education criticize not education itself; they call for even more of it with the "back to basics" demands. What they object to are higher than necessary property taxes to support the unnecessary "frills" of elective courses, poorly prepared students and declining test scores, the perceived lack of discipline in schools, and the proverbial "administrative fat" which can always be cut out of any budget. On the other hand, supporters of education call for higher teacher salaries to attract higher quality people into public school teaching, introduction of new technology into schools, and stronger mathematics and sciences curricula to prepare students to compete successfully with others in work and in the world.

The final budget represents a series of compromises among various segments of the community and within the school district organization as well. It requires negotiations and tradeoffs among various groups concerned with education—all of whom believe strongly in their programs and positions. Analyses and research evidence can be utilized during the process, but they are frequently used to make partisan points.

For districts requiring a budget election to fund their operations, two points should be kept in mind. First, the activities during the budget development process should be aimed at developing a consensus within the community about the programs to be funded and the funding amounts. Persons or groups alienated during the preparation of the budget may become nonsupporters or even active opponents at election time. Second, the final budget should be acceptable to a majority of voters in the school district.[5] It is probably not possible to please everyone, but there should be something in the budget to appeal to more than half of the expected voters in order to win the election. The traditional wisdom was that smaller voter turnouts resulted in higher percentage of Yes voters and a greater probability of winning the financial election.[6] However, more recent analyses have shown that this relationship is no longer consistent and that "the strategy adopted by most school districts . . . to maintain a low profile, avoid conflict, and hope for a normal—or smaller than normal—turnout" is now unreliable.[7]

BUDGET ELECTION PROCESS

The fiscal election held by a school district is the culmination of the budget approval process. Figure 7.1 illustrates the general election process.

Budget Development

During the budget development phase, the proposed budget is assembled by the school district personnel. The decisions concerning the overall level

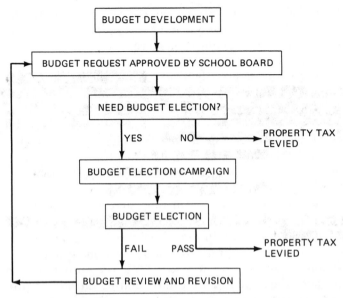

PROCESS CONTINUES UNTIL ELECTION PASSES OR BUDGET REQUEST IS LOWERED TO A POINT WHERE ELECTION IS NOT NEEDED.

FIGURE 7.1 School District Budget Election Process

of the budget request and particular program emphases are guided by school board directives and instructions. Further, a great deal of information, suggestions, and advocacy is provided by numerous other individuals and groups interested in shaping the final budget toward their programs or values. Such actions come both from inside the school district organization (for example, high school science teachers requesting new laboratory equipment, middle school principals seeking a greater share of the money allocated for supplies and equipment in the district, business manager asking for several new microcomputers to improve the efficiency of the fiscal office) and from groups in the community (such as parents of a particular elementary school insisting on new playground equipment, business groups suggesting greater emphasis on vocational skills for graduating students, an advocacy organization for the handicapped demanding improved access to school buildings and classrooms). Additionally, the employee associations or bargaining units in the district have a great deal of influence on the outcome of the budget request; settlements with teachers, classified staff, and administrators constrain the ability of the district to fund other types of expenditures.

School Board Approval

Once the budget has been developed, it is submitted to the school board for its approval. School board members, as either elected or appointed representatives of the public, must evaluate the budget request prepared by the school district. During the board's deliberation, they may allow public testimony on the budget at regular or special board meetings. Special interest groups again have an opportunity to make their case for funding their particular programs or activities, but this time in front of the school board members rather than district personnel. In addition to educational advocates, the board may also hear the views of groups and individuals concerned with the high cost of education and its impact on their property taxes; it is likely that these groups would advocate cutting the budget to reduce taxes.

If the board feels that the budget as presented is appropriate they may approve it without much question or controversy. Otherwise, they may ask for additional information or justification and may require some reductions in the proposed budget before giving it their approval. Occasionally, they may request increases in certain budget areas to initiate or augment popular programs. Once the school board is satisfied with the budget request they approve it with appropriate modifications.

Necessity for Election

The next step is to determine whether or not a budget election is required. As Table 7.1 illustrates, if the school district will have sufficient revenues from state, federal, and other locally raised funds (including property taxes which can be levied without an election), then it will not be necessary to hold a fiscal election. Otherwise, the district will need to have a fiscal election to obtain voter approval to levy additional property taxes to balance its budget.

An alternative to an election would be reducing the budget request (expenditures) to the level covered by available revenues. Some districts and their boards may choose this option if the amount of additional revenue requested is small and the budget cuts relatively minor. Other districts may not have this option if they are dependent on annual elections to approve property tax revenues which comprise a substantial portion of their total revenues. For example, some districts in Oregon have over half of

TABLE 7.1 Amount of Budget Election

Total District Budget		$20,000,000
Less:	State Aid	$11,000,000
	Federal Funds	$1,000,000
	Local Funds	
	Nonproperty Tax Revenues	$500,000
	Property Tax Revenues Not Requiring Voter Approval	$3,500,000
Equals:	Tax Levy Amount for Budget Election	$4,000,000

their budget dependent upon an annual tax levy election; a budget reduction of more than 50 percent would be required to avoid a tax levy election, an impossible situation if any semblance of adequate educational programs are to be maintained.

In reality, the district administrators and school board will have determined the necessity of a budget election prior to board approval. In addition to the size of the overall district budget and the programs which it represents, the amount of the election, if needed, will have been one of the key considerations of the board. What is believed to be a reasonable amount will vary from district to district and from year to year. The school board is a political body and the members generally attempt to represent the views of the majority of their supporters. The past history of the district's support of education, its voting record on budget elections, and the economic situation of the district and its patrons all contribute to the board's decision on approving the budget at a given level and the necessity of holding a budget election.

Election Campaign

If an election is to be held, the school district will need to conduct a campaign to convince the voters to support the tax levy request. This campaign is a political effort aimed at winning the election and consists of a series of activities aimed at obtaining passage of the budget election. However, the district is constrained in what activities it can undertake during the campaign. School districts are public, tax-supported institutions and their employees are paid from public funds; consequently, it is generally inappropriate (and in most states it is illegal) to use district funds or district employees during working hours in the budget election campaign. Nevertheless, it is generally proper for the district to furnish the public with factual information concerning the tax levy to be voted on and for district employees to work in the campaign on their own time.

In spite of these limitations, there are a variety of effective campaign strategies which are available to school districts. The particular campaign strategy chosen will vary with the school district's situation. Even within a district, circumstances can vary widely from election to election even during the same year; it is important to choose an appropriate combination of activities for specific district situations and characteristics of the likely voters.

Budget Election

The culmination of the election campaign is the election itself. If the district is successful in obtaining a majority of "Yes" votes, then the district has secured public approval to levy the needed property taxes to support its operations during the upcoming year. However, if the budget election fails, the district does not have the authority to levy the needed taxes and must begin again with the approval process.

Budget Review and Revision

What happens following a budget election defeat depends on the governing statutes of the state and the decisions of the school board. In some instances, state law specifies a particular process (for example, revert to last year's budget, tax levy, or tax rate; a mandatory percentage reduction in the levy request). In others, the local school board has discretion on what to do. This can include resubmitting the identical budget levy to the voters for another election attempt, reducing the budget levy and resubmitting a lower amount to an election, or accepting the voters' decision and operating the district within the available funds. This latter choice is only feasible when the district has sufficient funds to provide at least a minimally acceptable educational program for the school year.

To reach an appropriate decision, the district administrators and the school board members need to review the district's budget, educational programs, and the election results. A narrow defeat could indicate that passage of the election would be possible in another election if a more effective campaign were conducted. On the other hand, a large margin of defeat could readily be interpreted as a clear message from the voters that the budget and levy amount must be reduced before they will support them. If the election amount is to be reduced, then, unless additional revenues are found from state or federal sources, the total budget must be reduced and programs cut. If budget cuts are necessary, the usual procedure is for the district administrators (with input from district personnel, bargaining unit representatives, parents, and community members) to propose programs or parts of programs to be reduced, and to develop a revised budget to present to the school board for their approval. (See Chapter Six for a discussion of budget reductions.) The school board members must then review the revised budget and the proposed cuts, make any modifications that they think are appropriate, and approve the revised budget. From here the process reiterates until either a budget election passes or sufficient budget reductions are made so that an election is not necessary.

CAMPAIGN STRATEGY[8]

The primary responsibility for directing a budget election campaign and the related efforts and activities is with the district office. If the district is large enough to support an office and staff for public relations (also called community relations or public information), then most likely the management of the budget election campaign will be one of their responsibilities. In smaller districts the superintendent must either take on these responsibilities personally or delegate them to other staff members. In any event, management of the campaign is a district office responsibility even though many other persons may be involved in various campaign activities.

Year Round Effort

The first point most experienced school administrators will make about budget elections is that they are a year round effort, not just the few weeks or months before an election date. For maximum effectiveness at budget election time, the public should be involved with the school during the whole year. Another way of saying this is to give ownership of the schools to the public; the feeling of proprietorship leads to support and even active participation when budget elections are held.

This is an increasingly important task. "The number of people with a direct stake in education (e.g., parents) . . . is declining."[9] Conversely, the number of people who may perceive no immediate personal benefits from the taxes they pay to support schools is increasing and that group represents a majority in most communities. In addition to communicating the district's messages to its publics, the district should actively solicit the views of individuals and groups in the community. Such procedures should not be just a gimmick, but represent a genuine interest in what the public is thinking about the schools and a responsiveness to their concerns.

One important way of involving the community in school fiscal affairs is to include a variety of outside participants in the budget development process. This can be done at the school level with advisory councils or area meetings of parents and local residents, and at the district level with budget committees having representatives from major interest groups—parents, senior citizens, business community.

Another useful approach for both building community support and obtaining useful ideas is the creation of citizen task forces; these task forces are created to study particular problems facing the district and to recommend solutions. Financial topics for task force consideration could include achieving financial stability for the district, long-term facilities and equipment needs of the district, and school closures. At the conclusion of the task force's existence, some members may be willing to serve as spokespersons for the district to promote acceptance of their recommendations. For budget elections, this can mean public endorsements and even speaking engagements by task force members.

Before establishing citizen task forces, the district must be willing to put into practice at least some of the feasible recommendations which may result. Creating a committee to study a problem as a means of stalling for time in the hope that the problem will go away is very shortsighted and breeds lack of trust in the community.

Research and Analysis

To begin the actual activities associated with a budget election, one of the first steps is to collect and analyze information which can guide the remainder of the campaign. These research activities can give the district administrators vital information in planning and implementing an appropriate strategy. The results provide the means of understanding the attitudes and feelings of the community; they also can indicate the important messages which the district needs to communicate to the community in order to pass the election, and the means of delivering these messages.

Election data. Useful data for election campaigns can come in many forms. Some are readily available statistics from the county elections office (or other agency) which conducts the budget elections. Breakdowns of the percentage "Yes" and "No" votes by precinct over the past several elections can provide an indication of voting patterns in the district. A further grouping of the precincts by school attendance area within the district can also provide useful insights to interpret voting patterns as well as establishing a baseline to measure the results of school based campaign activities. For example, a controversy concerning a particular school—parental dissatisfaction with teachers or administrators—could result in a larger than usual "No" vote in the precincts surrounding the school.

The number of registered voters and the level of voter turnout by precinct (percentage of eligible voters who voted) is also information which the elections office should maintain. Voter turnout tends to vary by type of election. General elections, involving statewide and national elections, tend to have higher voter turnouts than those involving the district budget election alone or with other local elections. The general elections draw a wider variety of people with varying interests, while local elections tend to attract those particularly interested in the local issues on the ballot. This implies using a specific strategy to reach the particular mix of voters who are likely to participate in the type of election of which the budget will be a part.

It is important to identify the precincts with the highest possible payoff to the district in terms of winning the election. First, large precincts have more votes than do smaller ones. Second, the number of voters who cast ballots in a precinct is even more important than the number of registered voters. Third, the percentage yes votes combined with the turnout are the critical measures of the precinct's importance in winning the election. It is better to get a 60 percent yes vote in a precinct with a turnout of 1,000 voters (600 yes − 400 no = 200 yes vote margin) than to get a 100 percent yes vote in a precinct that turned out only 100 voters. Fourth, efforts should be concentrated on the activities most likely to maintain and increase the number of yes votes. It may be a waste of time, energy, and money to concentrate too many of the campaign resources on voters who already are going to vote yes or who will never vote yes. While the believed-to-be committed yes voters should not be ignored, it will generally be more fruitful to direct significant resources toward the uncommitted voter, the changeable no voter, and the nonvoter who is a likely yes voter.

Demographic data.   Data concerning the characteristics of the district's residents can also provide helpful information for the election campaign. Demographic data concerning the age, education levels, income levels, number of children of school age, family size, housing, and other characteristics can be compiled from census data and broken down by individual school boundaries or precincts. With the voting information, these data can be organized to develop profiles of district and precinct voters which can aid in selecting an overall campaign strategy and specific election activities.[10]

Economic data.   The economic conditions of the area must also be assessed. Frequently, the available economic data, such as employment or unemployment figures, personal income, and business starts and failures are reported for areas much larger than a single school district. However, a picture of the economic conditions facing the district can be assembled from a variety of local and regional or state indicators which may be available. These include newspaper reports of business activity (new starts, expansions, bankruptcies, closings), real estate information (new housing building permits, house sales, housing and apartment vacancies), county or region unemployment statistics. The economic condition of the district will have a significant influence on the choice of campaign strategies for the budget election. The chances of voters approving a budget election which will raise property taxes are much less in difficult economic times. Consequently, the message which the district needs to communicate to the voters in order to convince them of the necessity of passing the election may differ from robust economic times to poor ones.

Community surveys.   Another common approach to gathering information on community attitudes and concerns about the school district and its fiscal situation is by survey. Remember that this type of information costs money (in the form of staff time or an outside consultant) and it must be worth the price. Prior to conducting or commissioning a survey the school district must know why the information is wanted and how it will be used to improve the chances of winning the budget election.

There are many different types of surveys which school districts can use in their communities. Mail questionnaires are the least costly and can be sent to the greatest number of people. However, they are limited in the types of questions which can be asked and in the interpretation of the answers; further, a poor response rate may weaken the validity of the results. Telephone surveys are also limited in the number and type of questions which they can adequately ask, but they can be relatively inexpensive and include a large number of persons on the survey. Personal interviews can be the most intense survey method, but they are also the most time consuming and expensive, which limits the number of persons who can be surveyed. In selecting a survey method the district must balance the content of the survey questions, the number of people desired in the sample, the detail of the answers required or desired, the time available for the survey, the personnel available to conduct the survey, and the cost of the survey.

In preparing for a budget election, districts will often try to assess the voters' opinions on issues believed to be important. Examples include: their understanding of the financial situation facing the district; whether they believe that the district actually needs the money; whether they would support a tax levy and the amount of the levy; if their support is tied to using the money to accomplish certain things in the district (and what those things might be); whether the fiscal management and spending patterns of the district is seen as prudent and appropriate or excessive and wasteful; and their perceptions of the most critical problems facing the schools in the district.

The answers to these questions can be extremely helpful in developing a campaign strategy and message to communicate to the voters. If the survey also contains a section for personal information about the respondent (such as, age range, income range, type of employment, children in school, general location in district or perhaps zip code), it may be possible to develop profiles of various types of voters which will help target campaign efforts effectively.

Planning the Campaign

A successful election campaign requires careful planning of all of the activities involved and coordination of the many individuals and groups working in the campaign. Planning begins months before the actual election and is necessary to identify what specific activities are to be undertaken, to mobilize the necessary resources (people and money), and to direct the campaign.

Campaign leadership. Election campaigns need an individual or small group of individuals who serve as the core leadership body to decide upon strategy, raise and allocate resources, and direct the activities of others involved in the campaign. The primary responsibility for these tasks lies with one or more school district administrator assigned to manage activities associated with the budget election. However, state laws frequently prohibit school employees from working for the passage of budget elections or use of district resources in an advocacy role. Providing unbiased information about the budget election is generally permissible, but it must be done in a manner which neither supports or urges passage of the tax levy. Consequently, any advocacy work must be done either by school district employees after work hours or on their own time (vacation days, lunch hours) or by private citizens not employed by the school district.

Yes Committee.   To assist in the campaign and to work actively for the passage of the budget election, a "Vote Yes for Schools" committee (or some similarly named group) may be formed. Although the Yes committee is a private, nonprofit group organized to support the budget election, it certainly will have the encouragement of the school district. Typically, officers and members are well-known citizens in the community whose public endorsements will lend validity and prestige to the election campaign. Such a committee is a valuable tool to counter organized opposition to the budget election, to develop public support of education, and to refute any controversy over the size of the budget or tax levy proposed by the district.

The Yes committee serves as a partner to the school district in the election campaign doing things that the district is prohibited from doing—encouraging the public to vote for the budget election. If school district employees are members, they must not participate in any Yes committee activities during working hours because the committee is an advocacy organization established to campaign actively for passage of the budget election.

Election date.   One of the first steps in planning a budget election is to establish an election date. In some states the date is fixed and the district has no choice. In other states, there may be several election dates which are allowable and the district needs to select from the available alternatives.

Two major considerations are important in the selection of an election date. First is what type of election it will be. A date that coincides with a scheduled general election in the state will mean that the budget election will be on the ballot with a number of other races and issues. It is also likely that in the general election the voter turnout will be higher and the mix of voters will be somewhat more varied than those who would vote in a limited election involving only the district's budget measure.

The second consideration is: What happens if the budget fails in the election? Is there an opportunity for an additional election or elections? When could they be scheduled? Districts in states which permit multiple elections must have a contingency plan for their timing. Oregon, for example, permits a district to hold up to six tax levy elections per year; a district which fails to pass its levy in March (often too early in the budget process to know what the levy amount on the ballot must be) or May (a preferred date in the budget cycle for many districts) still has opportunities to submit another levy in elections in August (vacations, low voter turnouts), September, October, and November. The last three dates are all after school starts which means that the district would have to begin operation without an approved budget or tax levy to support expenditures for the entire year.

Timeline for election activities.   A useful device for planning and organizing all of the budget election activities is a timeline or schedule of all important events. Similar to the budget calendar, the timeline lists in chronological order all of the activities which need to be accomplished during the budget election campaign. An election campaign is generally a frantic undertaking and it becomes increasingly chaotic as the election date approaches. A well thought-out timeline can aid in keeping track of critical activities in the heat of the campaign. An example of a combined school district and Yes committee timeline for a mid-May budget election is shown in Table 7.2.

Target audiences.   Another important step in the planning phase is to specify the various audiences on which the school district will focus its campaign efforts. There are many groups of potential voters in the district and they often have different concerns about the district's educational pro-

TABLE 7.2 Timeline for Budget Election

ACTIVITIES OF SCHOOL DISTRICT PERSONNEL	DATE	ACTIVITIES OF YES COMMITTEE
	January 9	Hold organizational meeting for Yes committee.
	23	Contact community leaders to join & support.
		Contact employee & student groups for support.
	26	Plan budget & funding sources.
	28	Locate office space and furniture.
Set election date. (May 15)	February 7	Contact ad agency to develop campaign.
Launch voter registration drive at schools.	23	Outline major tasks and timeline.
		Contact parent advisory committee at each school.
		Begin work on brochure design & content.
	March 5	Identify key workers for each region.

TABLE 7.2 *(Continued)*

ACTIVITIES OF SCHOOL DISTRICT PERSONNEL	DATE	ACTIVITIES OF YES COMMITTEE
Arrange interviews on TV & radio.	8	
Locate speakers.		
Complete administrators' budget election handbook.	12	
Complete speakers' materials.		
Presentation to district administrators.	13	
Letter to district employees describing election.		
Complete media materials.	15	Firm up dates for speakers at parents' meetings.
Hold media briefings and provide material.	19	Solicit contributions from individuals, business community, district employees.
Board determines levy amount.	April 4	
Follow-up meeting with district administrators.	12	
Complete voter analysis.	15	
Establish "hotline" for budget or election information.	16	Draft of brochure completed.
Op-ed article by school board member in newspaper.		
Send voting reminder material to schools.	23	Print brochure.
Mail informational material to public.	May 7	
Send fact sheets to parents from schools.		
Promote school activities and open houses.	13	Distribute advocacy material.
		Canvas neighborhoods with regional workers.
		Run newspaper ad supporting budget election.
ELECTION DAY	May 15	ELECTION DAY

gram. Besides trying to reach the general public with the overall message of the need for support of the budget election, it is often effective to target selected messages for each important group in the district.

For each target audience selected, the district must identify the message to be emphasized. Examples of groups which may rate special attention and the possible message to communicate are shown below.

District teachers—emphasis on teaching positions and educational programs which would be maintained or restored if the budget is approved.

Classified employees—emphasis on jobs which would be maintained or restored and job security with passage of budget.

Parents with children in school—emphasis on classroom size and program restoration which would be possible with approved budget election.

Patrons with no school-age children, such as senior citizens, college students, young married couples—emphasis on benefits to the community of a quality educational system.

Business community/chamber of commerce—emphasis on sound business practices of the school district, recent money saving efficiencies in the district, and the role of good schools in economic development.

Communication Techniques

Once the planning phase is complete, work begins on implementing the strategy. This effort consists of communicating specified messages concerning the budget election to the general public and target audiences. Some of the more important communication techniques are discussed below.

District office tasks.   The tasks which the district office must accomplish fall into six categories: overall development of strategy and planning for the campaign; preparation of materials which will be used in the campaign; orchestration of centralized campaign activities; working with the news media; coordination and monitoring of campaign activities by other district personnel; and evaluation of the campaign results for use in the next budget election.

Voter registration.   An early and ongoing step in increasing the number of likely "Yes" voters is to conduct voter registration drives among groups believed to support education. This effort is promoted and encouraged by the district office, but most of the actual registration can be done at the school level.

The most obvious support group are parents of school age children, particularly elementary grades. Each school principal should encourage parents to register to vote. New community residents or those who have changed address and are registering their children in a new school should be provided with a voter registration form as a part of the school registration process.

A more systematic voter registration effort can be undertaken, perhaps by parent advisory council if they are active in each school. Voter registration lists can be compared with the names of the parents of students in the school. Those parents not registered to vote can be contacted and encouraged to register.

School based activities.   One of the keystones of an election campaign is the active involvement of personnel at the school building level. Principals play an important role in this effort and have the responsibility of leading their school's activities. Three things are necessary for effective school based election activities: procedures for encouraging the principals to participate actively in the campaign and to give campaign activities a high priority in their administration of the school; assistance to principals in formulating effective activities and developing appropriate materials; and coordination between the district office's overall campaign strategy and school based activities to avoid overlap, contradictions, and illegalities.

School level activities can be mandated by a directive from the district superintendent, but the most dedicated and innovative efforts come, not by fiat, but through school building personnel being positively involved in the campaign with a feeling of ownership of their activities and results. This can be accomplished by the district office establishing expectations and guidelines for the process of the school level activities in the campaign and then providing schools encouragement and assistance to building administrators in reaching those goals.

One useful procedure is for the district office to prepare an Administrator's Handbook for the upcoming budget election. The handbook could include two options for each principal: (1) Follow the list of campaign related activities specified by the district office in the handbook; or (2) Put together an individual plan for the particular school building which covers the required school level involvement. Even with the second option, the district office can provide assistance in preparing written materials and planning strategies for reaching voters.

The specific activities at the school level are limited only by the imagination of the district and school administrators. In general, they consist of trying to increase registration of likely Yes voters, of informing local patrons of the budget election and its likely results on the school's programs and students, of creating direct contact between the school and its neighbors to increase their knowledge about their local school, and of working to involve all building staff in the activities in a productive fashion. An example of an actual checklist of school level campaign activities prepared for building principals by the district community relations office is given in Table 7.3.

Speakers bureau.   An effective means of providing wide, personal coverage of the issues and concerns in a budget election is through a speakers bureau. This is a list of individuals—school district personnel and pri-

TABLE 7.3   Principals' Checklist for Budget Election

_____   Get parents registered to vote. Voter registration blanks are available from the County Elections Office or the school district office.

    _____   New residents.

    _____   Families who have moved to your school from another school in the district must re-register if their address has changed.

_____   Plan to involve as many parents as possible in registering voters and getting people out to vote. The Yes committee will probably contact your advisory committee to ask for volunteers to work on campaign projects.

_____   Review "profile" of people living in school area (census and election data) provided by district office to help plan for disseminating information about election.

_____   Send a letter to parents one week before the election date. A sample letter is included with this checklist, but you may want to develop your own. Tell them about all the good programs you have had this year and some of your plans for next year. Inform them of cuts made over the last several years and how those have affected your building. Include items such as staffing ratios of both classified and certified personnel, supplies, and so on, and tell them how the proposed budget would restore some of the cuts.

    _____   Send a draft of the letter to the district office to be checked for nonadvocacy. It can be sent to parents as soon as the approved copy is returned to you.

_____   Plan an open house or other event for parents between now and election day. Some other event ideas are:

    _____   Swap day (for high schools) where parents take their childrens' places in school for one day

    _____   An Education Celebration to let people know all the outstanding things that have been done in your school this year

    _____   Open house

    _____   Community Day with activities for people

    _____   Grandparents Day, inviting seniors from the neighborhood

    _____   A coffee for school neighbors in the school or in neighborhood homes. Invite people who are unfamiliar with schools.

_____   The district has developed a special brochure for parents. The brochure could be included in your next newsletter, sent home with students, or passed out at events.

_____   If you have volunteers other than parents, plan a coffee or event (possibly a "volunteer recognition") and discuss the election with them.

_____   Visit senior citizen groups, community groups, and other organizations in your area to tell them about the budget election and what it means for your school.

_____   If you belong to a service club or other community group, urge members to have a speaker on the budget election or offer to speak yourself. Because you are known and trusted by friends in that group, your participation in the discussion will be important.

_____   Plan a staff meeting before election day to present the facts about the budget. The district office has prepared fact sheets and transparencies for your use if you want them.

_____   Encourage staff members to participate in the canvassing campaign to distribute literature in selected precincts on the Saturday before the election. It will take about two hours.

_____   On election day, remind each of your staff members to vote.

vate citizens—who are available to speak to community groups about the school budget election. Speakers need to be briefed on their roles, the issues in the election, questions that are likely to be asked, and proper responses to them. Speakers should also be provided with written materials giving factual information about the district's financial situation, the amount of the budget and tax levy, how the money will be used in the district, and the consequences of not passing the levy.

A list of potential groups for speaking engagements can be compiled from the service clubs, civic clubs, professional and business associations, neighborhood groups, and other similar organizations in the district. These groups should be contacted well in advance to arrange speaking engagements shortly before the budget election.

For both information and advocacy in each speaking engagement two members of the speakers bureau should be utilized: a school district employee and a member of the Yes committee. With this arrangement a school district can legitimately give factual information about the district's financial condition, as well as the size and uses of the tax levy being requested in the election, while the accompanying Yes committee member can ask for support of the budget election.

Campaign materials.   A successful election campaign requires the development of a variety of informational materials. Materials prepared by the school district must be unbiased, present factual information, and not advocate passage of the budget election. Materials produced and financed by the Yes committee may promote the budget election and urge its approval.

If target audiences have been established in the research and planning phases of the campaign, it may be appropriate to create special materials with messages aimed at each audience. The messages in the material for each target audience should be accurate and fair, but they will contain different information and emphases depending on the concerns and interests of each audience. For example, materials for parents typically emphasize educational programs and the impact on students of the passage or failure of the budget election. They can take several forms and be distributed in several ways: a letter from the superintendent to all parents; articles in newsletters from each school; handouts at school events near the election date.

Employee groups are also important in any election campaign. Special information which illustrates the importance of the election to administrators, teachers and other professional staff, and classified staff can be prepared. A positive supportive attitude should be strongly encouraged from all employees; their jobs and those of their colleagues may depend on the outcome of the election. A disgruntled janitor, who complains publicly that "teachers waste too much paper and the schools really don't need all that money," can do untold damage; after hearing it from an "insider," citizens will rarely believe the administration's claims of efficiency and need for the tax levy.

Other materials for district employees include "Remember to Vote" posters for staff bulletin boards, "Ask Me" badges for district employees to wear, and school-specific information illustrating the results of winning or losing the election. The Yes committee can contact district employees to encourage them to support the budget election and to vote yes on election day. The Yes committee can also solicit assistance from district employees to help in the campaign. As private citizens, district employees may contribute money to help finance the election campaign, and, on their own time, they can volunteer to work in the campaign. Activities which require a number of people, such as preparing mailings in the evenings or canvassing neighborhoods on weekends to solicit support, are excellent opportunities for district personnel to assist the election campaign.

Other types of targeted materials to consider include: a special booklet for chamber of commerce members with detailed financial data; a separate mailing in traditionally high yes percentage voting precincts to voters who have no school-age children; and a general mailing to all district patrons emphasizing the importance to the community of a high quality system of public education. Each of these will be different and tailored to its intended audience.

News media. The news media present a special case for attention during the campaign. For many people much of their knowledge of the district and its educational programs comes through newspapers, television, and radio. Regular, routine reporting and news stories by the media are an ongoing part of a school district's communication effort; these activities are frequently stepped up as a budget election approaches because of the importance of the event. Consequently, the district should use media to publicize the upcoming election. Throughout the campaign the news media personnel need to be provided with sufficient factual information to enable them to report accurately the financial situation of the district and the circumstances of the budget election. If the district will be seeking editorial endorsements supporting the budget election, additional information about the importance of passing the levy, the financial requirements of the school district, and the likely programmatic results and effects on students may need to be prepared and presented to the editorial staffs of the local media.

There are a number of specific activities which can be undertaken to work successfully with the media. Each news editor for the newspapers and television and radio stations operating in the district's boundaries can be visited by the senior administrator responsible for media and supplied with printed and verbal information concerning the budget election; at this time upcoming events and topics can be suggested.

An organized "Letters to the Editor" effort in which citizens and representatives of organizations supporting the budget election submit letters giving their endorsements, can create the appearance of widespread community support. Talk shows on local television and radio stations offer excellent opportunities for presenting both the district's factual information and the Yes committee's advocacy position. •

If funds are available, the purchase of some media advertising to promote passage of the budget election can be considered. Newspaper advertising will reach a broad segment of the community and, consequently, most likely should present a message of general support and the need for quality schools. Radio and television spots, on the other hand, can be targeted to specific groups.

Election eve activities.   In an election campaign timing is critical. The objective is to orchestrate a crescendo of positive activities just prior to the election date to sweep the voters along with a real or perceived wave of support for the budget election. Reaching a peak too early allows the opposition time to gain strength and counter the district's and Yes committee's activities with anti-activities of its own. Reaching a peak too late means the election is over before adequate public support can be built.

Last minute activities are generally of three types: the final advertising, speaking, and information blitz; countering opposition efforts; and getting out the likely yes voters on election day. The final push by the district and Yes committee will be continuations of many of the ongoing activities during the campaign. Some of them, such as advertising, may be intensified during the last weeks. If a visible and active opposition has developed, it may be necessary to refute their claims and answer any questions that they may have raised. This could entail revising the district's messages and even preparing new materials to diffuse opposition activities.

"Get-out-the-vote" activities are concentrated during the last few days of the campaign, but the district and Yes committee must have planned them well in advance to ensure that they can be accomplished on time. These include such activities as telephone and door to door canvassing in targeted neighborhoods shortly before the election date to make people aware of the issue and to remind them to vote. For election day itself, other activities could include offering transportation to polling places for those who need it and calling registered voters in historically pro-education precincts who have not voted by late afternoon to remind them to vote.

Evaluation

The work is not over after election day. A precinct by precinct analysis of the results should be made. Compare the turnout, percent yes, and percent no votes on the budget election with past elections and with any other issues which were on the same ballot. Identify locations where there were changes in past budget election patterns. Then compare the precinct results with locations of specific campaign activities. Did the precincts with the largest percentage yes votes and the greatest improvement in percentage yes votes correspond to areas where the most work was done by individual schools and campaign workers? This is the expected result; if there are anomalies to this pattern they should be investigated to understand their cause.

Provide feedback to those who worked in the campaign. If the principal or parents at certain schools made a difference in the election results in their area, they should be told—either way. Principals who were active and directed a thorough and effective local campaign should be congratulated and their accomplishments lauded publicly. On the other hand, the shortcomings of principals who put forth a minimal effort can be exposed by a comparison of the voting results of their precincts with successful precincts.

Much information and experience is obtained by those working in the campaign. This knowledge should not go to waste. Post-election evaluation sessions should be held with campaign workers to discuss the effectiveness of the campaign organization, the fund-raising effort, the specification of appropriate target audiences and the messages for each, the advertising, the campaign literature, the direct mailing strategies, the speakers and the selection of audiences, and canvassing and telephone efforts. The recent campaign will not be the last one which the district has to conduct and the knowledge gained on this budget election campaign can be put to use in future elections.

CONCLUSIONS

If a school district needs to hold an election to obtain sufficient funds to balance its proposed budget and operate its programs for the upcoming year, it is critical that a maximum effort be devoted to winning the election. This effort culminates in the actual election, but it requires an ongoing program of communication between the district and its patrons. Voters who know about the school system, who have been told of its successes, who have had the opportunity to participate in deciding its direction, and who share its goals for improvement will be most likely to vote to support schools at an election. Regular communication from the district office to parents and other members of the community, but even more importantly communication from the individual schools, is the key to an informed and supportive public.

The actual campaign to win the budget election can be very time consuming, but it deserves top priority from school administrators. The district superintendent and other senior district administrators must take responsibility for planning and executing a winning campaign. This involves research and analysis to understand the district's past voting patterns and types of voters, the planning of an appropriate campaign strategy including the use of a Yes committee if needed, and the implementation of the various campaign activities to inform and convince the public to support the budget election.

PROBLEMS

7.1   Collect and organize election, demographic, and economic data relevant to a budget election in your district. Prepare a report highlighting your findings; use appendices, if necessary, to present extensive tabular data.

7.2   Prepare a campaign activity timeline for an April budget election in your district. Identify the major activities which need to take place, their sequence, and the appropriate dates for each.

7.3   Identify the important target groups for a budget election campaign in your district. Specify the message(s) most appropriate for each group and the means you would choose for communicating those messages.

7.4   Outline the activities for an effective speakers bureau for a budget election campaign in your district. Identify appropriate speakers from within the school district and from the community (positions, not individuals' names). Specify the groups, organizations, and situations to which you would plan to send a speaker and which speaker(s) from your bureau would be sent.

NOTES

1. Tax limitation measures are discussed in James Danziger and Peter Ring, "Fiscal Limitations: A Selective Review of Recent Research," *Public Administration Review* 42 (January/February 1982), pp. 47-55. An extensive listing of the research on this topic is provided by Deborah Thresher, "Annotated Bibliography of Tax and Expenditure Limitation Literature," Project Report No. 81-A6 (Stanford, CA: Institute for Research on Educational Finance and Governance, Stanford University, 1981).

2. For a discussion of how varying voter preferences for education are translated into voting behavior, see Thomas Jones, *Introduction to School Finance: Technique and Social Policy* (New York: MacMillan, 1985), pp. 26-32.

3. *Education Week*, December 17, 1986 and January 14, 1987.

4. Michael Kirst, "Loss of Support for Public Secondary Schools: Some Causes and Solutions," *Daedalus*, 110 (Summer 1981), pp. 45-68.

5. See Theodore Bergstrom and Robert Goodman, "Private Demands for Public Goods," *American Economic Review*, 63 (June 1973), pp. 280-296.

6. Philip Piele and John Stuart Hall, *Ballots, Budgets, and Bonds* (Lexington, MA: D. C. Heath, 1973).

7. Philip Piele, "Public Support for Public Schools: The Past, The Future, and The Federal Role," *Teachers College Record*, 84 (Spring 1983), p. 691.

8. This section is based on materials provided by Gay Campbell, Eugene School District 4J, Eugene, OR, describing two district fiscal election campaigns which were awarded Gold Medallions from the National School Public Relations Association for outstanding achievement.

9. Michael Kirst and Walter Garms, "The Political Environment of School Finance Policy in the 1980s," *School Finance Policies and Practices, The 1980s: A Decade of Conflict* James Guthrie, ed. (Cambridge, MA: Ballinger, 1980), p. 48.

10. For a review of voter support for public schools, see Piele, "Public Support for Public Schools," pp. 690-707.

8

BUDGET MANAGEMENT

During the preparation of a budget, the document itself serves as the vehicle for planning and resource allocation decisions in the district. After the budget is adopted by the school board and the appropriations made to the various accounts, it then becomes a tool for managing and controlling expenditures. *Budget management is the process of regulating expenditures during the budget year to ensure that they do not exceed authorized amounts and that they are for the proper purposes.*

The appropriated amounts established by the school board set the limits on what the district can spend in each budget area. These areas are usually fairly broad—the first function level (such as, Instruction or Support Services) in each fund in the district budget. The appropriation amounts provide only general guidance to manage district spending during the school year. This situation, however, is entirely appropriate; it is the role of the school board to establish general fiscal policy for the district and the role of the district administrators to implement that policy. It is generally not appropriate for school board members to involve themselves on an ongoing basis with the details of individual expenditures (unless they suspect some problem).

Expenditure Data

For administrative use in controlling district expenditures detailed budget data are utilized. These are the expenditure projections prepared by each school and district level department during the budget development process and aggregated into the summary budget document for the district. Within each accounting fund these original budget data are established at lower, more specific levels in the school accounting system. For example, a typical budget can be developed by *third level function accounts* (like elementary, middle, or high school instruction, special instructional programs for physically handicapped, educational media services, office of the principal, fiscal services, operation and maintenance of plant) and within each function by *second level object accounts* (like regular salaries, type of benefits, type of purchased services, type of supplies). In some districts the budget data are shown at even lower levels of detail to provide additional information. For example, regular salaries can be separated into those for certified personnel or for classified personnel.

Another budget classification dimension frequently used by school districts in conjunction with the function and object specifications is *cost center*. Every segment of the district's operation can be assigned to a specific cost center that has an administrator in charge of it. For example, each school building in the district could be a separate cost center with the building principal responsible for managing the expenditures of the building. Similarly, district level departments in the central office can be created and managed as cost centers. Each cost center would have an individual accounting code number assigned to it. During the operating year this number, along with the function and object of the expenditure, would be recorded for all expenditures incurred by the cost center. For example, the purchase of textbooks for a high school mathematics course would not only be recorded as an instructional expenditure for the regular high school program (and even for the mathematics area if the district maintained its function codes at this levels) and as a textbook object of expenditure, but also would be identified by the particular high school in the district which made the purchase. In this way, the financial accounting system would then be able to collect, maintain, and report all expenditures by each individual school and district level department separately.

By summing all of the expenditures for the same function and object account codes for each cost center it is possible to maintain a running total of the amount and types of expenditures to date in each area. The expenditure data should be updated regularly, and reports presenting this information prepared and distributed to the the district administrators. If the reports are available on a timely basis, all cost center administrators will have a report which can be used to monitor the expenditures of their operation.

Budget versus Actual Expenditure Comparisons

The first comparison to be made with this information is between the actual expenditures and those budgeted. Two questions can be answered which are significant to principals and department administrators concerned with cost control.

1. Are the actual expenditures for the particular area within the budgeted amount?
2. How much is left to spend?

If the budgeted expenditure amount is included in the expenditure report the comparison is readily available. Table 8.1 illustrates the simple comparison. In this case, this account had a budget of $100,000 and the year-to-date (YTD) expenditures totaled $80,000. The account is not overspent and has $20,000 or 20 percent of the original budget still available for further expenditures.

As a manager, how can you judge whether or not the situation illustrated in Table 8.1 is under proper control or in need of rapid attention to prevent exceeding the budget? More information is necessary to make this judgment. First, the type of budget account is important to know, and second, the date of the report is also critical. If the account is for expenditures which generally are expected to occur regularly and more or less equally throughout the year, then this report would indicate a problem if it is early in the school year. For example, if 80 percent of the money is gone in November, this account is in trouble. However, if the report is in May, with 20 percent of the money unspent, there may be funds left over at the end of the year.

Accounts with irregularly timed expenditures require knowledge of the spending patterns to be able to evaluate the budgetary status of the account. If the expenditures are in an account, such as instructional supplies, where items are purchased early and used throughout the year, then spending 80 percent of the money by September may be an appropriate action.

Another piece of information which is often provided in cost reports is the monthly expenditure amount. This is the amount spent in the last accounting period. The year-to-date amount is the total of all of the monthly amounts up to that time. It is a good idea to review the monthly

TABLE 8.1   Budget versus Actual Expenditure Comparison

BUDGETED APPROPRIATION	YEAR-TO-DATE EXPENDITURES	BALANCE REMAINING	PERCENT REMAINING
$100,000	$80,000	$20,000	20%

amounts that are reported for each of the accounts under your cost center to ensure that they are correct on two counts. On a managerial level, inspect the expenditures to confirm that the proper spending level or pattern is happening and that no unauthorized purchases have been made. On a mechanical level, check to see that there are no recording or reporting errors in the report, such as expenditures from other cost centers charged to your accounts or incorrect amounts charged for purchases. If the monthly expenditures are verified each month the year-to-date figures will be reliable also.

ENCUMBRANCES

Reliance on the budget versus actual comparison of expenditures may not be sufficient to provide adequate cost control and to prevent overspending. Not all of the balance remaining may actually be available to spend. Some of the remaining funds may have already been committed to expenditures that have not yet been made. The accounting system does not record expenditures until the time that they are incurred; only actual amounts are entered into the expenditure accounts, not planned or anticipated ones. If the district has made a commitment for a future expenditure, but has not actually made the expenditure yet, then that expenditure will not appear in either the monthly or year-to-date totals.

Without information on the money committed but not yet spent, as well as the actual expenditures to date, it would be possible for an administrator unknowingly to spend or approve an expenditure which would exceed the budget limit. For example with the information in Table 8.1, if a purchase order has been issued for $15,000 for an item which has not yet been delivered, then only $5,000 is really available in the account. However, this information does not appear in this simple budget versus actual comparison to inform or warn the administrator in charge of the account. So by looking at the balance remaining, an administrator could approve another $10,000 expenditure in the account with every expectation that it is appropriate and within the budget. Instead, the administrator would have caused the account to go over budget by $5,000.

As is clear from this example, another component is needed in the financial control and reporting system to prevent inadvertent overexpenditures due to lack of information about future commitments. The obligations against the budget amount need to be recorded and reported along with the actual expenditures. Administrators will then be informed of the real balance remaining that they can spend.

This is done through a method known as *encumbrances*. These are a separate set of accounting records which are used to record financial commitments made by the district before they are final and recorded as expenditures. Encumbrances are defined as:

> obligations in the form of purchase orders, contracts, or salary commitments chargeable to an appropriation and for which part of the appropriation is reserved.[1]

Encumbrances are different from expenditures. The obligations recorded in the encumbrance accounts are *estimated* amounts. The encumbrances are estimated at the time the obligation is made and are subject to change when finally settled. By contrast, expenditure accounts by definition are reserved for recording only the *actual* amounts of transactions; estimates are not permitted in these accounts. Consequently, expenditures can only be recorded in the accounting system when the amounts are known with certainty—only after the transaction is completed. The reason is that the actual amounts may be different from the originally estimated or anticipated amounts.

This is the case for many district commitments made for the future, even legally contracted obligations. For example, salary contract amounts are commitments by the district to pay employees agreed upon salaries. These amounts are established in the contracts and are obligations of the district. However, they are not actual expenditures until salaries are paid each month. Resignations, leaves, or other situations will come up during the year which will prevent some of the contracts from being fulfilled as originally written.

Another common example of differences between original commitments and actual expenditures occurs with purchase orders. When a purchase order is issued, it is an obligation on the district to pay for the specified items. However, sometimes the price of the items is not known precisely at the time of issue, or prices may change between the time the purchase order was prepared and when the goods were delivered, or different items were substituted for unavailable items in the purchase order, or freight will be added to the price of the item purchased. Use of the encumbrance accounts in these situations prevents the expenditure account from incorrectly recording estimates rather than actual amounts, but also provides information to administrators to prevent over-budget expenditures.

Encumbrance Accounting

When the district incurs an obligation for payment later in the year and wishes to keep track of its uncommitted and available remaining funds in that account, it may use the encumbrance accounting system. As noted above, encumbrance accounts are separate from expenditure accounts, but they are used in combination to record related financial information about district transactions.

The procedure begins when the district makes a financial commitment against a budget appropriation, but will not pay for the commitment until sometime later. The first step is to enter the estimated amount in an encumbrance account associated with the appropriation. This reduces the uncommitted funds still available in the appropriation and, in effect, reserves this part of the appropriation to pay off the commitment. When the commitment is paid, the actual amount is recorded as an expenditure against the appropriation and the associated encumbrance is canceled. The payment satisfies the obligation and the recorded expenditure for the actual amount now reduces the appropriation. The encumbrance amount is canceled since it is no longer needed to earmark those funds to pay for the obligation.

To accomplish this recording and reporting an extended format is required in order to include the encumbrance accounts. An example of a summary encumbrance and expenditure report format for a cost center is shown in Table 8.2. This simplified format illustrates the encumbrance concepts. Actual report formats will show financial information by specific account within the cost center and will aggregate transactions with the same account numbers, but the general design will be similar.

Each item or transaction in the report is given a separate line to illustrate its activity and status. The total appropriation for the accounts of the cost center is shown next. This is followed by columns to record individual encumbrance and expenditure amounts. The year-to-date columns for encumbrances and expenditures are the totals for the entire cost center and reflect the changes from the single transactions. The unencumbered balance column represents the amount of the original appropriation that is uncommitted and available for use. The relationship among the appropriation, the year-to-date encumbrances and expenditures, and the unencumbered balance is straightfoward and shown in the equation below.

$$
\begin{aligned}
&\ \text{APPROPRIATION}\\
&-\ \text{YTD ENCUMBRANCES}\\
&-\ \text{YTD EXPENDITURES}\\
&=\ \text{UNENCUMBERED BALANCE}
\end{aligned}
$$

The equation simply says that what you start out with (appropriation amount) less what you have committed to date (YTD encumbrances), less what you have spent to date (YTD expenditures) equals what you have left to spend (unencumbered balance).

Illustration of Encumbrance Procedures

An example of these procedures is shown in Table 8.3. The total appropriation of $100,000 is recorded on the first line as the first item. Since nothing has been charged against or spent from this account yet, the unencum-

TABLE 8.2 Encumbrance Reporting Format

ITEM	APPROPRIATION	SINGLE ENCUMBRANCE	SINGLE EXPENDITURE	YTD ENCUMBRANCES	YTD EXPENDITURES	UNENCUMBERED BALANCE

APPROPRIATION − YTD ENCUMBRANCES − YTD EXPENDITURES = UNENCUMBERED BALANCE

TABLE 8.3 Encumbrance Example Worksheet

ITEM	APPROPRIATION	SINGLE ENCUMBRANCE	SINGLE EXPENDITURE	− YTD ENCUMBRANCES	− YTD EXPENDITURES	= UNENCUMBERED BALANCE
	APPROPRIATION	SINGLE ENCUMBRANCE	SINGLE EXPENDITURE	YTD ENCUMBRANCES	YTD EXPENDITURES	UNENCUMBERED BALANCE
1. Record appropriation to start year	$100,000			$0	$0	$100,000
2. Record salary contracts of $80,000		$80,000		$80,000	$0	$20,000
3. Issue purchase order for equipment in amount of $10,000		$10,000		$90,000	$0	$10,000
4. Pay monthly salaries of $8,000		($8,000)	$8,000	$82,000	$8,000	$10,000
5. Receive equipment invoiced at $9,000		($10,000)	$9,000	$72,000	$17,000	$11,000
6. Cancel remaining contract of resigning staff member, $7,000		($7,000)		$65,000	$17,000	$18,000

bered balance is equal to the original appropriation. The second item is to record annual salary contracts of $80,000 against the appropriation. The amount is recorded in the single encumbrance column and in the year-to-date encumbrance column as well. (Since it is the first encumbrance, the single and year-to-date amounts are the same.) The unencumbered balance now changes to reflect the salary commitments which have to be paid. In accordance with the equation above, the $20,000 is the result of subtracting the salary contract amount ($80,000) from the original appropriation ($100,000). This indicates to the administrator of this operation that after staff salaries have been paid, $20,000 remains for other types of expenditures.

The third item is a purchase order for $10,000 for equipment. With the purchase order, the district has committed itself to pay for the equipment when it arrives, but at this point the actual expenditure amount is only estimated. Therefore, the purchase order amount is treated as an encumbrance until the equipment, accompanied by an invoice with the exact amount, is delivered to the district. To enter this transaction into the accounts, it is first necessary to record the purchase order amount in the single encumbrance column. The year-to-date encumbrance column is then updated for this new encumbrance giving a total of $90,000 in encumbered funds. This leaves $10,000 as the unencumbered balance after this transaction.

The fourth item is the payment of monthly salaries, a total of $8,000. This is an expenditure because it is an actual cash disbursement for a particular amount, and $8,000 is shown in the single expenditure column (and in the year-to-date expenditure column as this is the first expenditure of the year). However, the salary costs were encumbered at the start of the year, so this item does not represent a new transaction but rather a change from an encumbrance to an expenditure. Since the actual expenditure amount is now recorded, there is no need to reserve that amount in the encumbrances. Therefore, an $8,000 deduction is made in the single encumbrance column and the year-to-date encumbrance amount is likewise reduced. The unencumbered balance does not change in this instance since all that happened was that $8,000 in year-to-date encumbrances were shifted to year-to-date expenditures. As a check on this condition, Appropriations ($100,000) minus Year-to-date Encumbrances ($82,000) minus Year-to-date Expenditures ($8,000) equals Unencumbered Balance ($10,000).

For the fifth item the equipment previously ordered arrives, but the invoice is for $9,000 while the purchase order amount of $10,000 was encumbered. The procedures are the same as recording the monthly salaries in the previous item, but care must be taken to use the correct amounts for both the encumbrance and expenditure entries. In the single expenditure column the actual amount of the equipment or $9,000 is recorded. The year-to-date expenditure column is updated for this amount giving a total of $17,000. Since the equipment ordered in the purchase order has received and the actual amount entered as an expenditure, there is no need to maintain an encumbrance for this item. Therefore, the entire amount of the original encumbrance or $10,000 is deducted in the single encumbrance column and from year-to-date encumbrance amount as well. This leaves the year-to-date encumbrance total at $72,000. Notice that the unencumbered balance has increased by $1,000 to $11,000 in this transaction. The reason is easy to understand. Originally it was estimated that the equipment would cost $10,000 and the available money from the appropriation was reduced by this amount. When it arrived, however, the actual cost was only $9,000 and this amount was charged against the account. The $1,000 difference is money that was not needed for the equipment purchase and is once again available for other purposes.

The final item in this example is the cancellation of a contract for a staff member who is resigning and will not be replaced. At the beginning of the year the entire contract amount was encumbered as part of the total staff salaries (Item 2). Now $7,000 of that amount will not be used. To show this change a $7,000 deduction is made in the single encumbrance column and also from the year-to-date encumbrance amount. No change occurs in the expenditure amounts, but the unencumbered balance is increased by $7,000 to reflect that this amount is now free for other uses. With these changes, the basic equation remains in balance; Appropriations minus Year-to-date Encumbrances minus Year-to-date Expenditures equals the Unencumbered Balance.

While most school administrators will neither see nor work with encumbrances in this single-item format, they do need to understand both the concepts and mechanics of encumbrance accounting. As managers of programs, schools, and departments, they will deal with expenditure reports of their operations which incorporate aggregate encumbrances data for each budget account under their responsibility.

TRANSFERS BETWEEN BUDGET ACCOUNTS

Rarely, if ever, will all of the actual expenditures be equal to the detailed budget estimates. As the end of the year approaches, in particular, it will become obvious which accounts are going to spend more than was budgeted and which are going to spend less. This is not necessarily a cause for concern if the overages and shortfalls among the accounts balance each other out and the total expenditures do not exceed the total appropriation. This is the case for the district as a whole and generally true for each cost center within the district.

In order to manage effectively, school administrators need to have flexibility to transfer budgeted monies from one account to another within their cost center responsibility. This authority is not without its restrictions, but within district policies it can provide administrators with an effective device for reallocating monies under their control for improved programs.

The transfers can be explicit accounting transactions involving changes in the original budget allocations or implicit transfers where the administrator approves overspending by one department and restricts spending in another to compensate.[2] In either case, the results are the same: Spending approval is shifted from one area to another.

The rules for transfers among accounts will vary among school districts depending on their policies. Some examples of the restrictions different districts may place on an individual administrator's authority to implement transfers are shown in Figure 8.1. These rules illustrate varying degrees of freedom for individual administrators in managing their operations and control of expenditures by higher administrative levels in the school district.

The first example is clearly the least restrictive and gives administrators the maximum flexibility in controlling their operations. The restrictions on shifts among functions is intended to keep the monies used for the same general purposes as they were appropriated unless the school board is consulted about and approves the proposed changes in spending. Similarly, the restrictions on monies spent for personnel and equipment give district administration and the school board control over two key expenditure areas. The last example provides the maximum district control; the cost of exerting this extensive control can be additional administrative time for preparing and reviewing more paperwork.

FIGURE 8.1 Examples of Varying Budget Account Transfer Policies

---

1. No constraints except to stay within the total budget for the cost center.
2. No transfers among major functions. Appropriations for instruction cannot be transferred to support services or vice versa without board approval.
3. No transfers in or out of salary accounts. Appropriations for personnel cannot be shifted to other types of expenditures and vice versa without central office or board approval.
4. No transfers in or out of equipment. Appropriations for equipment cannot be shifted to other types of expenditures and vice versa without central office or board approval.
5. No transfers permitted without district office approval.

MANAGEMENT INFORMATION AND REPORTING FOR CONTROL

A wide variety of reports can be prepared to assist school board members, school administrators, other district staff, and district patrons in monitoring and understanding the implementation of the budget. They all provide information which is thought to be relevant in evaluating the financial condition of the district and the fiscal performance of administrators. The reports should be designed to fit specific district needs and meet any state or federal reporting requirements. They rely on information in the accounting system that is summarized, analyzed, and presented in a useful format. A report that no one understands or uses is a waste of time and money.

Expenditure Reports

Probably the most important type of report for budget control is the expenditure report. These reports generally are a comparison of the expenditures and encumbrances to date with the budget amount for the account. They allow the manager with responsibility for the account to monitor spending and prevent unwanted overexpenditures.

Expenditure reports can be prepared in a number of formats, depending on what emphasis is desired. They can feature expenditures summarized by function or subfunction, by object, or by cost center. Further they can provide reports which combine several of these dimensions to give more detailed expenditure information about particular aspects of the district's operations. This is possible because the accounting system records expenditures along function, object, and cost center dimensions. Expenditure records can be combined in any number of ways to produce different kinds of expenditure reports.

Expenditures by function. As one example, a report can summarize expenditures by function across the district—elementary instruction (function 1110), middle school instruction (function 1120), high school instruction (function 1130), and so forth through each of the functions in the district's accounts. Table 8.4 shows a sample expenditure report of this type, presenting the budgeted amount, the actual expenditures and encumbrances to date, and the remaining balance by function for a school district.

This report is an actual example of one prepared monthly by the district and presented to its school board to keep them informed of the expenditure status of the district. As shown in the report, with only one month remaining in the school year the district still has 17 percent of its budget unspent. Unless significant expenditures are planned during the last month, the district will most likely end up underspending its budget. If further detail about functions which are either under or over budget is desired, subreports which present expenditure data by by subfunction can be prepared. For example, to investigate why each of the instructional programs is substantially under budget, a report which presents expenditure data by instructional department within each instructional grouping (for

TABLE 8.4 **Expenditure Report, Budget Comparison by Function: Green Valley School District, Budget Balance for May 25, 1985**

FUNCTION

CODE	DESCRIPTOR	1984–85 BUDGET	EXPEND. TO DATE	DIFFERENCE	PERCENT REMAIN
1110	Elementary program	$1,387,023	$1,118,952	$268,071	19.3%
1120	Middle School program	757,613	638,646	118,967	15.7%
1130	High School program	1,087,885	921,285	166,600	15.3%
1210	Gifted & Talented	34,148	33,911	237	0.7%
1222	TMR Special Education	5,400	2,333	3,067	56.8%
1260	Learning Disabilities	90,919	61,426	29,493	32.4%
2110	Attendance	25,713	19,695	6,018	23.4%
2120	Counseling & Guidance	86,694	73,107	13,587	15.7%
2130	Health	15,440	12,676	2,764	17.9%
2210	Instruction Improvement	83,025	60,357	22,668	27.3%
2220	Media	278,545	233,715	44,830	16.1%
2312	Board Secretary	1,500	0	1,500	100.0%
2315	Legal Services	8,000	1,630	6,370	79.6%
2317	Audit Services	10,000	9,835	165	1.7%
2319	Board of Ed. Services	7,070	4,623	2,447	34.6%
2321	Superintendent's Office	101,324	82,558	18,766	18.5%
2339	Other Admin. Services	0	17,002	(17,002)	NA
2410	Principals' Offices	590,495	499,774	90,721	15.4%
2510	Business Office	97,139	80,781	16,358	16.8%
2524	Payroll Service Ins.	28,250	10,512	17,738	62.8%
2529	Early Retirement	21,600	15,708	5,892	27.3%
2535	Building Repair & Const.	86,635	83,840	2,795	3.2%
2536	Classroom Furniture	6,283	6,909	(626)	−10.0%
2542	Care/Upkeep of Bldg.	893,940	755,802	138,138	15.5%
2543	Care/Upkeep of Grounds	30,983	26,006	4,977	16.1%
2544	Care/Upkeep of Equip.	25,808	26,613	(805)	−3.1%
2545	Capital Out. (Vehicles)	13,000	9,370	3,630	27.9%
2550	Transportation	376,628	312,144	64,484	17.1%
4800	Gen. Fund Contingency	50,000	0	50,000	100.0%
	TOTALS	$6,201,060	$5,119,210	$1,081,850	17.4%

example, mathematics, language arts, or social studies within the high school) can be prepared. Depending on the circumstances, the situation could represent either an efficient use of district funds and a substantial savings to the taxpayers, or a serious shortchanging of the educational program through an unwise effort to reduce instructional expenditures more than necessary.

Expenditures by object.   Another type of expenditure report is a summary report by object. In this report the year-to-date expenditures and encumbrances in each object account are compared with the amount budgeted for that account. A report of this type presents data aggregated by each object account utilized by the district—regular certificated salaries (object 111), regular noncertificated salaries (object 112), temporary certificated salaries (object 121), temporary noncertificated salaries (object 122), overtime certificated salaries (object 131), overtime noncertificated salaries (object 132), and so forth through the entire list of object accounts. Similar reports can be developed for each cost center in the district's operation where the total expenditures of the cost center are summarized and compared with the budget allocation.

Expenditures by cost center.   While the function and object expenditure reports present aggregate information and can identify possible trouble spots, they do not provide sufficient detail for much specific management action. If the total supply expenditures in the district, for example, are approaching an overexpenditure condition, which cost centers are causing the problem? If a school is spending more than its budget, what types of expenditures are to blame and can the principal be held responsible? To answer these types of questions, expenditure reports are needed which present specific information about the operations in question and locate administrative responsibility for them. These are obtained by combining several of the accounting dimensions into a single report. In order to tie the report to specific administrative responsibility, one of the dimensions should be the cost center. For example, a cost center report could show expenditures for a single cost center broken down by object—salaries, benefits, purchased services, supplies, and equipment for a single school. While breadth is lost by focusing on a smaller segment of the operation, much more useful management information is gained for monitoring and understanding that component.

An example page from an actual expenditure report, combining function, object, and cost center data into a single report, is reproduced in Table 8.5. It is taken from a report prepared for an Oregon school district by the Oregon Total Information System (OTIS), a data processing consortium of school districts. This particular report is prepared every two weeks and distributed to the school district administrators.

The identifying information is at the top of the report. It is titled District Financial Summary and is for the General Fund. It was prepared on April 29, 1982 and is page seventeen of the total report. The column headings specify the information contained in the report. The function (FUNCT) is code number 1131 or high school instruction. There are several objects (OBJ) on this page for this function which are coded and described in two separate columns; for example object code 370 is for tuition and object 410 is for supplies. The next column is the cost center (CTR) and is for center number 031 which is a high school in the district. Since all the information is for this one center the report serves as a cost center expenditure report. The area of responsibility (ARA) is the next level of detail shown on the report. The ARA code numbers represent the instructional departments in the high school and are identified in the area description column.

The financial information presented in the budget follows a similar format to the previous example, but it is in summary form. The budget column provides the budgeted amount established for each object in each department. The year-to-date encumbrances and expenditures columns give the annual total that have been committed or spent. The monthly expenditures column shows the most recent expenditures, and the unencumbered balance columns show both the dollars and percent of budget which are remaining at the time of the report.

How would a manager use this report to help control expenditures in the school? Let's look at the supplies accounts first for they are frequently the largest discretionary expenditures at the school level. Reviewing the unencumbered balance column to check the status of past spending and available dollars for each department reveals a wide variety of results. With only about one month to go in the school year no department is precisely on budget. The first two departments, Language Arts and Social Studies are well under budget at this time. However, there are several other departments which have spent beyond their supplies budget, Industrial Arts and Physical Education in particular. The inexactness of departmental spending for supplies in not surprising and not a cause for serious concern. The reason is shown in the CENTER TOTAL row of the supplies section. This provides a summary of the supply expenditures for the entire school and indicates that the overspent departments have been largely balanced out by the departments which have underspent. If no large supply expenditures are anticipated in the final weeks of school, the principal appears to have done a reasonable job of balancing supply expenditures for the school as a whole. The slight overspent amount for supplies will most likely be offset by underspending in other areas of the school (for example, object 380, freight & drayage, which is underbudget).

The only possible problem area that is indicated on the report is textbooks. Here the school has spent over $25,000, but has no budget for this item. Given the magnitude of the expenditures involved, it is unlikely that this is an oversight. The more likely explanation is that the budgeted monies for textbooks are in another part of the budget, perhaps shown at district level, but that the expenditures are recorded in the school's cost center.

TABLE 8.5   District Financial Statement, Detailed Report by Function for General Fund

FUNCT	OBJ	CTR	ARA	OBJECT	/AREA	BUDGET
				DESCRIPTION		
1131				H.S. Instruction		
	370	031	79	Tuition	/Workexp/Dive	50.00
	380	031	12	Freight & Dra	/Science	800.00
	380	031	13	Freight & Dra	/Arts & Craft	200.00
	380	031	16	Freight & Dra	/Industrial A	100.00
	380	031	61	Freight & Dra	/Metal Occupa	50.00
	380	031		Center Total:		1,150.00
	390	031	12	Other Purchas	/Science	200.00
	3XX			Major Object Total:		40,034.65
	410	031		Supplies	/	
	410	031	10	Supplies	/Language Art	8,425.00
	410	031	11	Supplies	/Social Studi	4,492.00
	410	031	12	Supplies	/Science	5,000.00
	410	031	13	Supplies	/Arts & Craft	5,700.00
	410	031	15	Supplies	/Home Making	4,263.50
	410	031	16	Supplies	/Industrial A	3,920.00
	410	031	17	Supplies	/Traffic Safe	1,500.00
	410	031	18	Supplies	/Mathematics	1,779.00
	410	031	19	Supplies	/Health Educa	1,477.00
	410	031	20	Supplies	/Physical Edu	7,300.00
	410	031	21	Supplies	/Foreign Lang	650.00
	410	031	22	Supplies	/Business Edu	310.00
	410	031	26	Supplies	/Music	6,230.00
	410	031	53	Supplies	/Agriculture	1,800.00
	410	031	54	Supplies	/Office Occup	1,425.00
	410	031	55	Supplies	/Construction	1,455.00
	410	031	61	Supplies	/Metal Occupa	500.00
	410	031	63	Supplies	/Industrial M	840.00
	410	031	79	Supplies	/Workexp/Dive	520.00
	410	031		Center Total:		57,586.50
	420	031		Textbooks	/	
	420	031	10	Textbooks	/Language Art	
	420	031	15	Textbooks	/Home Making	
	420	031	16	Textbooks	/Industrial A	
	420	031	19	Textbooks	/Health Educa	
	420	031	63	Textbooks	/Industrial M	
	420	031		Center Total:		
	440	031	22	Periodicals	/Business Edu	150.00
	4XX			Major Object Total:		57,736.50
	541	031	10	Initial & Add	/Language Art	314.38
	541	031	11	Initial & Add	/Social Studi	679.76
	541	031	12	Initial & Add	/Science	1,104.61
	541	031	13	Initial & Add	/Arts & Craft	382.36
	541	031	15	Initial & Add	/Home Making	
	541	031	16	Initial & Add	/Industrial A	2,057.12
	541	031	18	Initial & Add	/Mathematics	1,919.48
	541	031	19	Initial & Add	/Health Educa	662.77
	541	031	20	Initial & Add	/Physical Edu	297.39

YEAR-TO-DATE ENCUMBRANCES	YEAR-TO-DATE EXPENDITURES	MONTHLY EXPENDITURES	UNENC/ACTUAL BALANCE	PERCENT REMAIN
			50.00	100.0
			800.00	100.0
			200.00	100.0
	20.27		79.73	79.7
			50.00	100.0
	20.27		1,129.73	98.2
			200.00	100.0
525.00	35,636.06	1,821.23	3,873.59	9.7
294.24	4,216.12	301.04	3,914.64	46.5
	2,200.67		2,291.33	51.0
559.03	5,238.43	30.00	797.46 −	15.9 −
108.70	6,066.12	595.58	474.82 −	8.3 −
600.00	2,722.97	254.68	940.53	22.1
840.94	6,940.83	164.59	3,861.77 −	98.5 −
	1,216.12	80.48	283.88	18.9
160.00	1,808.10	18.00	189.10 −	10.6 −
	1,543.27		66.27 −	4.5 −
1,275.00	9,289.34	347.50	3,264.34 −	44.7 −
	100.00		550.00	84.6
195.80	1,449.85	4.68	1,335.68 −	430.9 −
392.02	6,650.73	183.31	812.75 −	13.0 −
16.50	573.98	374.48	1,209.52	67.2
	315.00		1,110.00	77.9
	21.32		1,433.68	98.5
	695.42		195.42 −	39.1 −
908.13	1,617.06	30.60	1,685.19 −	200.6 −
			520.00	100.0
5,350.36	52,665.36	2,384.94	429.22 −	.7 −
104.90	25,618.47		25,723.37 −	
104.90	25,618.47		25,723.37 −	
			150.00	100.0
5,455.26	78,283.83	2,384.94	26,002.59 −	45.0 −
2,000.00			1,685.62 −	536.2 −
	1,610.94		931.18 −	137.0 −
150.00	4,020.21		3,065.60 −	277.5 −
	135.00		247.36	64.7
	180.00		180.00 −	
	9,876.08	427.85	7,818.96 −	380.1 −
	1,205.00		714.48	37.2
	560.36		102.41	15.5
	714.14		416.75 −	140.1 −

Revenue Reports

During the year it is also important to monitor the district's collection of revenues. The projection of revenues which was included in the budget is only an estimate. There is no guarantee that the actual revenues received by the district will equal those projected. If actual revenues are less than projected, expenditure reductions may be needed if the district does not have sufficient reserves or contingency funds to make up the differences. If actual revenues are greater than projected, additional expenditures beyond those authorized in the original budget may be possible if approved by the school board. In any event, the district needs to keep a close watch on the receipt of revenues during the year.

Revenue receipts. The basic revenue control report is a regular comparison of estimated revenues and actual revenues received to date by the district. The overall format provides a specification of each anticipated revenue source together with the amount in the original budget, the amount received year-to-date, and the difference between the two. Often a percentage column is also included for quick reference. An example revenue comparison report is shown in Table 8.6.

Interpretation of a report of this type depends on administrator's knowledge of the various sources of revenue, the likely timing of receipts,

TABLE 8.6   Revenue Comparison Report: Green Valley School District Revenue Received to June 3, 1985

	SOURCES				
CODE	DESCRIPTOR	ESTIMATED REVENUE	YR-TO-DATE RECEIPTS	DIFF.	PERCENT DIFF.
1000	Beginning Cash on Hand	$492,570	$1,148,276	$655,706	133.1%
1111	Current Year Taxes	3,073,095	2,850,154	(222,941)	−7.3%
1112	Prior Year Taxes	190,000	324,713	134,713	70.9%
1500	Interest on Investment	75,000	140,647	65,647	87.5%
1910	Rentals	3,500	4,357	857	24.5%
1930	Sale or Comp. for Loss	3,000	639	(2,361)	−78.7%
1990	Miscellaneous Revenue	25,000	45,327	20,327	81.3%
2111	County School Fund	25,000	26,901	1,901	7.6%
3111	Basic School Support	2,241,000	2,448,798	207,798	9.3%
3112	Common School Fund	50,600	56,645	6,045	11.9%
3123	Handicapped Child Fund	31,000	35,265	4,265	13.8%
3150	Vocational Ed Support	900	0	(900)	−100.0%
4800	Federal Timber Sales	110,000	307,040	197,040	179.1%
	TOTALS	$6,320,665	$7,388,762	1,068,097	16.9%

and the date of the report. Early in June, the final month of the school year, when the report in Table 8.6 is dated, it is probable that most of the revenues will have been collected. In this case, the district collected substantially more than was originally projected. A source-by-source comparison reveals that it is largely due to a much larger than anticipated beginning cash position, higher prior year tax collections than planned, and more state basic school support and federal timber sales revenue than were budgeted. These sources more than compensated for the shortfall in current year tax collections.

During the year, however, this report has its greatest value. Monthly (or more frequent) reports allow administrators to follow the actual collections, identify positive and negative collection trends early in their development, and to react quickly to any serious deviation. The administrator responsible for monitoring revenue collections must be knowledgeable about the revenue collection patterns for the important district sources—current and prior year taxes, state aid. In most states, aid is distributed according to state statute or regulation. For property taxes a comparison with past years' collection patterns can be useful. If, for example, 40 percent of current year property taxes are traditionally collected by the end of November, and the November revenue comparison report shows only 30 percent collected, district administrators should investigate to either explain the discrepancy (for example, the last collections were received too late to be included in the monthly report) or plan any necessary expenditure reductions.

Cash flow reports. School districts take in revenues at varying times during the year depending upon the dates which property taxes are due, state and federal aid payment schedules, and when other revenues are received. Expenditures require payment during the year, some at regular intervals and others at irregular times. The important aspect is that the receipt of cash and the need for cash to pay the district's expenditures frequently occur at different times. There are periods during the year when the district will have more cash on hand than it needs immediately, while at other times it will be short of cash needed to pay its bills.

Cash management attempts to smooth out the mismatch between the timing of receipts and expenditures. Excess funds can be invested for short periods of time to earn interest for the district and short term borrowing may be necessary to cover temporary cash shortages. A proper cash management program has two financially related objectives:

1 *Availability*—to maximize cash available to meet daily needs and to increase the cash available for investment
2. *Yield*—to earn the maximum return on cash invested[3]

Two aspects of cash management are particularly relevant for budget management. First is the investment income earned through the cash management program. This represents revenue which does not have to be raised from other sources and can keep property taxes lower than they otherwise might be. Since investment income is usually a specifically budgeted revenue source, the performance of the investment program can be monitored through the regular revenue comparison reports discussed above.

The second aspect is the cash position of the district during the year and most importantly at year end. The district's anticipated ending cash position will be used in budget planning as a revenue source in the upcoming year's budget. Significant deviations from planned amounts will cause disruptions in the budget for next year. Too much cash at year end can sometimes cause as many problems as a shortfall. An unfortunate, but true, episode concerns a district which ended the fiscal year with $1,000,000 more than originally projected in their ending cash balance. Unfortunately, this was discovered just before the end of the school year and only weeks before a tax levy election was scheduled. This was interpreted by the media and the district voters as the district suddenly finding an extra million dollars. The opponents of the levy election felt validated in their claims that the district did not need more money if they could find an extra million lying around. The outcomes were that the district lost the election and the superintendent lost his job. What is most unfortunate about this situation is that it was a failure of communication, not necessarily management. Normally, a million dollar savings would be a laudable event and the superintendent who created it would perhaps be deserving of a raise. Instead, it was interpreted as administrative incompetence and deceit.

The moral of this tale is not to be perfect in your projections; that is unrealistic. Rather, it is to keep district management informed of the current and projected ending cash position. This can be accomplished through regular reports to the top district administrators and the school board notifying them of the present amount of cash on hand and projecting what the ending cash balance will be at the end of the year. The ending cash balance is projected by taking the current amount, adding anticipated revenues still to be received, and deducting planned expenditures. Deviations from earlier projections should be identified and explained as early as they are known. In this way no unpleasant and avoidable surprises will occur.

Financial Reports

The expenditure and revenue reports discussed above are prepared for the principal purpose of management control. They are for *internal* use primarily and serve to keep administrators and school board members informed about the status of the district's spending and revenue collection activities as compared to the approved budget amounts. In addition to these types of reports, the district prepares another series of reports which have *external* uses as well. These are the district's financial statements and they are designed to present the financial condition of the school district not only to district staff and administrative officers, but to the school board and public at large.

At regular intervals during the year the district should prepare and submit to the school board *interim financial statements.* Separate financial statements are prepared for each fund used by the school district. These reports present the district's financial status as of the date which they are prepared. The timing of the interim statements is decided by the district; some districts will prepare them quarterly, although monthly preparation is the recommended frequency.[4] The reports, prepared on a regular schedule and in a consistent format, will allow the board members and district administrators to assess the strength of the district's financial condition.

At the end of the year the district should prepare a *comprehensive annual financial report* which summarizes the district's financial activities for the year and its financial position as of the last day of the fiscal year. Guidelines for preparing this report have been established by the Governmental Accounting Standards Board, the American Institute of Certified Public Accountants, and the Association of School Business Officials.[5] The financial statements required to be included are:

1) Combined balance sheet—all fund types
2) Combined statement of revenue, expenditure and changes in fund balances—all governmental funds
3) Combined statement of revenue, expenditures and changes in fund balances—budget and actual—general and special revenue types
4) Combined statement of revenue, expenditures and changes in retained earnings (or equity)—all proprietary fund types
5) Combined statement of changes in financial position—all proprietary fund types[6]

The statements must be prepared in accordance with generally accepted accounting principles. In addition to the specified financial statements, the annual report should contain an independent auditor's report of their examination of the district's financial statements and records. The auditor's report ensures that the information presented is valid, fairly stated, and accurately reflects the district's financial position.

USE OF MICROCOMPUTERS IN BUDGETING

There are many opportunities for using microcomputers in school district budgeting. They range from routine tasks which occur on a regular basis to special one-time analyses. This section will provide some examples of microcomputer applications in budgeting which can be used by individual administrators, such as a principal or a department director in the central office. These examples are for microcomputers and should be distinguished from the uses more appropriate for larger computers which would handle accounting, payroll, student records, and personnel data.[7]

Two points about the use of microcomputers are appropriate before the examples are discussed. First, the problems addressed are common administrative problems which an administrator will likely face; they are not "microcomputer" problems per se. The microcomputer is simply a tool for solving these problems with less effort and perhaps greater accuracy. Second, an administrator does *not* need to be a computer programmer to use a microcomputer to work on these problems. All of the problems can be dealt with using electronic spreadsheets and data base programs which are readily available and easily learned.

In most of the examples, an important analytical technique, *sensitivity analysis,* can be used to great advantage. The technique is simple and almost intuitive, but it can be very powerful. The basic idea is that the analysis or calculations are done the first time using the best available data, including the most likely case assumptions. The analysis is then redone one or more times, but now some assumptions are changed. The results of the two analyses are compared to see the difference in outcome the change in input assumptions made. For example, what would it cost the district if it negotiated a 5 percent increase in the teacher salary schedule instead of a 3 percent increase? This is the *what if?* approach and using a microcomputer to carry out the analyses can make it feasible to test many assumptions and try many alternatives. This provides administrators with a range of possible results and can aid in making better decisions.

Enrollment Forecasts

The cohort survival technique (Chapter Four) can easily be set up on an electronic spreadsheet and the numbers of students projected by grade, school, and special condition. Sensitivity analyses can test the results for different assumptions about survival rates and first year entering students.

Salary Schedules and Expenditure Projections

Each of the district salary schedules for teachers, administrators, and classified personnel can be input into a separate microcomputer file. The files should be constructed using the district's unique number of educational and experience steps in the salary schedules. Corresponding files with the number of personnel at each step in the schedule should be created for each type of schedule. The analysis consists of projecting the number of personnel at each step for the upcoming year and then projecting the salary expenditures based on the number of personnel at each step and the salary for that step next year.

Once the schedules are constructed, sensitivity analyses can be carried out to test the impact of different possible changes in the salary schedules for the next year. The most common change to examine would be an increase in the base salary level, perhaps associated with contract negotiations. Another type of sensitivity analysis could consider the financial impact of modifying the number of steps or changing the amounts between steps in any of the schedules.

An extension of salary expenditure projections would be inclusion of employee benefits. Many of the necessary data are common with the salary projections and by adding specific benefit information it would be possible to develop separate, but linked benefit estimates.

Expenditure Projections

Although there are special microcomputer software programs devoted to developing expenditure projections for budgets, it is not difficult to create an individual district program using an electronic spreadsheet. The format would be that of the budget document and will include: account code and description; past years' amounts; and budget request. Additional items may be appropriate for individual districts. For a complete district budget the initial development of the required format will involve considerable, but mostly clerical, effort to input the account codes and descriptions and past data. After that, however, the use of this budget format in the microcomputer will be rapid and save considerable time in revision.

To develop a new budget using the microcomputer budget format, the budget amount for each account is entered into its designated space in the budget request column. The spreadsheet will automatically add together subaccount amounts into account totals where formatted for this task. The real power of the budget format, however, comes when changes in any budget item or account are needed. The changes are entered into the microcomputer budget program; they are incorporated into the budget and the new totals and subtotals calculated instantly. Updating the budget for changes or modifications is accomplished automatically; no recalculating or retyping is required.

This rapid revision capability with a budget spreadsheet program also allows administrators and even board members to investigate the effects of potential budget changes before proposing or deciding upon them. Any number of sensitivity analyses can be performed to test the impact of different budget request levels or different allocation patterns. For example, what would be the increase in expenditure required to provide every elementary classroom with two microcomputers for instructional uses?

All organizational units in the district preparing budget requests should use the same microcomputer format. This allows their budget submissions to be combined electronically by the business office and the results to be automatically totaled for the entire district. This is most easily accomplished by providing each unit with a copy of the budget program for their use. They can make their budget submission either through a network or modem arrangement or deliver a diskette to the business office. Once the budget is complete and has been adopted by the school board, the data can be transferred electronically to the accounting records which are usually processed by a larger computer.

Revenue and Tax Projections

The revenue side of the budget can also be estimated using an electronic spreadsheet. The revenue projections also use the budget document format which lists the individual sources from which revenues are anticipated along with the account code for each and the amounts received in the past several years. Individual analyses for particular revenue sources can be created and the results incorporated into the overall revenue projections. For example, if the district has property which it is leasing to other organizations, the square footage and rental price per square foot of each property can be input into a electronic spreadsheet, the calculations performed, and the results transferred to the line for Local Revenues—Rentals in the main revenue projection listing. This type of analysis lends itself to sensitivity analyses as well. In the rental properties example above, it would be easy to test the impact of changes in price per square foot charged by the district, even on a property-by-property basis, and incorporate the results directly into the total revenue projections.

An important consequence of revenue projections is the amount of local property tax required to support the district budget. Whether the district has a maximum amount or rate it may levy or whether the local property tax levy is the amount needed to balance the budget after considering all other revenues, the property tax amount is significant to administrators, school board members, district patrons and voters, and the media. An additional analysis which would be highly useful is the determination of the property tax amount and tax rate. This can be accomplished with an extension to the revenue projections which calculate the amount of property tax required to be levied according to governing statutes and regulations. With an additional input of the district's assessed value (actual or estimated depending on data availability) the property tax rate can also be determined.

Budget Analyses

Once the proposed budget has been prepared, a microcomputer can be used to carry out several different analyses of the budget. One type of analysis is a baseline budget analysis of significant changes from the current to the proposed budget in any of the accounts. The baseline budget analysis technique is explained in Chapter Five and the use of a microcomputer for calculations will allow more accounts to be analyzed in greater detail.

Possible budget reductions or increases are also readily analyzed with a microcomputer, especially if the original budget has been prepared on an electronic spreadsheet. Proposed changes are input into the budget and the ramifications can be calculated instantaneously. If the revenue and tax projections are also linked into the program, the impact on the local property tax and the tax rate will also be displayed. An administrator with a full budgeting program in the microcomputer is capable of evaluating the fiscal implications of expenditure and revenue changes and illustrating the impact of those changes to district decision makers.

Budget Management Reports

Many, if not all, of the budget management reports discussed previously in this chapter can be developed on a microcomputer. However, some of them which utilize data from the financial accounting records can be prepared more efficiently on a larger mini or mainframe computer. The main reason is that accounting data are usually kept on a larger computer and to transfer the data back to a microcomputer is unnecessary.

However, other types of budget management reports can usefully be developed on a microcomputer. A cash flow analysis for the district's funds is a good example. Either a commercially developed or a district developed electronic spreadsheet based program will allow a district financial officer to project the anticipated inflows and outflows of cash and to plan the amount and timing of short-term investments.

At the school level a supplemental expenditure reporting system for supplies and equipment is often useful for building administrators if the district prepared reports are not received in a timely fashion. The school records can also be used to check the district reports for accuracy and completeness. Again, a relatively simple spreadsheet program can be developed. The report would be organized around school departments (such as, language arts, mathematics, counseling, or administration) and would maintain for each department a record of the original budget, each expenditure and encumbrance charged against that department's account, and the amount remaining in the account. The departmental data can be combined into a school summary. Prior to approving a departmental expenditure request during the year, administrators can check the department's account to make sure that sufficient money remains in the account.

Special Analyses and Reports

At times during the school year there is a need for some special analysis or study of a particular issue. These are not routine events, but occur sporadically and in response to a special situation. If the investigation involves quantitative analysis it may be helpful to carry out that portion of it with a microcomputer. If appropriate, graphic displays can be developed to demonstrate important points. While the four examples discussed below are illustrative only and not intended to be exhaustive, they do provide an indication of the possibilities.

New-program cost estimation.   When a new program is proposed for the district one necessary piece of information for decision makers is the estimated cost. One cost estimation method is the resource-cost model approach which requires the analyst to specify the appropriate resources for the new program and the prices of those resources, and then uses these data to derive the resultant program cost.[8] The format of this methodology fits naturally into an electronic spreadsheet and the analysis can be enhanced by utilizing a microcomputer. Estimates of not only the first year cost, but of following year costs as well can be developed to provide an indication of ongoing operating costs. Similar analyses can be carried out for major modifications proposed to existing programs.

Cost-effectiveness comparisons.   When the district is faced with deciding among alternative approaches for solving the same problem or accomplishing the same objective, a standard course is to conduct a cost-effectiveness analysis. This consists of collecting all of the comparable costs of each approach along with the anticipated results produced by each one. The approaches are compared to see which produces the greatest results for the same amount of expenditure or equivalent results for the least expenditure. Setting this type of analysis up on an electronic spreadsheet facilitates not only the calculations, but, more importantly, requires the thorough delineation of the relevant costs and results. Cost-effectiveness analyses can be developed not only for support service and administrative operations, but are also quite helpful in examining instructional alternatives.

Make or buy decisions.   At times the district may be trying to decide whether to perform an activity itself or to contract with an outside vendor for the service. This is the classic make (do it internally) or buy (purchase it externally) decision situation. While not all of the important factors in the decision are quantifiable, many of them are, particularly the costs. An electronic spreadsheet developed for the specific problem can identify and compare the costs and the anticipated results for each internal or external alternative.

Election analysis.   For those district needing elections for budget approval, tax levies, or bond issues, post-election analysis of voter behavior can be very enlightening and prove quite helpful in future elections. An analysis of precincts to correlate the percentage yes voters with voter characteristics, such as number of voters with children in school, age, income,

and average assessed value of residential property will identify possible relationships which could be utilized in upcoming elections. Also, if different
tactics were tried in different precincts, an analysis of the results could reveal those which were most effective in reaching certain types of voters.

FINAL COMMENTS

The district budget and the management reports generated from the accounting system and from special analyses provide vital information to administrators. The reports serve as a fiscal scorecard to tell how the operation is performing. Administrators can keep track of what is happening
financially through a regular review and analysis of expenditure and revenue reports. However, to be able to do this administrators need to understand the format and language of the reports and be able to interpret the
data presented.

While administrators need to utilize the management reports which
may be available to them, it is not necessary that they personally study each
number in detail. Someone else can be delegated the task of reviewing the
reports for an administrator, but he or she should be aware of the critical
elements to monitor. For example, a school principal may delegate to an
administrative assistant or budget clerk the task of reviewing the specific
items on the building expenditure report, but the principal should be informed of the overall situation—total expenditures for supplies versus the
school budget amount—and of any possible trouble areas.

An efficient way of using management reports is on an *exception basis.*
The idea is that one should focus on potential problem situations and leave
the others alone. Areas which are performing according to expectations
financially do not need management attention. Rather administrators
should concentrate their time on those areas which deviate from planned
performance. Consistent with this approach, reports should be looked at to
identify areas in which the results are out of line with expectations. Look
for red flags which will identify problem areas and do not use limited administrative time on areas that have no need of it.

Another suggestion for using the management reports is to concentrate on the large amounts. Be more concerned about the absolute dollar
amount of the deviation than the percentage deviation. It is much better to
have a $100 account overspend by 100% than to have a $20,000 account
overspend by 2%.

Above all, administrators need to be able to use the information which
they have to manage and improve their programs. Financial reports are a
means to an end. Expenditure reports, in particular, identify the budgetary
constraints under which administrators work and how close to reaching
those constraints the operation is. With information about the balance re-

maining in each of the accounts, an administrator can make informed decisions and tradeoffs among different program areas. For example, in a high school overexpenditures can be approved for the foreign language department if the mathematics department is sufficiently under budget. Or, the student transportation office may be permitted to purchase a microcomputer if lower fuel costs have resulted in less expenditures than budgeted for gasoline for the buses.

The point to remember is that the budget and the related management reports are simply tools for administrators to utilize. Dollars are obtained through the budgeting process to carry out educational programs. Resources are reallocated during the year to meet newly emerging needs, to take advantage of opportunities, and to motivate staff. The budgets and reports are a blueprint for educational planning and a language for describing operations and activities of the district. Consequently, administrators must know what budgets and management reports are, what content is included in each, and how to interpret and use the information they contain. If, as an administrator, you don't control your budget, then it will control you. The best administrators know this secret and use budgets and financial information to achieve the maximum for their educational programs.

PROBLEMS

1. TRAPPER POINT UNION HIGH SCHOOL DISTRICT
   In the first two months of the 1987-88 school year, Trapper Point UHSD experienced the transactions listed below in the General Fund Support Services area. Using an encumbrance reporting format (see Table 8.2), calculate the effect of each transaction on expenditures, encumbrances, and unencumbered balance.

   1. The district school board appropriated $3,440,000 for support services in the General Fund.
   2. Personnel contracts in the amount of $2,230,000 were encumbered.
   3. Benefits associated with the personnel contracts were also encumbered in the amount of $670,000.
   4. Purchase orders for educational media supplies were issued for $130,000.
   5. Salaries were paid in the amount of $220,000.
   6. Three new staff members were hired and their personnel contracts and associated benefits were encumbered in the amount of $90,000.
   7. The educational media supplies were delivered with an invoice totaled $120,000. They were distributed for immediate use.
   8. A contract for psychological services was made with the local Mental Health office for an amount not to exceed $40,000.
   9. Two staff members resigned and their salaries and associated benefits were released from encumbrances in the amount of $60,000.

10. Salaries were paid in the amount of $230,000.

11. Quarterly payments for employee benefits were made to various governmental agencies totaling $180,000.

12. Payment was made to the Mental Health office for $10,000.

13. A purchase order was issued for maintenance supplies and materials for $50,000.

14. The contract with the Mental Health office was canceled by mutual consent.

15. Maintenance supplies and materials delivered at a cost of $55,000.

At this point what is the maximum amount for which the school district could contract for new data processing equipment?

2. EXPENDITURE REPORTING IN ORION HIGH SCHOOL

During the early portion of the school year, Orion High School had the following transactions:

1. The allocation to Orion High School of the General Fund appropriation for instruction was set at $1,500,000.

2. The business office reported contracts for certificated and noncertificated personnel were $950,000 and these were encumbered.

3. Benefits associated with these staff were calculated at $290,000 and these were also encumbered.

4. Shop equipment was ordered for $40,000 on a district purchase order.

5. The first month's salaries of $90,000 were paid.

6. A purchase order was issued for office equipment for $10,000.

7. The shop equipment arrived and the final price was $43,000.

8. The second month's salaries of $90,000 were paid.

9. The office equipment was delivered at a final cost of $9,000.

Show the cumulative effects of each of these transactions using the encumbrance reporting format shown in Table 8.2. At each step determine the year-to-date encumbrances, year-to-date expenditures, and unencumbered balance remaining.

3. Specify the budget account transfer policies utilized in your district. Do they vary by type of expenditure? What authority and constraints do principals have in making transfers between accounts in their schools?

4. Collect a sample of the reports used in your school district to monitor and control expenditures. Who in the district receives them and how often? Are they understandable, useful, and appropriate? Why or why not? What suggestions do you have for improvements?

5. Using a spreadsheet with a microcomputer, construct your district's current salary schedule for teachers. (Use formulas to relate all other salary levels to the base/entry salary amount.) Show what the schedule would be next year with increases of 2 percent, 5 percent, and 10 percent in the base salary level.

6. Using a spreadsheet with a microcomputer, design an expenditure reporting system to keep track of departmental expenditures and encumbrances in a high school in your district. Illustrate its operation with actual or hypothetical data from one academic or administrative department.

NOTES

1. *Financial Accounting for Local and State School Systems* (Washington, DC: National Center for Educational Statistics, 1980), p. 118.

2. William Hartman, "Resource Allocation in High Schools" (Eugene, OR: Center for Educational Policy and Management, College of Education, University of Oregon, 1985), pp. 81-85.

3. Frederick Dembowski, "Cash Management" in Guilbert Hentschke, *School Business Administration: A Comparative Perspective* (Berkeley, CA: McCutchan, 1986), pp. 214-215.

4. Sam Tidwell, *Financial and Managerial Accounting for Elementary and Secondary School Systems*, 3rd ed. (Reston, VA: Association of School Business Officials, 1985), p. 550.

5. Sam Tidwell, *Financial and Managerial Accounting*, Chap. 20 has a thorough discussion of the comprehensive annual report.

6. Association of School Business Officials, "Certificate of Excellence in Financial Reporting by School Systems" (Reston, VA: Association of School Business Officials).

7. E. Ronald Carruth and Gayden Carruth, "Use of Computers in School Business Management" in L. Dean Webb and Van D. Mueller, eds., *Managing Limited Resources: New Demands on Public School Management* (Cambridge, MA: Ballinger, 1984).

8. William Hartman, "Projecting Special Education Costs," in Jay Chambers and William Hartman, eds., *Special Education Policies: Their History, Implementation, and Finance* (Philadelphia, PA: Temple University Press, 1983).

SCHOOL
DISTRICT
BUDGETING

INDEX